THE ROLE OF TARIFF QUOTAS IN COMMERCIAL POLICY

Also published for the Trade Policy Research Centre by Macmillan

TOWARDS AN OPEN WORLD ECONOMY
by Frank McFadzean *et al.*

WORLD AGRICULTURE IN DISARRAY
by D. Gale Johnson

THE ESSENTIALS OF ECONOMIC INTEGRATION
by Victoria Curzon

NEGOTIATING ON NON-TARIFF DISTORTIONS OF TRADE
by Robert Middleton

TRADE EFFECTS OF PUBLIC SUBSIDIES TO PRIVATE ENTERPRISE
by Geoffrey Denton, Seamus O'Cleireacain and Sally Ash

INVISIBLE BARRIERS TO INVISIBLE TRADE
by Brian Griffiths

TECHNOLOGY AND ECONOMIC INTERDEPENDENCE
by Harry G. Johnson

THE ECONOMICS OF THE OIL CRISIS
edited by T. M. Rybczynski

PUBLIC ASSISTANCE TO INDUSTRY
edited by W. M. Corden and Gerhard Fels

MEETING THE THIRD WORLD CHALLENGE
by Alasdair MacBean and V. N. Balasubramanyam

AGRICULTURE AND THE STATE
edited by Brian Davey, T. E. Josling and Alister McFarquhar

PRICE ELASTICITIES IN INTERNATIONAL TRADE
by Robert M. Stern, Jonathan Francis and Bruce Schumacher

TARIFF PREFERENCES IN MEDITERRANEAN DIPLOMACY
by Alfred Tovias

NUCLEAR POWER AND THE ENERGY CRISIS
by Duncan Burn

The Role of Tariff Quotas in Commercial Policy

MICHAEL ROM

with a Foreword by
GERARD CURZON

for the
Trade Policy Research Centre
London

© Michael Rom and the Trade Policy Research Centre 1979

All rights reserved. No part of this publication may be reproduced or transmitted, in any form or by any means, without permission

First published 1979 by
THE MACMILLAN PRESS LTD
*London and Basingstoke
Associated companies in Delhi
Dublin Hong Kong Johannesburg Lagos
Melbourne New York Singapore Tokyo*

*Printed in Great Britain by
Unwin Brothers Limited
The Gresham Press Old Woking Surrey*

British Library Cataloguing in Publication Data

Rom, Michael
   The role of tariff quotas in commercial policy
   1. Tariff quotas
   I. Title II. Trade Policy Research Centre
   382.7   HF1713

ISBN 0–333–17638–3

To Sheila, Ruthie and Ofra

*This book is sold subject
to the standard conditions
of the Net Book Agreement*

Trade Policy Research Centre

The Trade Policy Research Centre in London was established in 1968 to promote independent analysis and public discussion of commercial and other international economic policy issues. It is a non-profit organisation which is privately sponsored and serves as an entrepreneurial centre under the auspices of which a variety of activities are conducted. In general, the Centre provides a focal point for those in business, the universities and public affairs who are interested in international economic questions.

The Centre is managed by a Council which is headed by Sir Frank McFadzean. The members of the Council, set out below, represent a wide range of European experience and expertise.

SIR FRANK MCFADZEAN
Chairman

PROFESSOR JOHN ASHTON
SIR ALEC CAIRNCROSS
JAMES A. CLAY
PROFESSOR W. M. CORDEN
PROFESSOR GERARD CURZON
DIRK DE BRUYNE
PROFESSOR HERBERT GIERSCH
SIDNEY GOLT
PROFESSOR T. H. HEIDHUES
PROFESSOR ASSAR LINDBECK
HARALD B. MALMGREN

FRANCO MATTEI
PETER OPPENHEIMER
PROFESSOR THEO PEETERS
ALAN F. PETERS
T. M. RYBCZYNSKI
HON. MAXWELL STAMP
PROFESSOR LIONEL STOLERU
PAUL STREETEN
SIR ERIC WYNDHAM WHITE
MAURICE ZINKIN

HUGH CORBET
Director

Having general terms of reference, the Centre does not represent any consensus of opinion. Intense international competition, technological advances in industry and agriculture and new and expanding markets, together with large-scale capital flows, are having profound and continuing effects on international production and trading patterns. With the increasing integration and interdependence of the world economy there is thus a growing necessity to increase public understanding of the problems now being posed and of the kind of solutions that will be required to overcome them.

The principal function of the Centre is the sponsorship of research programmes on policy problems of national and international importance. Specialists in universities and private firms are commissioned to carry out the research and the results are published and circulated in academic, business and government circles throughout the European Community and in other countries. Meetings and seminars are also organised from time to time.

Publications are presented as professionally competent studies worthy of public consideration. The interpretations and conclusions in them are those of their authors and do not purport to represent the views of the Council and others associated with the Centre.

The Centre is registered in the United Kingdom as an educational trust under the Charities Act 1960. It and its research programmes are financed by foundation grants, corporate donations and membership subscriptions.

Contents

Trade Policy Research Centre	v
List of Tables	xi
Biographical Note	xiii
Preface	xv
Foreword by *Gerard Curzon*	xvii
Abbreviations	xxiv

1 INTRODUCTION TO TARIFF QUOTAS	1
Tariff Quotas Defined	2
Unallocated and Allocated	2
Discriminatory and Non-discriminatory	2
Categorisation by Method of Administration	3
Specific and General	3
Contractual and Autonomous	3
Common and National	4
Effective, Prohibitive and Ineffective	4
Ordinary versus Reduced Tariff within the Tariff Quota	5
Absolute and Relative	5
Type of Tariff	5
Other Classifications	5
Uses of Tariff Quotas	5
To Facilitate Border Trade	6
For National Specialities	6
To Promote New Trade	6
To Reduce Prices	7
To Supplement Domestic Output	7
For Harmonisation in a Customs Union	7
For Liberalising Trade	8
For Protective Purposes	9
Reduction or Avoidance of Trade Diversion	9
For Preferential Treatment	10
To permit Finishing Trade	10
Other Purposes	10
Notes and References	11

Contents

PART I PLACE IN THE GATT

2 TREATMENT OF TARIFF QUOTAS UNDER THE GATT 15
    Waivers under the GATT 19
    Equal and Equitable Treatment 21
    Allocation of Country Quotas 23
    Article XIII of the GATT 26
    Waivers under Article XXV 28
    Tariff Quota Exceptions to the MFN Clause 29
    Conclusions 31
    Notes and References 31

3 CUSTOMS UNIONS AND THIRD COUNTRIES:
   THE TARIFF QUOTA SOLUTION 34
    Problems of Interpretation 34
    Customs Unions in Economic Theory 37
    Proposed Solution 44
    Notes and References 46

PART II PRACTICE AND THEORY

4 TARIFF QUOTAS IN THE EUROPEAN COMMUNITY 53
    National Tariff Quotas in the European
      Coal and Steel Community 53
    Basis for National Tariff Quotas 55
      Basis for Application of Tariff Quotas in the Treaty 55
      The Agreement of 1960 regarding 'List G' 59
    National Tariff Quotas in Association and
      Trade Agreements 62
    Tariff Quotas and European Community Institutions 65
    National Tariff Quotas during the Transition Period 66
      Procedure for Granting Tariff Quotas 71
      Tariff Quota Administration 79
    Summary 82
    Community Tariff Quotas 85
      Types of Community Tariff Quotas 93
      Community Tariff Quotas and New Member States 94
    Notes and References 96

5 TARIFF QUOTAS IN THE UNITED STATES 102
    Character of United States Quotas 103
    Experience with Tariff Quotas 104
    Administration of Tariff Quotas 105
    Woollen and Worsted Fabrics 107
      Difficulties in Interpreting the Note 107

Concept of the Tariff Quota	114
Invocation of the Tariff Quota	115
Suggestions for Change	126
Developments after the Termination of the Tariff Quota	128
Stainless Steel Table Flatware	130
Comparison of the Cases	134
Notes and References	136

6   TARIFF QUOTAS: A PARTIAL EQUILIBRIUM ANALYSIS   140
    Notes and References   151

PART III   GENERALISED TARIFF PREFERENCES

7   TARIFF QUOTAS UNDER THE GENERALISED SYSTEM OF PREFERENCES   155

Introduction	155
Use of Tariff Quotas as a Tool for Preferential Treatment	158
Early Suggestions of Preference Schemes based on Tariff Quotas	159
The ECE Scheme of 1960	159
Proposal of the Author	160
Draft Proposal of the Latin American Countries	170
Tariff Quotas in UNCTAD Discussions	172
Notes and References	174

8   SYSTEMS OF GENERALISED TARIFF PREFERENCES FOR DEVELOPING COUNTRIES   178

Australian Scheme	178
Administration of the Scheme	181
Actual Experience with the Scheme	182
The European Community's Scheme	186
Administration of the Tariff Quota	189
The Scheme from 1971 (2nd half) to 1973	196
Main Changes in 1974	205
Proposed Changes for 1975	206
Japanese Scheme	207
Products falling within Chapters 25–99 of the Brussels Tariff Nomenclature	207
Products falling within Chapters 1–24 of the BTN	207
Administration of Ceilings	208
Changes in the Scheme	212
Operation of the Scheme	213
Notes and References	214

PART IV SOME FINAL THOUGHTS

9 RESPONSES OF EXPORTING COUNTRIES TO
   TARIFF QUOTAS   223
   Notes and References   229

10 SUMMING UP   231
   General Conclusions   234
   Notes and References   235

APPENDIX I MATHEMATICAL NOTE TO CHAPTER 9   236
        II TARIFF QUOTAS AND RATES OF DUTY, 1973   238

Selected Bibliography   242

Index   245

List of Tables

2.1	United States Reservation to the 1947 GATT Trade Agreement	17
2.2	Tariff Quotas Bound in the GATT by the European Community, 1969	17
4.1	European Community Imports by Volume, 1960	68
4.2	European Community Imports by Value, 1960	68
4.3	Tariff Quota Applications by European Community Member States, 1961–66	70
4.4	National Tariff Quotas in the European Community, 1961–70	71
4.5	Tariff Quotas in the European Community for Tunny, 1964–69	77
5.1	Estimated United States Production and Imports of Woollen and Worsted Fabrics, 1952–56	110
5.2	Wool Cloth Production in the United States, 1947–58	111
5.3	United States Imports of Woollen and Worsted Fabrics, 1957–60	
	(a) by value	117
	(b) by weight	118
	(c) by area	119
5.4	Utilisation of the United States Woollen and Worsted Fabrics Tariff Quota, 1957–59	121
5.5	United States Imports of Woollen and Worsted Fabrics after Break-point	122
5.6	A Comparison of Woven Cloth Imports into the United States in 1955 and 1958 from Main Suppliers, by Weight and Price	125
5.7	Utilisation of United States Stainless Steel Table Flatware Tariff Quota, 1960–66	134
8.1	Australian Trade under GSP, 1966–71	183
8.2	European Community Imports, 1967	191
8.3	European Community Imports subject to Tariff Quotas, 1969	195
8.4	European Community Tariff Quotas, 1971–73	197
8.5	European Community Tariff Quotas, 1971–73, by Value and Weight	198
8.6	Limitations on European Community Tariff Quotas, 1971–73	199

8.7	European Community Imports in 1970 subject to 1972 Ceilings or Tariff Quotas	200
8.8	European Community Imports in 1970 of Sensitive and Semi-sensitive Products as defined by the 1972 Scheme	202
8.9	European Community Imports, 1970, by Source	204
8.10	European Community Tariff Quotas and Ceilings, 1973–74	205
8.11	Japanese Imports of Products in 1970 under the 1971 System of Ceilings, annualised	211
8.12	Number of Product Groups for Ceilings in Japan, 1972–73	213
9.1	Optimising Export Receipts	227

Biographical Note

MICHAEL ROM (Rozenberg) has been, since 1967, Director of the Research Institute for International Trade at the Leon Recanati Graduate School of Business Administration, University of Tel-Aviv, where he is also a Senior Lecturer in International Trade. As a senior economist in the Israeli Ministry of Commerce and Industry, specialising in commercial policy and export market research, Dr Rom has been a consultant to the United Nations and was a member of the Israeli delegations to various sessions of the United Nations Conference on Trade and Development (UNCTAD) and other international organisations. Raised in Israel, he obtained his doctorate, in 1953, at the Graduate Faculty for Political and Social Sciences, of the New School for Social Research, New York.

Preface

This volume is based on a number of articles I have written over the last twelve years on different aspects of the tariff quota as an instrument of commercial policy. The material has been revised in places and supplemented with further analyses.

I first became interested in the subject in 1962 in the course of examining the justification for permitting, as a departure from the principle of most-favoured-nation treatment (the cornerstone of the General Agreement on Tariffs and Trade), the establishment of customs unions and free trade associations. It occurred to me that the tariff quota might provide a solution to the problem of trade diversion. In the latter part of 1963, while acting as a consultant to the United Nations Secretariat, I returned to the subject, but this time in the context of tariff preferences for developing countries in the markets of the industrialised world.

These two possible applications of tariff quotas provoked my curiosity in a more general way, but very few readily available references to the subject appeared in the literature of the economics profession. I therefore set about my own research. Naturally, points of interest, and of emphasis, have changed over the years since then and this is reflected in the varying degrees of detail found in the chapters. Rather than labour to produce a thoroughly balanced treatment of the subject, it has seemed that a better service would be done by including as much as possible, given that there is no reference book on tariff quotas. A start has been made towards filling a gap in the literature on international economic policy.

I have thus been at pains to provide as much information as possible about primary and secondary sources, even though this makes some of the reading rather hard going, for I hope the reader may be guided to material not otherwise known. In spite of all that is presented, much remains to be done. Absence of data has prevented empirical investigation into the economic effects of specific tariff quotas. Similarly, theoretical discussion has hardly begun, for extended analysis – under conditions of increasing returns to scale and monopoly, for example – may prove valuable.

As an instrument of commercial policy, the tariff quota has many applications and, as such, is 'neutral'. Its success or failure depends on specific purposes and conditions and on how it is applied. With greater experience and knowledge, the tariff quota should become more useful, albeit in very special situations.

Over the long period in which I have been studying the subject, I have had considerable assistance from officials in many countries, too numerous to name even if convention allowed such a thing. But I want to thank Raziel Haimi-Cohen, who contributed the mathematical appendix. Thanks are due to the editors of *Kyklos*, the *Journal of World Trade Law* and *Aussenwirtschaft* for their permission to reproduce those parts of this book which originally appeared in their publications. The articles concerned are: 'Customs Unions and Third Countries in the GATT', *Kyklos*, Vol. XVII, 1964; 'The Tariff Quota and its Treatment in the GATT', *Journal of World Trade Law*, March/April 1971; 'The Tariff Quota: a Partial Equilibrium Analysis', *Journal of World Trade Law*, July/August 1973; 'A Suggestion for a Preferential Scheme in the Developed Countries for Imports of Manufactures from Developing Countries', *Aussenwirtschaft*, No. 1, 1966; and, 'The National Tariff Quota in the EEC', *Aussenwirtschaft*, No. 1, 1972.

Support for my work was provided by the Israel National Union of Graduates in the Social Sciences and Humanities and also by the Leon Racanati Graduate School of Business Administration, where my colleagues Seev Hirsch, Seev Neuman and Yair Orgler have shown much interest in the study and helped, through the Institute of Business Research of the University Campus of Ramat Aviv, to finance the preparation of the typescript.

Turning to the Trade Policy Research Centre, which has sponsored the later stages of the study, I am especially indebted to Cedric Watts who has laboured patiently to improve the presentation of the material and the language in which it is expressed.

Gerard Curzon has very kindly written a Foreword to the volume for which I am most grateful. As he points out, 'economists fall desperately apart when they draw policy conclusions', and although I do not necessarily agree with all he says, I find his foreword stimulating.

Finally, I would like to thank Israel Galed who, in spite of his changing roles inside and outside government, has continued to lend active and moral support at various stages in my research.

Notwithstanding the help I have enjoyed, I am entirely responsible for the views and conclusions reached in this volume, which does not necessarily reflect the views of any of the organisations or institutions associated with the study.

Tel-Aviv   MICHAEL ROM
Autumn 1975

Foreword

One of the most intractable issues in international economic relations since 1964, when the first United Nations Conference on Trade and Development was held, has been the problem of access to the rich markets of the developed world for the goods manufactured in less developed countries. The tariff structures of most developed countries have all the appearance of liberality. Tariffs are low for the most part, and quotas are rarely used, even in emergencies. Developing countries have seen tariffs in the industrial world diminish steadily without any particular effort on their part. In the course of successive rounds of multilateral tariff negotiations, held under the auspices of the General Agreement on Tariffs and Trade (GATT), they have not been asked to contribute much in the form of 'concessions' on their own tariffs. As a result the less developed world presents to the rest of the world a high-tariff and somewhat illiberal picture, which has remained largely untouched by the wave of post-war trade liberalisation, while the developed world projects, in the main, a fairly low-tariff and fairly liberal image.

Despite the success of developing countries in hanging on to their own tariffs while those protecting their principal export markets have diminished steadily – in terms of tariff bargaining a considerable achievement – they have not been able to make the inroads into the markets of the developed countries that they and their well-wishers (of whom the author is one) would have hoped. Since the idea of growth by import substitution, so fashionable in the 1950s and early 1960s, has met a richly deserved fate, the problem of access to the markets of developed countries for the industrial exports of developing countries has become acute.

Many hypotheses have been put forward to explain the comparatively poor export performance of manufactured goods produced in developing countries. Some emphasise the illiberal attitude of developed importing countries, which impose emergency trade restrictions the minute developing countries achieve a major breakthrough in a 'sensitive' market, by producing efficiently what consumers there want to buy. Others emphasise the lack of infrastructure and external economies for the production of manufactures in developing countries, or inadequate access to appropriate technology, and argue that, because inefficient production is endemic, developing countries should be granted generalised tariff preferences. The two schools of thought cannot both be right: either developing countries cannot produce efficiently, in which case developed countries do not need to protect themselves, or they can produce efficiently, in which case they do not need preferences. The fact of the matter is that the group of developing countries breaks down into those which do produce efficiently, and against which various trade restrictive measures are applied, and those which do not produce manufactures efficiently, and which need tariff preferences, at the very least, to make their goods exportable. The interesting question is what distinguishes these two groups of developing countries.

Actual evidence in the form of published trade figures suggests that the picture may not be as black as it is usually painted. Thus, the export performance of manufactured products from developing countries is quite impressive. Their share in the total exports of developing countries rose from only 8 per cent in 1955 to an estimated 25 per cent in 1973 and they are considered by the GATT Secretariat to be 'the most dynamic export category of developing countries in volume terms'.

Be this as it may, the school of thought which considers that developing countries need generalised tariff preferences, in order to offset their inherent inefficiency, has been the most successful to date. Thus, after strong resistance on the part of the United States, generalised tariff preferences have finally been accepted by the majority of developed countries. Many, however, consider that this has proved an empty victory, since the extent of the tariff preferences in favour of developing countries is severely limited by tariff quotas. Thus, the European Community grants duty-free entry to manufactured goods originating in developing countries to the value of some $2300m out of a total of $7500m worth of manufactured goods from less developed countries, after which normal rates of duty are applied. This tariff quota represents about 30 per cent of the value of all manufactured goods imported by the European Community from developing countries, but only some 2 per cent of the value of manufactured goods imported by the Community from the world as a whole. Whether or not such tariff preferences limited by quotas actually succeed in raising the share of developing countries in the markets of developed countries remains to be seen.

Such is the strength of the lobby in favour of preferences, however, that it is likely that they, and the tariff quotas associated with them, will become a salient feature of the international trade system for some years to come. Thus Dr Rom's study of tariff quotas is most timely. It is the first theoretical analysis of tariff quotas to appear and it helps to formulate some normative conclusions of relevance to contemporary problems of commercial policy.

Economists, while united as long as they keep firmly to the straight and narrow path of economic theory, fall desperately apart when they try to draw policy conclusions therefrom – indeed, this is part of the fun of the subject and there is nothing the profession welcomes more than a good controversy.

Tariff quotas are likely to meet this fate and Dr Rom's work could well be at the origin of a wide-ranging and fascinating debate on the pros and cons of this ambiguous method of trade control. The following remarks are made in this spirit.

A tariff quota may be summarily defined as a progressive tax on trade the more is imported, the higher the rate of duty and the less the amount of trade (a degressive tax on trade would have the effect of discouraging trade altogether, since importers would put off importing as long as possible in the hope of benefiting from a lower rate of duty: an 'Alice Through the Looking-Glass' type of policy). Tariff quotas are a new hybrid, combining the characteristics of the tariff, which acts through the price mechanism to reduce trade, and the features of the quota, which reduces trade by means of quantitative controls.

Tariff quotas allow a country to be free-trading – up to a point. A scientifically determined tariff-quota policy would allow a country to decide what an 'acceptable' level of imports might be, and to subject all imports beyond this point to steeply progressive rates of duty, based on estimated price elasticities of demand and calculated to shut off imports, or maximise government revenue, after a predetermined point. What flexibility! At last we have an instrument of trade policy capable of fine-tuning the rate of import penetration in a national economy. Is this not the type of instrument of trade control that generations of trade ministers have been looking for?

The history of trade liberalisation under the GATT's auspices since the end of World War II shows that even the staunchest supporters of an open world economy have been unwilling to contemplate the idea of unqualified free trade. Theirs has been a cautious 'yes-but' approach. What could be more suited to their needs than the tariff quota, the yes-but policy instrument *par excellence*? Why has this delightfully ambiguous and sophisticated instrument of trade control languished for so long in comparative obscurity? Is the generalisation of the use of tariff quotas, should it occur, to be welcomed or not? These are the type of questions that Dr Rom's study inspires.

First, why have tariff quotas been little used in the past? Dr Rom shows that they have been favoured at various times by the United States Department of the Treasury as a unilateral safeguard measure taken at the behest of local producers who claimed that they were suffering, or about to suffer, serious injury due to imports (see Chapter 5). The European Community also used tariff quotas when establishing its common external tariff, so that some low-tariff countries could continue to import essential raw materials and tropical foodstuffs at their previous low or non-existent rates of duty. These tariff quotas not only reconciled the low-tariff members to the higher Community tariff, but helped to minimise trade diversion in certain cases and for certain products. But the real breakthrough for tariff quotas came with the introduction of the Generalised Scheme of Preferences agreed to in 1971. Dr Rom has assembled and analysed a vast quantity of information on these tariff quotas and their application.

What is their status under GATT rules? The GATT permits the use of tariffs to restrict trade, but not the use of quantitative restrictions. The reason for this is that whereas tariffs can be used in a non-discriminatory fashion, quotas, in practice, cannot. If quotas are administered on the basis of first come, first served, then one country may scoop up the whole quota, leaving others with none. If quotas are administered on a basis of historical market shares, newcomers will be discriminated against. Finally, to the extent that import licences are granted at the discretion of the authorities of the importing country, there may be hidden discrimination in favour of goods from certain countries and against others.

Administering tariff quotas raises all these thorny issues, but they are in fact legal under the GATT rules. Thus Article XIII(5) mentions in passing that tariff quotas should be administered in a non-discriminatory fashion, but the main article prohibiting quotas does not mention them and, indeed, since tariff quotas operate nominally through the price mechanism, this is not surprising.

The problems raised by the practical application of tariff quotas deserve to be examined more closely. How, without re-establishing the complex machinery to administer quantitative restrictions, which most developed countries were glad enough to disband in the 1960s, are customs officials to know when one tariff quota is filled and a new tariff rate is to be applied? As most countries have considerably more than one point of entry, close surveillance is needed on a daily, if not hourly, basis. Dr Rom tells us that in the United States 'elaborate arrangements have been made to monitor imports exactly and accurately – with the help of computers and a whole system of clocks showing the different hours in particular ports of entry – in order to determine which will enjoy the tariff quota advantage and which will have to pay the higher duty'. Other countries, occupying a shorter longitudinal area of the globe, might be able to dispense with the clocks, but not with the computers. In short, it is the computer revolution that has put the tariff quota on the map.

In the European Community a method of 'automatic' licensing has been adopted; that is, imports subject to tariff quotas must be accompanied by an import licence, which is issued automatically, its only purpose being to monitor the rate of import penetration so as to know exactly when the tariff quota is filled. The United States, however, has complained that these 'automatic' licences should be abolished, since they not only add to the red tape that deters trade, but may sometimes be used to restrict trade. The idea is that since the same objective could be accomplished by other means – such as the computerisation of import data – countries which insist on retaining an automatic licensing system do so with an ulterior motive in mind: for instance, in order to be able to slap on quantitative restrictions overnight in a crisis.

GATT work on non-tariff measures includes a draft code on automatic licensing which, if adopted, would establish rules for the administration of automatic licensing in cases where it can be shown to be the most effective method of achieving an innocent objective. Otherwise, licensing, automatic or not, would be proscribed. This draft code is very far from being accepted by all important trading countries, and, even if it were, it would not resolve all the problems connected with the practical application of tariff quotas. Thus, even if computers can exercise sufficiently precise and prompt control of imports to be able to dispense with prior licensing, they cannot do away with the potential for discrimination inherent in a system which permits identical batches of goods to be treated in different ways.

In order to cope with the inherent unfairness of administering tariff quotas on a basis of first come, first served, the European Community has placed an upper limit on what any one country can supply under a given tariff quota. These *butoirs* (or trip-wires), as they are called, add to an already complex administrative machinery and take tariff quotas well out of the realm of trade policies acting through the price mechanism and well into the world of administered trade patterns.

My personal view is that the tariff quota is the thin end of the wedge. It permits the reinstatement of planned and possibly discriminatory trade patterns while masquerading as an instrument of trade policy acting through the price mechanism. This makes it an excellent candidate for use in the round of multilateral trade negotiations in Geneva. The history of the GATT is also the history of techniques of tariff negotiation. The bilateralism of the 1930s was replaced by multilateral item-by-item negotiation of tariffs from 1947 to 1962. During the Kennedy Round negitiations, the latter was replaced by across-the-board, or 'linear', tariff cutting although there was a reversion to item-by-item bargaining on 'sensitive' items. Perhaps the present round of talks will see the emergence of the tariff quota as a new bargaining technique.

The tariff quota reflects both the mood of protectionism, which has illogically swept the world since the disintegration of the Bretton Woods monetary system, and the disenchantment with the market economy which has spread since the appearance of double-digit inflation and higher-than-usual unemployment.

More specifically, the tariff quota is tailormade to meet the needs of the developed market economies in their dealings with the less developed nations. The latter continue to seek the magic formula which will make their manufactured goods competitive in the developed world, while the former find ever more devious ways of stopping the really competitive products from developing countries from making large inroads into their home territories. Thus there developed in the 1960s the insidious technique of 'voluntary' export restraints applied by efficient low-cost exporting countries, which acted in this manner in order to avoid the introduction of emergency safeguards (in the form of extra tariffs or quotas) by developed importing countries. Compared with outright quotas, 'voluntary' export restraints were deemed the lesser evil. This belief is now being questioned and there is a move to open up the whole problem of safeguards during the Tokyo Round of multilateral trade negotiations in Geneva. The problem is important, and not just a technical point, because it is improbable that developed countries will liberalise their external trade any further without a reliable system of safeguards which will permit them to respond to SOS signals from their own people should the rate of import penetration be 'excessive'. As can be readily seen, the problem is one of nuance and interpretation, and an international code would have to be very carefully worded indeed.

The interesting point, however, is that tariff quotas are capable of accomplishing much the same objective without the negotiation of a complex code of behaviour. Thus a developed country could by negotiation establish a low or nil-duty quota on light manufactures of the type produced efficiently by less developed countries – equal, say, to the total quantity imported from the whole world in 1975 – but leave its tariff unchanged for imports in excess of this amount and lay down an 'emergency' rate for imports entering above a pre-established 'threshold of disruption'. Developing countries could either compete for the low-tariff quota with other suppliers in developed or socialist countries, or could ask for a precise share of low-tariff quota. In any event, the importing country would be sure of being legally and automatically entitled to apply higher rates of duty once the critical point of predetermined import-penetration had been reached. In terms of tariff bargaining, the right to apply the 'emergency' rate could be exchanged for a substantial cut in the tariff applied to the first tranche of imports.

Whether this type of development is desirable or not is another matter altogether and depends on various assumptions. For instance, if tariff quotas are viewed as alternatives to 'voluntary' export restraints, then they certainly appear preferable. Whereas 'voluntary' export restraints are applied in response to a direct threat, usually issued only after the situation has deteriorated beyond repair and therefore in a tense and crisis-laden atmosphere, tariff quotas would be established in advance of any crisis and thus might avoid potential conflict situations altogether. Also, whereas 'voluntary' export restraints are hardly negotiated, but dictated by the importing country, tariff quotas could very well be negotiated multilaterally under the GATT and their non-discriminatory application placed under international surveillance.

Used in this fashion tariff quotas could well be a means of opening up larger developed-country markets to the goods of the less developed nations in a manner acceptable to both parties. On the other hand, tariff quotas can also be used in a restrictive fashion, as in the generalised system of preferences currently in force in most developed countries. Here, the tariff quotas are generally so small that the benefits intended to accrue to the developing countries tend to end up in the importer's pocket.

Thus, a generous system of tariff quotas cum safeguards could go a long way towards achieving fair and liberal access to developed countries' markets for the manufactures of developing countries by reconciling the divergent interests of both parties, but a stingy tariff quota system achieves the opposite. Furthermore, even a generous tariff quota system would only cope with half the problem.

The other half of the problem is to make developing countries' manufactured goods internationally competitive so that they can dispense with tariff preferences. Preferences are an attempt to cure the sickness by attacking the symptoms. They reflect the uncompetitive nature of much manufacturing activity in developing countries, but do nothing to cure it. Indeed, preferences encourage inefficiency, or they would if they were more generous.

This huge and complex problem can only be touched on here, but one startling inconsistency can nevertheless be pointed out, as it has a direct bearing on the points discussed above, namely: how can a country expect to export successfully from an industrial base established behind huge import barriers? Its manufactures can only be inefficient by international standards and the degree of import protection is a fair measure of the extent of its inefficiency. Small wonder, therefore, that such products need tariff preferences in order to penetrate other markets successfully if they do not need export subsidies as well. Thus, the problem of access to developed countries' markets for the manufactured goods of developing countries needs to be attacked from two sides, both by progressively reducing the level of protection in developing countries, and by negotiating freer access to developed countries' markets, coupled with a better system of safeguards against 'excessive' flows of imports which might cause social and political unrest in the importing countries. Developing countries should make the most of the current round of multilateral trade negotiations to establish a viable long-term North-South economic order of this type instead of wasting resources in 'improving' the preference system.

Geneva GERARD CURZON
Autumn 1976

Abbreviations

BTN	Brussels Tariff Nomenclature
CET	common external tariff of the European Community
CRI	United States Committee on Reciprocity Information
ECSC	European Coal and Steel Community
ECE	United Nations' Economic Commission for Europe
EFTA	European Free Trade Association
EWG	Europäischer Wirtschaftsgemeinschaft
FAO	United Nations Food and Agriculture Organisation
f.o.b.	free on board prices
GATT	General Agreement on Tariffs and Trade
GNP	gross national product
HEW	United States Department of Health, Education and Welfare
ITO	International Trade Organisation
MFN	most favoured nation
OAS	Organisation of American States
OECD	Organisation for European Cooperation and Development
SITC	Standard International Tariff Classification
TC	United States Tariff Commission
TSUS	Tariff Schedule of the United States
UN	United Nations
UNCTAD	United Nations Conference on Trade and Development

CHAPTER 1
Introduction to Tariff Quotas

The concept of the tariff quota is essentially very simple, but in practice it can take many forms; and there are many reasons why it is introduced. This introductory chapter defines a tariff quota. And it identifies and classifies the various forms it can take and the uses to which it can be put. The following chapters are grouped into four parts.

The first part discusses the permissibility of tariff quotas under the General Agreement on Tariffs and Trade (GATT), the instrument by which the commerce of the free-enterprise world has been governed since the end of World War II, and examines, the justification of customs union in the GATT from the point of view of third countries.

The next part gives details of two areas where tariff quotas have been used in practice. The first of these studies deals with the European Community and demonstrates how the adoption of tariff quotas helped to smooth out differences in import practices between individual member countries during the establishment of the Community. The second describes how the United States introduced tariff quotas as a protective device for two industries and the contrary developments that followed. This part also analyses the theoretical application of tariff quotas under a range of alternatives which goes somewhat beyond the two actual case studies examined in detail.

Part III deals with the desire of the developing countries to obtain access to the markets of the industrialised world and outlines various proposals based on tariff quotas that could bring this about. It comments on three individual schemes those of Australia, the European Community and Japan.

In the final part an attempt has been made to see whether (a) there has been sufficient experience in the commercial use of tariff quotas to produce any useful general conclusions, and (b) to develop certain notions as to the way exporting countries might react when faced with the imposition of tariff quotas, an aspect of the subject which is frequently overlooked.

TARIFF QUOTAS DEFINED

A tariff quota, unlike an ordinary quota (guillotine), sets no absolute maximum to the total amount of imports of a product or products permitted into a customs area during a given period. Instead it provides that a specified quantity, value or share of this import may enter during a given period into all or part of the area free of duty or at a lower rate of duty than imports in excess of that limit.[1]

This definition is much wider in scope than many of the customary definitions,[2] since it tries to take into account all possible forms of tariff quotas. Most of the definitions given are usually directed to one or other type of a tariff quota; but while these differ in detail from case to case, they have common characteristics.

Unallocated and Allocated

The most important distinction to bear in mind is the difference between an unallocated and an allocated quota.[3] An unallocated tariff quota establishes an overall limit for the import at the lower duty of a certain commodity or group of commodities, but it does not determine the respective shares of the various exporting countries in that overall quota. Each country may share in it according to its competitive strength. On the other hand, an allocated quota is an overall (sometimes called global)[4] quota, which is subdivided into country quotas.

The wool and worsted fabrics tariff quota of the United States, which was in force during the period 1956–60, is an example of an unallocated quota. It permitted imports at a lower tariff duty from any source up to a specified limit beyond which a higher tariff had to be paid. Examples of allocated quotas can be seen in the case of the cotton yarns customs quotas allotted to various countries.[5]

Discriminatory and Non-discriminatory

Closely related to this difference between allocated and unallocated tariff quotas is a classification according to their discriminatory or non-discriminatory nature. A tariff quota can be allocated so as to exclude some countries interested in the export of the particular commodity and it is then discriminatory. On the other hand, if the overall tariff quota is either unallocated or allocated equitably into country tariff quotas it is non-discriminatory.

In the past there has been considerable discussion as to what constitutes an equitable principle of distributing tariff quotas: whether it is more just for a particular country to allocate equal country quotas to all exporting countries or to distribute quotas according to their past relative share in exporting. Today it is customary to consider as non-discriminatory an allocation of quotas on the basis of an agreement with all partners, or on the basis of past relative shares in imports of the commodity into the particular country, taking into account 'special factors' which are more closely defined. The quotas covering imports of citrus fruits from Greece and various products from Turkey into the European Community are discriminatory. So are the specific quotas in commercial bilateral treaties, such as the tariff quotas for certain types of tobacco, cigars, coconut oil and pearl or shell buttons in the United States trade agreement with the Philippines.[6] There is no discrimination between the 120-odd developing countries and territories in the Australian waiver:[7] the principle of equal treatment and non-allocation of the quota among member countries within the developing country group is adhered to. The tariff quota, however, is discriminatory with respect to the developed countries adhering to the General Agreement on Tariffs and Trade (GATT).

Categorisation by Method of Administration
Very similar to the preceding classification are the specific methods of administration of tariff quotas. Broadly speaking, there are two major categories. The first is known as the 'greyhound' process, the other the prior licensing system; and both can be applied to unallocated tariff quotas. Within the quotas, the first includes the quantities of an imported commodity which physically have crossed the border, on a first-come-first-served basis. The second includes those quantities for which applications for licences have been submitted first. This second system may easily be misused and licensing may be of a discriminating nature even though the quota itself is not.[8]

Specific and General
Specific tariff quotas relate to an individual commodity or group of commodities. A general tariff quota (for lack of a better phrase) includes all commodities up to a certain value of total imports. Such a tariff quota has not yet been established in practice, but it has featured[9] in discussions of preferences for developing countries.

Contractual and Autonomous
A distinction can be made between those tariff quotas determined[10] by one state alone and those made on a contractual basis after bilateral[11] or multilateral negotiations with other states. This seemed a relevant distinction to the members of the Economic Committee of the League of Nations:[12] 'We do think it necessary to call attention to the difference in the character of customs quotas according as they are established by a bilateral commercial agreement or by an alteration introduced in the general tariff of a country by an autonomous act.'

According to that committee, the chances of compatibility of a tariff quota with most-favoured-nation (MFN), or equal, treatment are greater in the second case than in the first, but practical considerations prevent the use of this differentiation. If autonomous tariff quotas are considered compatible with MFN treatment, then any country wishing to avoid obligations arising out of the clause would merely have to avoid fixing a quota by commercial treaty. It might even, to the point of making it illusory, limit specific customs concessions extended in a commercial agreement arbitrarily, by fixing a quota to an autonomous act. As a consequence, the concession to that contracting party might be reduced, or even disappear entirely.

In recent years, discussions within the European Community over the internal distribution of a common quota have revived the distinction. When an autonomous quota is in force, unutilised shares resulting from internal misallocation may create no external difficulties. The same is not true with regard to a contractual quota where the outside country or countries, who are parties to the agreement, have a right to demand the utilisation of the whole quota.

Common and National
The previous classification indicated that within the European Community there is a distinction between common tariff quotas, which are extended to outsiders by the Community as a whole, and 'national' tariff quotas, which are granted by individual member countries with the consent of the Community. The first type are determined by the Community according to Article 28 of the Treaty of Rome and are becoming the more accepted form. Nevertheless, national tariff quotas, which at the beginning of the transitional period were much more numerous, still exist. These are granted by the Community under Article 25 of the Treaty.

Some national quotas were also established at the initiation of the Treaty of Rome and are included in the Treaty as special Protocols or were agreed upon during the negotiation of List G (see p. 59).

Effective, Prohibitive and Ineffective
If a tariff quota is being utilised beyond its limit, so that imports continue to take place even at a higher rate of duty, then it is 'effective'. The wool tariff quota of the United States is an example. If the quota is not fully utilised, the quota is deemed 'ineffective'. (Examples of this are many of the Australian tariff quotas for developing countries.) In an ineffective quota, no problem of allocation can arise: it is only with an effective quota that the issue arises of who receives the special benefits within the quota.

When imports are exactly at the quota limits, but not beyond them, then the tariff quota is prohibitive. It has been argued[13] that prohibitive tariff quotas should be considered in the same manner as quantitative restrictions and should be considered incompatible with MFN treatment. As will be explained[14] later, this interpretation could be incorrect.

Ordinary versus Reduced Tariff within the Tariff Quota
A further distinction has been made[15] between those cases where there is a reduction in the ordinary tariff inside the tariff quota, and those where the tariff duty has been increased above the ordinary tariff for quantities outside the tariff quota, although this seems to be of relatively minor importance.

Absolute and Relative
Whereas an absolute tariff quota stipulates a specific quantity or value, a relative tariff quota limits the import permitted under the quota to a percentage of total imports, consumption, or production. These can be based either on value or quantity. As an example, the United States wool fabrics tariff quota was stipulated in terms of 5 per cent of domestic production by weight.

A curiosity is the tariff quota bound in the GATT by the European Community. Some of these are defined on the principle that the size of the quota would be determined by the gap between local production and consumption.

Type of Tariff
The tariff itself, within and outside the tariff quota, can be a specific or *ad valorem* duty. It can also be a mixed tariff of the two rates; there are also cases where the mixed tariff is used alternatively, whichever is bigger or smaller.

Other Classifications
There are other categories into which tariff quotas could be divided: those which distinguish between one-time quotas granted for a specific period, automatically renewable ones, and permanent ones; between those which are renewed at the same size, increasing, decreasing, or a combination of a fixed part and a changing part in an automatic manner; and between those in which the tendency of the duty is to change and those in which it is to remain the same.

USES OF TARIFF QUOTAS

Classifying the various forms of tariff quotas rarely explains the purpose for which they are used, as they are manifold and sometimes even contradictory. To discuss their various uses in the past is therefore more useful.

To Facilitate Border Trade

It has been argued, for instance by Professor H. K. Heuser in his 1939 book,[16] that one of the purposes of the inclusion of tariff quotas in trade agreements is to facilitate border trade, and as an example he quotes the agreement between Belgium and Luxemburg in 1839, which permitted the import of 4000 tons of cast iron at a lower duty than normal. The report of the League of Nations[17] also tries to distinguish tariff quotas according to their object and importance and cites as the first category those customs quotas 'which have no other purpose than to regulate the traffic in certain goods between neighbouring zones in adjacent countries. This is not frontier traffic in the strict sense because the range of ten to fifteen kilometers is greatly exceeded, nor on the other hand is it a traffic that concerns the entire territory of the two adjacent states. Still less is it likely to be of any interest to third countries.'

Examples are given from the Treaty of Switzerland with Austria (6 January 1926), and the example of tariff quotas for mirabelles and strawberries in the commercial agreement between Belgium and France of 23 February 1926, where the tariff in these commodities was limited to certain parts of the territory only.

Professor Heuser thinks, too, that tariff quotas of this kind, which are indeed intended to facilitate border trade, are 'evasions of the MFN clause, but the nations not parties to the particular contract have generally not considered their exclusion from them important enough to renounce existing treaties'.[18] On the other hand, the impression derived from the League's report is that such border trade tariff quotas are compatible with the MFN clause. This will be further discussed at a later stage.

For National Specialities

The report of the League classified, as a special category, tariff quotas designed to limit the import of a commodity which no other country produces, but which may compete with close, or less close, substitutes produced elsewhere, in particular domestically. An example of such a quota given in the report was the tariff quota in the Italian-German Treaty of 3 October 1925 for maraschino spirits: 'Seeing that other countries do not produce that liquor but do supply the importing country with other liquors, it seems clear that the quota in question may be more to their advantage than to their detriment and so the question of the compatibility of the quota with the clause cannot arise.'[19]

To Promote New Trade

While the philosophy of free trade is based on the idea of competition between equals, the reality is that countries are unequal, being at different stages of economic development and competitive ability. Most countries have accepted that it is desirable to help to stimulate the economic progress of developing countries by providing them with an advantage in comparison with developed countries, facilitating the promotion of their exports and the development of new export industries. Accordingly, tariff quotas have been established for developing countries, as for instance in the case of the Australian waiver in the GATT,[20] and of the European Community's and Japanese General Scheme of Preference (GSP) presented to the United Nations Conference on Trade and Development (UNCTAD).[21]

The same purpose was also probably behind some of the country tariff quotas extended by the European Community to countries such as India and Pakistan for handicrafts of various kinds.[22]

To Reduce Prices
An attempt to use tariff quotas to reduce prices to the consumer was made by Germany in the 1920s. A non-discriminatory tariff quota was established in Germany for frozen meat in order to provide the needy classes with cheap meat, but the scheme failed completely, as the importers pocketed a substantial quota profit.[23]

To Supplement Domestic Output
A problem arises where, for some reason, local production of a raw material or a semi-finished product is insufficient. While its unlimited import from abroad would undermine the local producers, the prohibition of its import, or its import at a higher rate of duty, could be to the detriment of the local processing industries using that raw material or semi-processed product. A tariff quota supplementing domestic output has been tried as a solution. An example is the tariff quota for aluminium which was in effect for many years in Germany prior to the establishment of the Common Market.[24]

For Harmonisation in a Customs Union
Similar to the previous purpose are tariff quotas designed to permit the harmonisation of the common external tariff of a customs union. Such a tariff, which is brought about gradually during a transitional period, is very often determined by averaging the national duty rates of individual member countries, and this means an increase in the level of the external tariffs of low tariff countries.

Where such an increase in the tariff may bring about substantial dislocations in production and trade, tariff quotas have been found to constitute an adequate solution to the problem. Under this system, a low-tariff country can continue to import from third countries the quantities that it needs for its own use under the same conditions as before the establishment of the union, applying the external tariff to the rest of the imports. Examples of such tariff quotas can be found in the Benelux customs union,[25] as well as in the European Coal and Steel

Community (ECSC) and in the European Community [26] itself.

It has been argued[27] that experience with tariff quotas for the purpose of the harmonisation of the external tariff has been much more favourable than with those introduced for protective purposes. Tariff quotas can be established at the level of the normal imports originating in third countries without seriously affecting the harmonisation of the tariff, and even a possible increase of imports at the higher external tariff will not constitute a failure of the scheme, as is the case with tariff quotas established for the purpose of protection. Moreover, since the tariff quotas established permit the normal import, there is no pressure to utilise the quota, no abuses and, therefore, no need for state intervention and licensing.

For Liberalising Trade

According to Jacob Viner,[28] 'in most cases (from 1839 to the crisis of the 1920s and 1930s, as well as in the United States Trade Agreements Programme), tariff quotas were not intended to be restrictive of imports as compared to the situation prior to the introduction and were set at levels high enough to permit imports in somewhat greater values than prevailed prior to the introduction'.

Introduction of tariff quotas instead of absolute quotas as a means of liberalising trade has been suggested.[29] This takes into account their differentiating feature which permits the continuation of imports beyond the quota limits provided a higher tariff is paid, whereas with ordinary quotas no such imports could materialise.

For the purpose of liberalisation, however, tariff quotas may have a third advantage. Within the Trade Agreements Programme of 1934 of the United States, which was intended to bring about mutual liberalisation of trade through extensions of tariff concessions, a number of tariff quotas were granted by the United States to Canada in return for tariff concessions granted by the latter. These concessions in the field of agriculture by the United States could not have been made had they not been accompanied by safeguards 'which make it virtually certain that the effects will not be seriously felt by the domestic industry concerned, even when looking at the matter exclusively from the point of view of the share of domestic market which it will continue to enjoy'.[30] Thus, for instance, tariff quotas for cattle, cream and whole milk were established in the agreement with Canada, which took care not to injure the domestic market.[31]

Another example of tariff quotas whose object was to facilitate liberalisation of trade can be found in the United States concession on wool and worsted fabrics. This stipulated that a reduced rate of duty would apply only as long as imports did not exceed 5 per cent of the domestic output by weight of the same commodities. It can be argued that such a tariff concession could not have taken place unless it had been safeguarded by the above limitation. Three different ways can therefore be distinguished whereby trade can be liberalised through tariff quotas:

(a) quotas, established at a lower rate than the ordinary duty, may increase the total imports of the product itself into that country;

(b) the transition from quantitative regulations to cost restrictions may be a move towards more liberal practices of commercial policy; and

(c) the use of the device of tariff quotas permits the extension of concessions which make it possible to liberalise trade in an all-round effort of multilateral negotiations.

For Protective Purposes
Tariff quotas have also been used for the opposite purpose of increasing protection. The most elaborate example was a tariff quota system instituted during the early 1930s by Switzerland. The world crisis threatened to ruin individual economic sectors,[32] and the Swiss desired to protect the threatened sectors without generally raising tariffs, considered inopportune because of trade agreements. On the other hand, the use of ordinary quota restrictions seemed too extreme.[33] Accordingly, a surcharge duty, imposed once imports exceeded certain specified quantities was introduced. Such a surcharge was also considered by the Swiss authorities to be more compatible with the MFN clause,[34] in particular since it was thought that no substantial state intervention would be needed to administer the scheme.[35]

It soon became clear that this method did not fulfil expectations. In the first place, it was evident very quickly that state intervention and licensing were an essential condition for the proper functioning of the scheme. Secondly, the tariff quotas were found to be a weak tool for protective purposes, since imports increased well beyond the quota limits, despite the surcharge. This was largely the result of the price fall abroad which compensated for the increase in the tariff. Thus the Swiss authorities were forced to switch increasingly to ordinary quotas.[36]

Reduction or Avoidance of Trade Diversion
Tariff quotas have been used to maintain customary trade flows, or to reduce the danger of trade diversion which could result, or which did actually result, from the creation of a customs union. An example of the first type, which has been approved by GATT under a waiver, is the tariff quota granted by Italy to Libya.[37] Another example that may be cited is the tariff quota for bananas into Germany, agreed upon in the Treaty of Rome.[38] In Chapter 3 there is a fuller examination of the

possibility of using tariff quotas to solve the trade diversion effect of the establishment of a customs union.

For Preferential Treatment
By contrast to the use of tariff quotas for the purposes mentioned in the preceding paragraph are those occasions where they have been included in trade agreements and treaties as preferential concessions, with the explicit purpose of giving a particular country more favourable treatment than that accorded to other countries. This kind of tariff quota has been quite prevalent in the past,[39] and there are also present-day examples. For instance, it can be argued that tariff quotas extended to Turkey and Greece, for raisins or citrus fruits respectively, are of this nature. In this case the intention is that, through association with the European Community during the transition period, some advantage should be created for these countries, but that this should be limited lest they disrupt the local market too seriously.

To Permit Finishing Trade
Under the recommendations of the League of Nations' Economic Committee, ' "passive" finishing trade arises when a country authorises the temporary export of certain goods and readmits them free of duty when they return to the country after being finished abroad. The goods concerned in "passive" finishing trade are, as a rule, articles already partly finished, or almost completely finished, which merely have to undergo a final process, for example, fabrics which have to be dyed or embroidered. This trade cannot therefore take place without the consent of two parties: the exporting state, which promises to readmit the finished article free of duty, and the importing state, which offers exemption from duty for the article when it is brought to be finished.'[40]

Furthermore, this finishing trade is usually explained by very specific conditions in the two respective countries which account for this phenomenon. Consequently, the Committee of the League dealing with the matter did not feel able to advocate the application of the MFN clause to this type of trade, provided these particular specific conditions did not exist in other countries not parties to this particular agreement. An example of finishing trade which limits this trade within a specified tariff quota is that between the European Community and Switzerland,[41] where a tariff quota of up to a value of $1.87m has been established for imports of such commodities into the Community from Switzerland, as well as vice versa. Switzerland will reciprocate with concessions of similar value.

Other Purposes
The categories that have already been mentioned by no means exhaust all the purposes, uses and possibilities of tariff quotas. They have been

established for seasonal or temporary shortages, as well as to stabilise prices, and there are also cases where they were introduced for political considerations.[42] They may at times be used to achieve a number of purposes at once: their desirability and adequacy as a tool of economic policy depend on specific conditions and aims, and must be judged from case to case in the particular setting in which they are being applied.

NOTES AND REFERENCES

1. According to this definition complete waivers of tariffs for a part of the customs area – for example, Italy and the European Community in respect of list G in Protocol III.
2. See, for example, H. C. Hawkins, *Commercial Treaties and Agreements, Principles and Practices* (New York: Rheinhart, 1951) p. 277, note 2. 'A tariff quota is a specified quantity of a product during a particular period (for example, a calendar year) at a reduced rate, imports in excess of that quantity are subject to the original or sometimes a still higher rate.' Also see H. K. Heuser, *Control of International Trade* (London: Routledge, 1939) p. 77. 'Under a tariff quota a specified quantity of a particular commodity is permitted to enter the country under a lower tariff than any quantity beyond this specified maximum.'
3. Recommendations of the Economic Committee Relating to Tariff Policy and the Most-Favoured-Nation Clause, E805 (Geneva: League of Nations, 1933), Economic and Financial Series, II Bl, p. 10 (hereafter cited as League of Nations E805). Summarised in 'Commercial Policy in the Post-war Period', League of Nations, Annex I, IIA, April 1945, pp. 67–104.
4. According to Hawkins, *op. cit.*, p. 158, an allocated quota is called a global quota; but the specified shares given to each country are called country quotas. The term global may refer to the overall nature of the quota, whether allocated or unallocated.
5. League of Nations E 805, *op. cit.*, p. 10.
6. See United States Tariff Commission, *Quantitative Restrictions and Tariff Quotas on United States Imports as Provided for or Cited in the Tariff Schedules of the United States* (Washington. US Government Printing Office, 1965) pp. 17–18.
7. See *Basic Instruments and Selected Documents*, 14th Supplement (Geneva: GATT, 1966).
8. For a detailed description of examples of these non-discriminatory systems, see *Deutscher Gebrauchs Zolltarif*, Herausgegeben vom Bundesminister der Finanzen für die Dienststellen der Bundeszollverwaltung, Bonn, 1 January 1970, Part Vc, pp. 9–19.
9. See Raul Prebish, *Towards a New Trade Policy for Development* (New York: United Nations, 1964) p. 70. Also see Michael Rom, 'A Suggestion for a Preferential Scheme in the Developed Countries for Imports of Manufactures and Semi-manufactures from Developing Countries', *Aussenwirtschaft*, 1966.
10. Examples of autonomous tariff quotas in recent years are contained in the list of tariff quotas which have been established, unilaterally, within the European Community. One example – that of the tariff quota on aluminium oxide – was increased autonomously by changes in the German customs tariff from 25,000 tons to 50,000 tons on 30 March 1967. This action was taken within the rules of the Treaty of Rome, Article 15(1). See *Nachrichten für Aussenhandel*, 19 April 1967.
11. Bilaterally agreed tariff quotas are numerous. One example that caused some commotion in the GATT was the bilateral tariff quota concluded by a contracting party and the Soviet Union where, up to the value of $4.25m, various commodities pay only half the price. See *Neue Zürcher Zeitung*, Zürich, 17 July 1970.

12. See League of Nations E 805, *op. cit.*, p. 14.
13. Robert Zinser, *Das GATT und Die Meistbegünstigung* (Baden-Baden and Bonn: August Lutzeyer, 1962) p. 135.
14. See discussion on page 20.
15. Zinser, *op. cit.*, p. 135.
16. Heuser, *op. cit.*, pp. 77–8.
17. League of Nations, E 805, *op. cit.*, p. 9.
18. Heuser, *op. cit.*, p. 77.
19. League of Nations E 805, *op. cit.*, p. 10.
20. See *Basic Instruments and Selected Documents, op. cit.*, pp. 23–31.
21. See *Special Committee on Preferences of UNCTAD*, 4th Session (Geneva: United Nations, 31 March 1970).
22. See *Amtsblatt der Europaischen Gemeinschaften*, 31 July 1969.
23. See M. Häfner, 'Die Politik der Mengenmassigen Einfuhrregulirung', *Weltwirtschaftliches Archiv*, No. 40, 1934, p. 213.
24. Isaiah Frank, *The European Common Market* (London: Stevens, 1961) p. 107, note 14.
25. *Ibid.*, pp. 76–7 and pp. 103–7.
26. See Protocols II, V–VII, IX–XV and XVII of the Treaty of Rome; and list G.
27. Hans Binswanger, 'Zollkontingente in Rahmen eines harmonisierten Zolltarifs', *Aussenwirtschaft*, 1961, p. 163.
28. Jacob Viner, 'Trade Relations between Free Market and Controlled Economies', League of Nations., II A4, 1943, p. 50.
29. M. Van Zeeland, 'Commercial Policy in the Inter-war Period', League of Nations., II A6, 1942, p. 84. See also *Non-tariff Obstacles to Trade* (Paris: International Chamber of Commerce, 28 April 1969) p. 34.
30. Lynn R. Edminster, 'Agriculture's Stake in the British Agreement and the Trade Agreement Program', *International Conciliation*, February 1939, No. 347, pp. 92–3.
31. *Ibid.*, p. 91.
32. Binswanger, *op. cit.*, p. 152.
33. Viner, *op. cit.*, p. 55. As tariff quotas still allowed imports to enter if a higher duty was paid, they were considered to constitute a lesser deviation from the principle of regulation of imports by the free market process, subject only to the impact of ordinary import duties. Gottfried Haberler, 'Quantitative Trade Controls: their Causes and Nature', League of Nations., II A5, 1943, p. 20, states that 'import duties, even high ones, are "comformable" interference which do not destroy the price mechanism on the functioning of which a private enterprise must depend.'
34. Heuser, *op. cit.*, p. 78.
35. Binswanger, *op. cit.*, p. 157.
36. *Ibid.*, p. 158.
37. *Basic Instruments and Selected Documents*, 1st Supplement (Geneva: GATT, 1953) pp. 14–15.
38. *Treaty Establishing the European Economic Community, Rome, 25 March 1957* (London: HM Stationery Office, 1962) pp. 145 and 147.
39. See George De Leener, 'Les Systèmes de Contigentement Douanier', *Bulletin d'Information et de Documentation*, Banque Nationale de Belgique, 10 February 1932, where he gives the example of the British-Spanish Trade Agreement signed in Madrid on 31 October 1922. Under this Agreement Spain granted Britain a tariff quota of 750,000 tons of coal free of duty. Also the Agreement between France and Spain signed on 23 October 1931, which permitted Spain to export 1,880,000 hectolitres of wine at a minimum rate of duty of 84 francs per hectolitre.
40. 'Recommendations of the Economic Committee relating to Commercial Policy', League of Nations., II 15, 1929, p. 9.
41. See *Amtsblatt der Europaishen Gemeinschaften*, 24 September 1969, Rechtsvorschriften L240/6, paras 2–3.
42. De Leener, *op. cit.*, p. 66.

PART I
Place in the GATT

CHAPTER 2

Treatment of Tariff Quotas under the GATT

Before embarking on the detailed examination of the application of tariff quotas in practice with which the later chapters are largely concerned, it is necessary to see how their use can be reconciled with the principles underlying the institutional requirements that govern the GATT, for considerable doubts and conflicting views have been expressed on this point.

On the one hand, there are statements such as that made by John H. Jackson: 'Nothing in Article XI, nor for that matter in Articles XII through XIV, prohibits the use of a "tariff quota", whereby a product may be imported under one tariff rate up to a total amount specified and all amounts over that at a higher rate. But by paragraph 5 of Article XIII, when tariff quotas are used, they must also comply with the provisions of Article XIII.'[1] Similarly, Werner Reichwald[2] has said: 'Tariff quotas do not contravene the rules of GATT as long as they are applied in a non-discriminatory manner.' On the other hand, there is the opposite view, such as that of Seyid Muhammad:[3] 'Whatever may be the purpose of tariff quotas, they involve an evasion of the MFN clause.'

There are also intermediate positions, such as the statement by Robert Zinser:[4] 'A tariff quota is accordingly compatible with the most-favoured-nation clause only if the imports at the original duty are permitted without limitation, and provided that only a surplus of imports at the lower tariff, which would disrupt home production, is discouraged. A tariff quota should therefore facilitate imports even if only within limits.'

These differences of opinion are nothing new, and existed as early as the 1920s and 1930s, when the problem first arose. The League of Nations, according to a resolution of the Eleventh Assembly, requested its Economic Committee to resume the study of the most-favoured-nation clause, devoting its attention to, among other problems, the compatibility of the customs quotas (tariff quotas) with the MFN clause. The Committee produced a report[5] which came to a unanimous conclusion, although this seems to be rather vague and can be interpreted in contradictory ways. The report, submitted to the Council in September 1931 by the *rapporteur* of economic questions and approved by the Council, stated: '. . . The Economic Committee has been able to reach a unanimous opinion on the subject of customs quotas in their relation to the most-favoured-nation clause, a subject which has recently become of particular importance and has given rise to animated discussions. The opinion of the Committee constitutes a compromise between two opposite theories, namely that of the supporters of the *unlimited clause*, who consider that any customs quota is *incompatible with the spirit* of the clause, and the opinion of these who regard such quotas, either equal or proportional, as permissible.'[6]

An examination of the actual treatment given to tariff quotas in the General Agreement on Tariffs and Trade produces a variety of different examples. In the first place, there are tariff quotas which have been bound in the tariff negotiations of the General Agreement, or which have been included in the schedule of concessions. One early example, included in the United States Schedule of Concessions, was the reservation with regard to wool fabrics which the United States made in the multilateral Trade Agreement of 1947 at Geneva. This reservation, which was introduced with regard to a tariff concession granted by the United States to the United Kingdom – and was extended to other countries on the basis of the MFN clause – applies to woollen and worsted fabrics dutiable under paragraphs 1108 and 1109(a) of the Tariff Act of 1930, as modified. A similar agreement was reached with Belgium at Torquay in 1951. Thus, under items 1108 and 1109(a), and the appropriate headings in part I of Schedule XX annexed to the General Agreement on Tariffs and Trade, a note was included which reads: 'The United States reserves the right to increase the *ad valorem* part of the rate applicable to any of the fabrics provided for in item 1108 and 1109(a) of this part to 45 per centum *ad valorem* on any of such fabrics which are entered in any calendar year in excess of an aggregate quantity by weight of 5 per centum of the average annual production of similar fabrics in the United States during the three immediately preceding calendar years.' For the rates of duty up to that quantity, see Table 2.1.[7]

The reservation with regard to the quantity that would be permitted at the agreed rates mentioned above has been known as the 'Geneva wool and worsted fabrics reservation'. It was invoked (as has been discussed earlier) in 1956 and was applied by the United States for four years. The quota was operated in an unallocated form, and is reviewed in more detail in Chapter 5. Examples of more recent origin are the tariff quotas which have been bound in the GATT by the European Community. Thus, in 1969, tariff quotas were bound in the GATT for the tariff headings[8] listed in Table 2.2.

These concessions were included in the schedules of the Community

TABLE 2.1
United States Reservation to 1947 GATT Trade Agreement

Paragraph[a]	Product	Duty
1108	Woven fabrics under 4 oz per sq.yd, wholly or in chief value of wool, regardless of value. If warp is of vegetable fibre	$0.3 per lb., and 25% *ad valorem*.
	Other Note...[b]	$0.375 per lb., and 25% *ad valorem*.
1109(a)	Woven fabrics over 4 oz. per sq.yd wholly or in chief value of wool, regardless of value.	as 1108 Other above.
	Woven green billiard cloths in the piece, 11 to 15 oz per sq.yd., all wool, regardless of value.[c]	$0.375 per lb., and 20% *ad valorem*.

Source: Press release, 26 September 1956, by James C. Hagerty, Press Secretary to the President, and annexed text of the President's Proclamation as well as further Supplementing Proclamation 2761A of 16 December 1947.

[a] Paragraph of the Tariff Act of 1930.
[b] Here was included the note quoted on page 16, paragraph 2.
[c] This concession was added at Torquay in 1951. It shall be subject to the note in item 1108 in Part I of Schedule XX (original).

TABLE 2.2
Tariff Quotas Bound in the GATT by the European Community, 1969

Tariff No.	Product	Tariff Autonomous	Tariff Conv.
01.02 A II b 2	Heifers and cows not for slaughter, mountain race grey, brown, yellow, Simmental and Pinzgau	16% +P[a]	20,000 head at 6%
01.02 A II b 2	Bulls, cows and heifers, not for slaughter, Alpine race, Simmental, Schwyz, Friboug	16% +P	5,000 head at 4%[b]

TABLE 2.2—continued

Tariff No.	Product	Tariff Autonomous	Tariff Conv.
02.01 A II d 2	Frozen beef	20% +P	22,000 tons at 20%
03.01 B I a 2 aa	Herrings, cooled, fresh or frozen[c]	20%	46,000 tons exempt (ref. price) Others: 15%[a]
03.01 B I b	Tunny fresh, cooled or frozen for tinning	25%	30,000 tons exempt (ref. price) Others: 25%[b]
	Cod salted or dried, cleaned and cut	13%	34,000 tons exempt
32.01	Eucalyptus Extrali	9%	8% 250 tons at 4%[a]
48.01	News prints	7%	625,000 tons[b]
54.03	Flax or ramie yarn measuring at least 30,000 meters per kg for the production of thread or cables in the shoe or cable industries (not from waste)	10%	500 tons at 2% others 6.5%[b]
73.02 C	Ferro-silicon	10%	20,000 tons[b]
	Supplementary		11,5000 tons
73.02 E	Ferro-chromium containing in weight 0.1% or less of carbon and from 30% to 90% of chromium	8%	3,000 tons[b]
76.01 A	Unwrought aluminium	10%	9% 130,000 tons at 5%[b]

TABLE 2.2—continued

Tariff No.	Product	Tariff Autonomous	Conv.
77.01 A	Unwrought magnesium	10%	8% within tariff quota consumption not covered by home production exempt

Source: *Liste des contigents tarifaires communautaires par le Conseil pour l'année 1969* (Brussels: European Commission, 1970).
[a] A levy in addition to customs duty.
[b] Final result of the Kennedy Round.
[c] From 16 June 1969 to 14 February 1970.

to the Kennedy Round negotiations,[9] concluded in 1967. Here, too, agreement has been concluded with the principal suppliers and extended as customary to the other countries on the basis of the MFN clause. The quota is an unallocated one.

WAIVERS UNDER THE GATT

The opposite case to the one discussed in the previous paragraph covers those instances in GATT where special waivers had to be granted in order to permit a member country to apply tariff quotas. One of the earliest examples is the waiver granted to Italy for the continued application of special customs treatment to certain products from Libya, some thirty-seven tariff quotas being included in the waiver.[10] Another example is the tariff quotas granted at the same time and needed by Belgium, Luxemburg and the Netherlands in connection with the creation of the European Coal and Steel Community.[11]

A waiver, requested by the United States with regard to the import restrictions which it imposed under Section 22 of the United States Agricultural Adjustment Act, refers among other things to tariff quotas. In the list of commodities were included the following:

Filberts – During the period 1 October 1954–30 September 1955 a fee of 10 cents per pound on imports in excess of £6 million.
Almonds – During the period 1 October 1954–30 September 1955, a fee of 10 cents per pound on imports in excess of £5 million.
Peanut oil – *Ad valorem* fee of 25 per cent on imports in excess of £5 million.[12]

Almonds and peanut oil were not listed items in Schedule XX.

An example of a waiver which was specifically granted for the application of tariff quotas is that granted to Australia by the contracting parties on 28 March 1966.[13]

To complicate the actual state of affairs still further, a specific reference to tariff quotas is included in Article XIII of the General Agreement. Paragraph 5 states that the provisions in that Article which relate to the non-discriminatory application of ordinary quotas apply also to tariff quotas. Since, however, quantitative restrictions are permitted only in exceptional cases, and usually are not compatible with the MFN clause, the question arises whether tariff quotas have to be judged in the same way. In other words, should their application under the Agreement be permitted only in the same exceptional circumstances as permit the application of ordinary quotas?

In order to clarify this question, it is necessary first to distinguish a tariff quota from a tariff or an ordinary quota. In principle, an autonomous increase, or reduction, of a tariff rate is not contrary to the rules of the GATT, if no concession has been granted by a country for a specific item. Just as an increase in duty can reduce imports substantially, or even prohibit them, there can be no objection against the tariff being raised, not on the whole quantity, but only beyond a given quota.[14] As long as the treatment of all countries enjoying the MFN clause is absolutely equal, both within the quota and beyond it, there can be no objection on the part of the member countries.

This is in line with the statement of the Economic Committee[15] of the League of Nations:

> The total advantages assured by the clause are not fixed or immutable. They may be increased if the State that grants the most-favoured-nation treatment concludes new commercial treaties making new or greater concessions in favour of other States or grants fresh privileges or advantages by autonomous act. They may decrease if one of the former commercial agreements becomes null and void, or if one of the privileges granted by autonomous act is withdrawn. For that reason, a State, which in virtue of the clause has had the right to import an unlimited amount of certain goods at a given Customs duty, cannot claim that the clause has been merely violated because the duty in question has been raised later by means of an autonomous provision and it only continues to benefit from the former duty for quantities corresponding to a Customs quota.
>
> But, if a State is not entitled to preserve unchanged the original advantages of the clause, it certainly has the right of insisting that the principle of equality of treatment which is assured by the clause, and which consists in guaranteeing every country equal

conditions where international commercial competition is concerned, should not be departed from.

EQUAL AND EQUITABLE TREATMENT

This is precisely the crux of the problem. Can tariff quotas in principle secure the absolute equality which is required by the MFN treatment? In this connection it is necessary to clarify the distinction between equal treatment and equitable treatment. As has been pointed out by Zinser,[16] countries entitled to the MFN treatment enjoy absolute equality, which means they receive the same concessions as have been granted to another third country. On the other hand, equitable treatment is also a concept of equal treatment. It refers, however, only to a relative concept, which tries to secure non-discrimination. An example of non-discrimination may be the treatment of countries in accordance with the principle of past trade, although under absolute equality of treatment each country would have been free to try to obtain the entire quota for itself.

It is evident, therefore, that a crucial factor in determining whether a tariff quota is compatible with the MFN treatment is the administrative form the tariff quota takes. If the quota is of an unallocated nature, open to free competition from all countries enjoying the MFN clause, then the quota is compatible with the MFN clause. This conclusion is corroborated by the Economic Committee of the League, which states, 'if the quota is established on an aggregate, all countries may share in it according to their competitive strength. The condition of equality guaranteed by the [MFN] clause is not infringed. The aggregate quota may injure the position of all third countries, but it would not constitute a breach of the most-favoured-nation clause.'[17]

Some have argued that the establishment of an unallocated quota adversely affects equality of treatment since competitors cannot gain sales by price competition but only by getting within the quota. If first come first served should be the prevailing rule, this may be a discrimination in favour of neighbouring countries that can ship quickly. It may be unfairly disruptive to established trade patterns and also damage the most efficient producer.[18] This argument seems unacceptable for the simple reason that geographic proximity is one of the comparative advantages which is a factor in competition. Furthermore, to the extent that the tariff quota's time limit is extended, renewed or broken into sub-periods, the disadvantage mentioned above disappears. It seems clear that the examples mentioned in the beginning of this chapter, namely the 'Geneva Reservation' and the quotas bound in the GATT by the European Community, are typical of unallocated quotas compatible with the MFN. It can be assumed that this type of quota can be applied whenever desired.

Unfortunately, past experience with the unallocated tariff quota in commodities which interested a number of exporting countries has not been favourable, and a number of difficulties and problems have arisen. For instance, the 'Geneva Reservation' of the woollens and worsted fabrics tariff quota caused serious difficulties in application, as can be seen from a statement made by the United States Department of State on 9 November 1960.[19] 'The operation of the tariff quota system has disrupted normal marketing practices in the woollen goods trade. United States importers, and clothing manufacturers, and retailers were faced with many difficulties resulting from the need to place orders far in advance of delivery and from the uncertainty over the applicable tariff rates at the time of importation of the fabric.'

Similar difficulties were evidently experienced in the 1930s.[20] At this time attempts were made to introduce prior licensing, and in some cases new trade agreements demanded the allocation into country quotas of the overall quota. This aspect will be dealt with later. More recent experience is apparently more favourable, not only in the European Community, for instance, but also in the case of the Australian Preference Scheme which has been in operation for some years.

Before moving on to the question of country quotas and the allocation of the overall quota, it seems worth while to mention that trade agreements in the 1920s did not refer explicitly to quantitative restrictions and tariff quotas. The most-favoured-nation clause was assumed to refer implicitly to these instruments of commercial policy. With respect to these newer forms of trade control there was substantial disagreement between the parties to trade agreements as to whether or not they came under the MFN clause. Since these were extensively used to defeat the MFN practice, it became highly necessary – according to the United States point of view – to define with considerable precision what was meant with respect to each of these new devices, in order to guarantee MFN treatment.

'One of the really difficult problems, therefore, which had to be faced in the negotiations of trade agreements under the new programme was how to secure equality of treatment for American goods in the face of the growing number of foreign quota restrictions, exchange controls, and government monopolies which were being widely used for discriminatory and other purposes. Upon these the American negotiators made a frontal attack by insisting upon the insertion of carefully devised formulae in the general provisions so as to confine the use of these devices to legitimate and non-discriminatory purposes.'[21]

At an early stage an attempt was made to apply the MFN treatment explicitly to the allocation of quotas – 'Thus the Brazil-United States Agreement of 1935 stated that quotas or quantitative control should be operated in accordance with the most-favoured-nation principle.'[22]

Another specific requirement for unallocated global quotas in trade agreements of the United States was full information about the total amount of the quota, the extent to which it had been filled at any time within the period of its existence, and the amount which had entered, or been authorised, from other supplying countries. This requirement was an attempt to safeguard against possible favouritism in those cases where prior licensing for each shipment within the global quota was required,[23] in order to prevent concentration of shipments in the beginning of the period. According to Hawkins, these specific requirements, which were included in the United States trade agreements, were in the draft of the International Trade Organisation (ITO) charter and from there taken over by the GATT, as will be discussed later.

ALLOCATION OF COUNTRY QUOTAS

Practical difficulties with the unallocated quota induced the United States administration to try to establish country quotas in their trade agreements. Such an attempt, however, required decisions on the criteria for determining the country quotas. As has been said, the mere fact that quotas are being fixed is in itself contrary to the MFN clause, since, instead of having the equal right to compete in a particular market, each country gets a fixed predetermined share of that market, thus upsetting the equal terms of international competition.[24] It was therefore considered preferable to accept the interpretation that the MFN clause should not apply to quantitative restrictions and similar other new devices. For these, the concept of non-discrimination based on equitable treatment, and not equal treatment, seemed to be a more proper principle.[25]

At the same time, it was argued by the League that, if the quotas could have been allocated on the basis of negotiations with all the countries concerned in such a way as to give to all states, whatever was the proportional share of their trade under free competition, and provided all the countries agreed and were satisfied with their quotas, then such a fixing of quotas could be compatible with the MFN clause.[26] In 1959, Western Germany provided a rare example.[27]

In compliance with the requirements of GATT, a non-discriminatory duty-free quota for coal of 5.13m metric tons was established by the Bundestag on 4 November 1959. This was on condition that the High Authority of the European Coal and Steel Community and the German Government should maintain permanent contact with the principal exporting countries, particularly the United States and the United Kingdom. During these negotiations the United Kingdom expressed the view that the German Draft Law on the allocation of imports did not take sufficient account of the traditional pattern of the United Kingdom's exports. On 26 October 1959, the United Kingdom, by adopting a new reference period, succeeded in obtaining an increase of 100,000 tons for its exports in 1959–60, within an allocation schedule acceptable to the other major supplier country.[28]

Another possible way of allocating national quotas is by providing equal quotas to each exporting country. But the League pointed out that equal sized quotas to all interested exporting countries would be an unjust principle of allocation. It would be contrary to the MFN clause since no account would be taken of the relative sizes of individual countries, their state of economic development, agricultural and industrial potential, geographical situation and so on. In other words, natural endowments, competitive advantage, as well as past performance, are completely ignored, while those countries which have a larger share in that particular market are more severely hit and discriminated against.[29]

Therefore, a more just or equitable principle of allocation would be to fix country quotas in accordance with the relative share held by exporting countries in an historic period. The League, however, pointed out one drawback prevalent during the 1920s. This arose when proportional country quotas were fixed after negotiations in bilateral trade agreements with the least interested country in that particular quota, so that a relatively small quota could be established with it. Then, on the basis of the non-discrimination principle, proportional tariff quotas were extended to all countries enjoying MFN treatment. It was argued that in order to secure the interests of the parties most directly concerned, the best solution was to decide that quotas should be fixed 'by agreement with the country which occupies the first rank among the countries exporting the goods in question'.[30]

But even if proportional country quotas are determined by negotiations with the principal supplier, they still are a far cry from MFN treatment. An attempt was made in the United States trade agreements of the 1930s to prevent, as far as possible, the use of country quotas as well as other devices which were contrary to the MFN. Thus trade agreements included specific articles which did not permit, as a general rule, the application of these devices to concessions agreed upon. Naturally this does not apply to customs quotas agreed as concessions in the trade agreements themselves. An attempt was made to limit the use of such devices, including customs quotas, to exceptional cases requiring prior notification.

These tariff quotas were to be applied on the basis of the proportional share in past trade unless otherwise agreed upon. Furthermore, there was an obligation to announce the allocation of the national quotas, and report on the current state of imports with regard to these quotas. An example of such a trade agreement is the agreement between the United States and Finland.[31]

The application of the past-trade principle to the allocation of country quotas has serious drawbacks as it does not take into account any possible changes in the competitive position of member countries, particularly the economic development of newcomers. This problem became particularly acute following World War II, when reference periods were established in respect of trade patterns that existed before the war.

Obviously the further back one goes in selecting a base period, the less representative the allocation becomes, especially as the intervening war years in many instances greatly and perhaps permanently disturbed existing relationships. It was therefore particularly important in formulating post-war agreements to take account of the idea of the United States–Canada Trade Agreement which stated that account should be taken 'in so far as practicable in appropriate cases of any special factors which may have affected or may be affecting the trade in that article.' This idea was embodied in the ITO Charter as drawn up in 1948 and was included in Article 22 of the Charter. It was then taken over from there into GATT; however, in both of these documents attempts have been made to specify more precisely the special factors that should be taken into account.[32] It will, however, be evident that despite all efforts which have gone into devising means of preventing discrimination in the allocation of quotas, the best that can be hoped for is that flagrant discrimination can be prevented.[33]

Attempts have therefore been made in GATT to make use of this second-best alternative only in special circumstances and, in general, to create conditions where only the MFN rule will apply. This is the reason for the general prohibition against the use of quantitative restrictions in GATT (Article XI, paragraph 1). Only in exceptional cases, which are set out in the Agreement, can the application of quantitative restrictions be permitted, and then only on a non-discriminatory basis. But whether, or to what extent, the same approach is true with regard to country tariff quotas is a question that needs further discussion. Article XIII of the GATT, which is the relevant Article of the Agreement dealing with the principle of non-discriminatory application of quantitative restrictions, explicitly states in paragraph 5 that the provisions of *this Article* should apply to any tariff quota instituted, or maintained, by any contracting parties. But if it is obvious that the non-discriminatory application of allocations of country quotas should be maintained, as well as all the other instructions with regard to the treatment to be given in the case of the institution of the tariff quota, it is less certain that the reference to equating tariff quota treatment with ordinary quota treatment also relates to the general prohibition mentioned in Article XI.

ARTICLE XIII OF THE GATT

What, then, are the provisions of Article XIII that have particular relevance for tariff quotas?

Paragraph 1 obliges a country to avoid the imposition of any kind of prohibition or restriction, unless the same prohibition or restriction is applied to all third countries – this is the MFN *clause of absolute equality of treatment*.

Paragraph 2 gives instructions on how import restrictions should be applied so that the result should approach as closely as possible 'the shares which the various contracting parties might be expected to obtain in the absence of such restrictions'. These are the instructions in order of preference:

(*a*) Paragraph 2(a) requires the fixing of an overall quota wherever possible, and the announcement of such a quota by public notice – in accordance with the instructions included in paragraph 3(b).

(*b*) According to paragraph 2(c) there is a requirement not to allocate the overall quota, except in accordance with 2(d); paragraph 2(b) is not applicable to tariff quotas.

(*c*) Paragraph 2(d) states that 'in cases in which a quota is allocated among supplying countries' – *the first preference* is the possibility that the imposing country 'may seek agreement with respect to the allocation of shares in the quota, with all other contracting parties having a substantial interest in supplying the product concerned'. If this method is not reasonably practicable shares should be allocated to 'the contracting parties having a substantial interest in supplying the products . . . based upon the proportions, supplied by such contracting parties during a previous representative period . . . due account being taken of any special factors[34] which may have affected or may be affecting the trade in the product.' Furthermore, no obstacles should be imposed which might prevent each contracting party from fully utilising its share, subject of course to the limitation that importation is being made within the prescribed period of the quota.

Should the administration of the quota require the institution of a licensing procedure, paragraph 3(a) provides that the imposing country should make available upon request all the relevant information concerning the administration of the restrictions, including details of import licences granted over the recent period, as well as their distribution to supplying countries. Paragraph 3(b) requires that public notice of the quota, and any changes, should be given, and detailed instructions for the treatment of supplies which might be *en route*.

Paragraph 3(c) lays down that all other countries with an interest in supplying the product should be promptly notified of the shares currently allocated among supplying countries.

Paragraph 4 refers to the method of selecting the representative period for the purposes of paragraph 2(d) of this Article (and for paragraph 2(c) of Article XI), as well as the appraisal of any special factors. It states that these should be made initially by the imposing country which, however, is required to consult on the need for adjustment of the relative shares if requested to do so by a contracting party with a substantial interest in such a product, or by the contracting parties.

While Article XIII of GATT embraces all the elements discussed earlier and evolved in trade agreement practices, in particular of the United States over an extensive period, and then incorporated in the GATT,[35] it contains nothing that prohibits the use of tariff quotas of any kind, as long as they are applied in accordance with the rules of this particular article. On the other hand, the only explicit reference to tariff quotas in GATT relates to this Article. It is for this reason that Jackson has deduced that there is nothing in the GATT which prohibits the use of tariff quotas, but that, when they are used, they must comply with the provisions of Article XIII.[36]

From a strictly formal point of view, this interpretation may be true. An examination of the general prohibition of the use of quantitative restrictions in Article XI, paragraph 1, indicates that 'no prohibition or restriction other than duties, taxes or other charges, whether made effective through quotas, import or export licences or other measures should be instituted'. Since a tariff quota restricts additional imports by higher *duties*, and not by other means, it may be argued that this is in line with the philosophy of the International Trade Organisation and the GATT, which considers tariff duties the most liberal method of restricting trade.[37] It is the only method acceptable in principle to the GATT, as it permits autonomous decisions by importers and exporters and provides more freedom to adjust to changing conditions at home and abroad.

In the case of ordinary quotas, on the other hand, decisions are made by the bureaucracy, and the quantities determined impose rigid limits on the volume of trade. For these reasons tariff quotas are more liberal than ordinary quotas and may be looked upon less severely. While this argument is true for the quantities imported beyond the quota limits, neither type of quota, within the quota limits, allows absolute equality of treatment, or of the right to compete. Thus, a tariff quota, too, would seem to be a contravention of the MFN clause, although this is only true to the extent that it is allocated into country quotas.

It would, therefore, seem logical to suppose that the treatment of an allocated overall tariff quota into country quotas should be no less objectionable than the allocation of ordinary quotas. In principle, tariff quotas of this kind should be prohibited, and permitted only in those cases where ordinary quotas would be justified, or where exceptional circumstances justify the use of the principle of non-discrimination, instead of the MFN clause. It seems that the position of Seyid Muhammad – that tariff quotas always constitute an evasion of the MFN clause – refers to quotas allocated into country quotas.

WAIVERS UNDER ARTICLE XXV

Mention has been made earlier in this chapter of another way of dealing with tariff quotas within the GATT. This requires the application of a waiver by the contracting parties under Article XXV, paragraph 5. An examination of such waivers in the past indicates that they were applied whenever a particular tariff quota was in contradiction to the formal rules of the Agreement, despite the fact that in the specific circumstances the introduction of such a tariff quota might be desirable, or permissible.[38] For instance, examination of the specific reasons for the application of a waiver in the case of the European Coal and Steel Community (ECSC), show that it was needed, in the first place, for products on which concessions had previously been made in the General Agreement.[39] Once a concession has been given on an unlimited quantity of a particular product any restriction of this concession constitutes a reduction which requires a waiver. No such requirement would be needed if the quantity had been fixed ahead of the concession being given (as was the case with the 'Geneva Reservation' mentioned earlier) or if, on the particular item, no concession had been granted.

In the case of the ECSC, another reason applies. The entire Coal and Steel Community is a preferential arrangement, and one that cannot strictly be considered a full customs union in the sense of Article XXIV of the GATT. Consequently the entire arrangement needed to be exempted by a waiver by the contracting parties. One of the reasons for the waiver, given in the report of the working party, was that the establishment of the Coal and Steel Community seemed worth while and desirable, even though the arrangement was contrary to the specific GATT rules. A waiver was granted because the proposal for the Community seemed to be in line with the General Agreement. Similar considerations seem also to have applied in the case of tariff quotas granted under a waiver to Libya in Italy, as well as in the case of the Australian preferences. In both these cases, discrimination exists in the application of tariff quotas since it does not apply to all contracting parties. In the case of Italy the tariff quota applied to Libya alone. In the case of the preferences for the developing countries, they apply to a substantial group of countries, but still exclude all the developed countries who are members of the GATT.

Since these quotas are applied contrary to the GATT rules, they required a waiver, which was given in view of the overall desirability of such measures from the GATT point of view. In the case of Libya, the waiver was intended to avoid disrupting a situation which existed before the establishment of the Agreement, due to the responsibility given to Italy with respect to the economic development of Libya. In the case of the Australian preferences, it was realised that some measure of encouragement to developing countries was desirable, so that they could develop their industrial exports on a preferential basis. Therefore the GATT approved the arrangement despite its incompatibility with the MFN clause.

TARIFF QUOTA EXCEPTIONS TO THE MFN CLAUSE

There are, however, a number of tariff quotas of a discriminatory nature which have not received a waiver in the GATT. A fourth type of tariff quota may not be contrary to the GATT despite its discriminatory nature, namely the tariff quota which relates to an exception to the MFN clause in the Agreement. The first of these exceptions to the MFN clause covers border trade. For it seems logical to permit border trade and 'finishing trade' between adjacent territories on a limited basis if, in principle, it is permitted in unlimited quantities.[40] Other exceptions relate to customs unions and free trade areas, as well as the interim agreement towards the creation of such a regional arrangement. In this particular case, two aspects need to be distinguished.

First are those tariff quotas which are created during the interim period of transition between the member parties to the regional arrangement. There seems to be no possible objection to these. Just as there can be a gradual elimination of internal barriers over a period of years, so there can be no argument against the expansion of a quota which from the start reduces the tariff substantially, or even to zero. The aim is to increase this quota gradually over the transition period until trade flows quite freely within the customs union. Many of the examples of tariff quotas, which have been introduced in the association agreements of the European Community, fall under this heading. For instance, in Protocol 15 of the Agreement of Association of Greece with the Community,[41] there is an arrangement for tariff quotas for citrus fruits, grapes and peaches to be increased gradually over the transition period. Similarly, tariff quotas for various products, including some textiles, are also included in the Turkish Association Agreement.[42] Even the more limited Association Agreement of Nigeria with the Community contains a number of tariff quotas which are annexed to Protocol 1 to that agreement.[43]

While the above seems logical, it must be emphasised that to the best knowledge of the author, no discussions have taken place in GATT with regard to the whole subject of national tariff quotas within a customs union, or an interim agreement towards its establishment. This applies equally to the second kind of tariff quota within this category: a national tariff quota established in the interim period by a member country of the regional arrangement in relation to a third country, or countries, outside the regional arrangement. Here, however, the question cannot be answered in such a clear-cut manner, for discrimination may be involved, not between member countries and third countries, but between different third countries.

The particular tariff quota established with regard to third countries could be an overall unallocated quota, permitted by the customs union to a member country, in order to facilitate the harmonisation of an external tariff while avoiding internal difficulties in that particular country during the transition period. Such a case creates no problem[44] from the point of view of the Agreement. Another possibility is the case where the third country's quota relates to border trade. This should create no problem either.

More serious is the case when a specific tariff quota, permitted by the customs union to a member country, is allocated to a specific country or group of countries, sometimes for specific commodities and sometimes even for a given volume of trade. An example of such a case is the permission granted in Article 21 of the Association Agreement of the Community with Greece, which permits Greece to establish tariff quotas with countries with which it maintains trade agreements. The Greek Government availed itself of the opportunity provided by this clause and concluded a tariff-quota agreement with the Soviet Union in 1970. As was to be expected, the Greek position was based, first, on Article 21 of the Association Agreement, which had already been discussed by the contracting parties; and second, on the importance of maintaining established bilateral trade links, which were unfavourably affected by the progressive tariff disarmament of Greece *vis-à-vis* the Community.

Furthermore, it was pointed out that these tariff quotas were insignificant in terms of total Greek trade, amounting to a small fraction of 1 per cent. Nevertheless, the Council received a formal request from the Greek Government for a waiver under Article XXV(5) and set up a working party. This strongly criticised the Greek action, both on principle and as a precedent. Several members did not share the Greek view that no trade diversion had, or would, occur and most members were not convinced that the exceptional circumstances required under Article XXV(5) existed. On 2 December 1970, the GATT Council of Representatives refused to grant the waiver.[45]

This kind of tariff quota clearly discriminates against third countries with which the member country of a regional community has MFN obligations. On the other hand, the introduction of the harmonised external tariff may injure precisely those trade relations with the third country which cannot be solved by the customary procedure provided for in the agreement. Such disruption of trade relations may be to the serious detriment of both countries, or one of them, while having no substantial effect on third parties. Furthermore, as will be argued in the next chapter, the basic philosophy of the GATT in fact justifies a reform of Article XXIV, with regard to the exception of customs unions and free trade areas from the MFN clause, if the intention is to avoid the trade diversion effect of the creation of a customs union.

CONCLUSIONS

Tariff quotas in the GATT have received little attention. There is no explicit and clear set of rules. Rules, therefore, have to be deduced from the general principles of the GATT, and sporadic references in the Agreement as well as from concrete precedents of treatment given to tariff quotas in the GATT. An examination of these sources shows that the following questions become relevant when determining treatment:

(a) Is the tariff quota related to a product for which a concession has been given?
(b) Is the tariff quota unallocated or allocated?
(c) If allocated, is it allocated in a discriminatory manner?
(d) If it is discriminatory, does it relate to exceptions from the MFN clause?

From the answers to the above questions will follow the treatment applied by the GATT.

A tariff quota will be compatible with the MFN principle if it relates to a product for which no concession has been given, or the quantity of which has been limited by agreement with the other contracting parties at the time of granting of the concession, provided that the tariff quota itself is an unallocated one, open to competition from all. A tariff quota might also be compatible with the MFN clause if agreement can be reached with all contracting parties as to their individual shares, using as a basis the expected shares under competitive conditions. Furthermore, tariff quotas based on the exceptions from the MFN clause permitted by GATT may also be considered compatible with the MFN treatment. If, however, quotas are allocated into national quotas they are permitted only in exceptional cases[46] (except in the case of agreement mentioned above). Treatment is exactly the same as for quantitative restrictions, with the principle of non-discrimination in Article XIII applying. If neither of the above takes place a waiver is needed in order to use a tariff quota.

NOTES AND REFERENCES

1. John H. Jackson, *World Trade and the Law of GATT* (New York: Bobbs-Merril, 1969) p. 321.
2. Werner Reichwald, *Die Deutschen Zollvorschriften* (Köln: B.F.A., 1966), Sonderveröfientlichung des Zoll dienstes, p. 19.
3. V. A. Seyid Muhammad, *The Legal Framework of World Trade* (London: Stevens, 1958) p. 202.
4. Robert Zinser, *op. cit.*, p. 135.
5. League of Nations E805, *op. cit.*, pp. 9–14. Summarised in 'Commercial Policy in the Post-war Period', *op. cit.*, pp. 67–104.
6. League of Nations E805, *op. cit.*, p. 23.
7. Press release by James C. Hagerty, Press Secretary to the President, and the annexed text of the President's Proclamation as well as the supplementing Proclamation 2761A of 16 December 1947.
8. Source: 'Liste des contingents tarifaires communautaires par le conseil pour l'année 1969', *Direction générale des Affaires Industrielles*, III/D/3, Paris, 1970, pp. 3–5.
9. See *Les perspectives après le Kennedy Round* (Geneva: Bureau de Presse et d'Information de Genève, May 1967).
10. *Basic Instruments and Selected Documents*, 1st Supplement, *op. cit.*, pp. 14–17.
11. *Ibid.*, p. 20.
12. *Basic Instruments and Selected Documents*, 3rd Supplement (Geneva: GATT, 1955) p. 146.
13. *Basic Instruments and Selected Documents*, 14th Supplement *op. cit.*, pp. 23–31.
14. The Economic Committee of the League of Nations presented an argument to the effect that the existence of a quota can permit a higher customs duty than would be the case otherwise. They maintained that without the existence of the quota the objections of domestic importers would create a stronger lobby against the raising of the tariff. The same Committee put forward the counter-argument that, without the tariff quotas, tariffs would have been applied to the whole quantities of the product. Furthermore, liberalisation of imports, even on a limited scale, would very often not have been possible. See League of Nations, E805, *op. cit.*, p. 13.
15. *Ibid.*, p. 12.
16. Zinser, *op. cit.*, p. 54.
17. League of Nations, E805, *op. cit.*, p. 11.
18. Jackson, *op. cit.*, p. 323.
19. Press statement, No. 636.
20. Hawkins, *op. cit.*, p. 169.
21. Francis Bowes Sayre, *The Way Forward – The American Trade Agreements Program* (New York: Macmillan, 1939) pp. 121–2.
22. Seyid Muhammad, *op. cit.,* p. 150.
23. Hawkins, *op. cit.*, pp. 169–70.
24. League of Nations E805, *op. cit.*, p. 10.
25. Seyid Muhammad, *op. cit.,* pp. 49–51; and Zinser, *op. cit.*, p. 59.
26. League of Nations E805, *op. cit.*
27. Seyid Muhammad, *op. cit.*, p. 20, points out that, even in recent times, the possibility of accepting, by multilateral negotiations, an agreed allocation of quotas did not exist. No agreement has been sought among supplying countries, primarily since Article XIV, which permits discriminatory application of quotas in certain circumstances, was used extensively during the early post-war period.
28. *Eighth General Report* (Luxemburg: High Authority of the European Coal and Steel Community, 1960) pp. 51–2 and 60.
29. League of Nations E805, *op. cit.*, p. 13.
30. *Ibid.*, pp. 13–14.

31. Sayre, *op. cit.*, pp. 218–20; in particular Articles VII and VIII.
32. Seyid Muhammad, *op. cit.* See note 27 above.
33. Hawkins, *op. cit.*, p. 163. Also Wilcox, *op. cit.*, p. 81.
34. Where Addenda Annex XI mentioned in Addenda Annex XIII reads as follows: 'the term "special factors" includes changes in relative productive efficiency as between domestic and foreign producers or as between different foreign producers but not changes artificially brought about by means not permitted by the Agreement'.
35. William Adams Brown, *The United States and the Restoration of World Trade* (Washington: Brookings Institution, 1950) pp. 21–2.
36. Jackson, *op. cit.*, p. 131.
37. Clair Wilcox, *A Charter for World Trade* (New York: Macmillan, 1949) p. 81.
38. *Basic Instruments and Selected Documents*, 1st Supplement, *op. cit.*, pp. 14–15.
39. *Ibid.*, pp. 20–1 and 88.
40. See the Agreement between Switzerland and the European Community.
41. 'Abkommen zur Gründung einer Assoziation zwischen der Europaischen Wirtschaftsgemeinschaft und Griechenland', *op. cit.*, pp. 121–2.
42. Issued in Bonn, 21 May 1964, *Bundergesetzblatt* Vol. II., 1964, Protocol 1 (2–8), pp. 532–8.
43. See Agreement establishing an Association between the European Community and the Republic of Nigeria, Protocol 1, *The European Year Book* (The Hague: Martin Nijhoff, 1969) Vol. XIV, 1966, p. 547, which contains tariff quotas established for cocoa beans, ground nuts, oils, palm oil and plywood black boards.
44. The same is also true with regard to unallocated Community tariff quotas. Examples of such Community quotas are given above. Examples of the national quotas are those granted by the Community during the transition period; for examples see Protocols annexed to list G.
45. *GATT* L/3384, L/3387, L/3406 (Spec. (70) 104), and L/3447.
46. Zinser, *op. cit.*, p. 54. There he states that, for those exceptional cases in which the application of ordinary quotas and tariff quotas is possible, the GATT provides the principle of non-discrimination (Article XIII), despite the formal interpretation to the contrary. It is in line with the spirit of the Agreement to permit these tariff quotas.

CHAPTER 3

Customs Unions and Third Countries: the Tariff Quota Solution

When customs unions are created third countries suffer from trade-diverting effects. The justification under the GATT for permitting this customs-union and free-trade-area exception from the MFN clause, embodied in Article XXIV appears to warrant further discussion.

This is so, particularly in the light of the developments in the sphere of regional integration over recent years which have threatened the freer world trading system[1] established since World War II, rendering unconditional most-favoured-nation treatment and non-discrimination devoid of any real meaning. Third countries which do not belong to such regional groups find it more difficult to develop or even maintain their exports.

That this is not in accord with the spirit of the Agreement, the intention of the legislator or the real interest of the contracting parties in the long run seems beyond doubt.

PROBLEMS OF INTERPRETATION

Article XXIV, paragraphs 4 and 5 of the Agreement, provide *inter alia* as follows:

> 4. The contracting parties recognise the desirability of increasing freedom of trade by the development through voluntary agreements of closer integration between the economies of countries parties to such agreements. They also recognise that the *purpose of a customs union or a free-trade area should be to facilitate trade between the parties (to such agreements) and not to raise barriers in the trade of other contracting parties with such parties.*
>
> 5. Accordingly, the provisions of this Agreement shall not prevent as between the territories of contracting parties, the formation of a customs union or of a free-trade area or the

adoption of an interim agreement necessary for the formation of a customs union or of a free trade area; provided that:

(a) with respect to a customs union, or an interim agreement leading to the formation of a customs union, the duties and other regulations of commerce imposed on the institution of any such union or interim agreement in respect of trade with contracting parties not parties to such union or agreement shall not on the whole be higher or more restrictive than the general incidence of the duties and regulations of commerce applicable to the constituent territories prior to the formation of such union or the adoption of such interim agreement, as the case may be.

Application and interpretation of the Article in general, and the above-mentioned paragraphs in particular, have raised a number of serious problems and controversies[2] particularly in the case of the European Community. Thus, during the debate in the subcommittee examining the Community's plan in accordance with the GATT's requirements, the relative importance of paragraph 4 was a point at issue,[3] and is of particular relevance here. Since paragraphs 5–9 of Article XXIV specifically prescribe the conditions which have to be complied with, the question arose as to what would happen if contracting parties desiring to form a customs union comply with the requirements of these paragraphs, and yet the result is in fact the raising of barriers to the trade of other contracting parties.

Community representatives argued that in such cases the customs union 'would automatically and necessarily satisfy the requirements of paragraph 4, since paragraphs 5–9 merely spell out the implications of paragraph 4'. The majority of the subcommittee was not prepared to accept this interpretation. They considered that paragraph 4 established the basic principle which a customs union should apply to be consistent with the objectives of the GATT. Some members even went so far[4] as to argue that the contracting parties would have to verify whether the application of paragraphs 5–9 was *consistent* with the aims of a customs union as defined in paragraph 4, and to adjust them accordingly.

The subcommittee did not reach any conclusions in its debate on this and other points, and decided to leave open the legal aspects, first trying to find solutions for the substantive problems. This approach is consistent with the way in which the GATT operates generally, as has been pointed out by G. Jaenicke:[5]

> The GATT is not the appropriate body for this, and it has tried as far as possible to avoid playing the role of judge between the conflicting legal standpoints of its contracting parties. It has regarded its main task as being much more the bringing about of an agreement between the contracting parties by the preservation

or re-creation of the equilibrium in the sphere of foreign trade and the world economy, because the participation of States in the GATT is based, as has already been mentioned, less on the legal obligations of the Agreement, which can always be resolved, but rather more on the all-round interest in the foreign trade economic advantages arising from the Agreement. Therefore, the preservation of this equilibrium has special significance for the maintenance of the GATT. [Translated from the German.]

If this approach is accepted, then it would seem that the last-mentioned interpretation of the relation between paragraphs 4 and 5–9 is justified.[6] It is not the letter of the Agreement but rather its spirit and purpose which should be taken into account.

This can be illustrated by the case of a contracting party which is a small country – not a main supplier – and which has not received any prior concessions requiring compensation. If the imposition of the common external tariff of the Common Market raises the level of duties on its products, the Agreement, and in particular paragraphs 5–9 of Article XXIV, do not provide any effective protection within the existing framework. The aggrieved country cannot claim compensation within the scope of paragraph 6. It cannot negotiate concessions nor ask for compensation in respect of its products by reason of it being a main supplier, nor is it interested in the products which are the subject of negotiations with other countries. That a way should be found to give at least adequate automatic compensation in such cases within the framework of the GATT is obviously desirable.[7] Moreover, the above discussion rests on a narrow interpretation of the phrase 'not to raise barriers to trade', meaning thereby not to raise the level of customs duties higher than it was before the formation of the customs union. The trade of third countries, however, may also be hindered merely by the widening gap of preference and discrimination. The question therefore arises whether this increase in preference cannot be considered and interpreted as 'raising barriers to trade'. Naturally, such interpretation immediately brings to the fore the purpose and meaning of the customs union exception clause since at first glance, the whole object of such a clause is to permit the creation of preference and discrimination.

The first explanation of the exception is simply that a tradition existed from earlier times; and that legal[8] recognition was given to this custom by including the exception in an international document ensuring that a customs union should be a genuine one and not serve as a means for evading a prohibition against preference.[9] This was achieved by the more severe conditions stipulated in the document.

Moreover, historically, customs unions have often related to the unification of small states, or to the attachment of small regions to larger states.[10] Most plans for large customs unions did not materialise because of the political and economic difficulties involved. The effect of an exception discriminating against non-members of the customs union therefore did not appear to be so dangerous as to undermine the principle of MFN. Moreover, it could be expected that 'trade in larger part would persist if the duties on imports from third countries were also abolished because they were adjoining territories, and therefore such customs union could be considered a step towards freer trade'.[11]

Secondly, in the course of the discussions on the Havana Charter, and especially at the time of the deliberations in Geneva[12] the question of European integration was already being considered, and it was found desirable to provide an exception in the case of customs unions in order to facilitate the creation of free trade, at least on a regional basis, during a period when universal free trade was regarded as unrealisable.

Thirdly, generally speaking, the theoretical analysis on which the exception clause was based was somewhat inadequate. The argument proceeded along the lines that customs unions are related to the formation of a larger free-trade area within a unified customs structure, and therefore tend to promote international trade. The theoretical discussion is of some importance and needs to be dealt with in detail.

CUSTOMS UNIONS IN ECONOMIC THEORY

Theoretical discussion of customs unions principally centres on the problem of whether it expands or contracts free trade from a world point of view. That there exists an identity between universal free trade and the maximisation of world welfare is assumed.[13]

It is noteworthy that the earliest customs union theory was largely embodied in oral tradition for it hardly seemed worth while to state it explicitly,[14] probably because of the unimportance of the customs union in reality. Few economists dealt with the economics of customs unions in any detail, and to a large extent it is necessary to resort to inference from the implications of brief *dicta*, and to draw conclusions from the few sentences which relate to the subject.[15]

The main argument prevailing among free traders who look favourably upon the formation of customs unions can be summarised in the words of Gottfried Haberler, who says that 'this partial reduction of tariffs is to be judged in principle in the same way as a general reduction, namely, as a means of extending the international division of labour and increasing the social product'. A partial reduction is better than none at all (although of course a general reduction would be better still from an economic standpoint). It thus follows that customs unions should be accepted and welcomed wholeheartedly from an economic point of view based on the principles of free trade.[16]

Jacob Viner disputed this and stressed that a partial reduction, that is to say, with regard to certain countries only, can at least in certain cases show a definitely protectionist trend, if inefficient production in both countries is of a complementary nature.

Thus, an inefficient industry in one country may extend its activities to other members of the union under the protection of the common external tariff. Viner therefore distinguished between two effects which operate in a customs union. One, stressed by the free trader, is the trade-creating effect, and relates to the shift in the locus of production from a high-cost to a low-cost production point. This is a change in accord with the principles of free trade, which lay down that movement in the direction of international specialisation in production in accordance with comparative costs is desirable from an economic point of view, even if universal free trade would divert production to sources with still lower cost.[17] The second effect is the trade-diverting effect, and is contrary to the principles of free trade. It refers to a shift from a cheaper source of production outside the area to a more expensive locus inside the area. After the formation of the customs union it becomes worth while to import a product duty-free from another member of the union in spite of its higher cost of production there, than in third countries which previously exported, but on whose products duty is still levied.

A customs union is a step in the direction of freer trade, or in the direction of protectionism, depending upon which of the two above-mentioned effects is predominant. Jacob Viner stressed the fact that it is difficult to determine which effect will predominate, because, in the absence of actual or even possible measurement, the matter involves personal judgement and estimation.[18]

His ideas were a turning-point in theoretical thought on the subject, and a number of economists critically examined and developed them. James Meade[19] emphasised, first of all, the difficulty − not dealt with by Viner − of weighing elements of gain against elements of loss. Such a method is necessary since these effects exist simultaneously, but the solution which first comes to mind, that of comparing the total diversion expressed in money terms with the total trade created expressed in money terms, does not provide an answer. In making a comparison, account must also be taken of the effect of the differing costs of manufacturing the same products in various countries. Thus, for instance, the gain from trade creation may be very substantial, even if the trade expressed in money terms is small. The gain can be derived from the substantial reduction in the cost of production of the same commodity. However, this answer is only a partial one, because it is most appropriate for the specific case where the quantity demanded is completely inelastic and the costs of production are constant.

Indeed, this presumption is unrealistic, because both quantity demanded and supplied change with price. Assuming for a moment that costs of production are fixed per unit, then, with the cheapening of the product as a result of the abolition of the duty in a member-country, the quantity demanded will increase. That is to say, in addition to the original quantity diverted from outside to the customs union, consumers will buy an additional quantity of the product. This addition is not a diversion from another place where it was bought previously at a known price, but is a net addition to both consumers and producers. In order to determine if there is a gain, the worth or value to the consumer has to be compared with the cost of production. Not only does the comparison between the cost of production of commodities manufactured in different geographical areas have to be considered, which is relatively easy, but also account has to be taken of the utility, satisfaction, pleasure, happiness or well-being of the person inside the customs union, with more of one thing and less of other things to consume;[20] and this is a much more difficult assessment.

Meade makes use of the old-fashioned utilitarian calculus which is almost, if not quite, of the cardinal instead of the ordinal variety.[21] Starting with a more realistic model of the world he tries to measure and weigh quantitatively the marginal gains and losses of welfare which result from the formations of a customs union.

Assuming for a moment that the economies within the various countries are perfectly competitive,[22] that no divergence exists between social and private marginal costs, and that income is distributed between countries in such a manner that the marginal value of money is equal for all income-earners in all countries, then if the countries are protected by import duties a divergence will exist between the marginal value of the product to the buyer in the importing country and to the seller in the exporting country, which, abstracting from transportion costs, approximates the customs duty.[23] This can best be indicated by an example.[24]

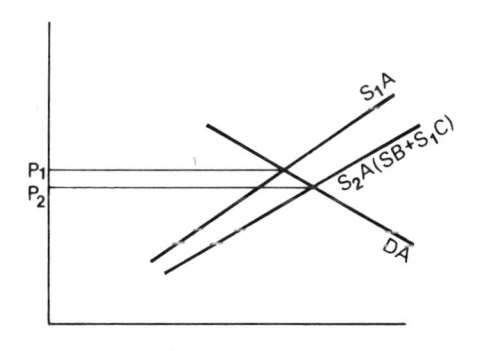

FIGURE 3.1

Country A, represented in Figure 3.1, which does not produce a particular commodity itself, imports it from countries B and C, shown in Figures 3.2 and 3.3, while imposing an *ad valorem* duty on it. *SB* and *SC* represent the export supply curve of countries B and C (assuming increasing costs), and S_1B and S_1C represent the supply curves of the importing country A, taking account of the tariff; S_1A represents the total supply curve of B and C in A, taking account of the tariff, while DA represents the demand for the product in A.

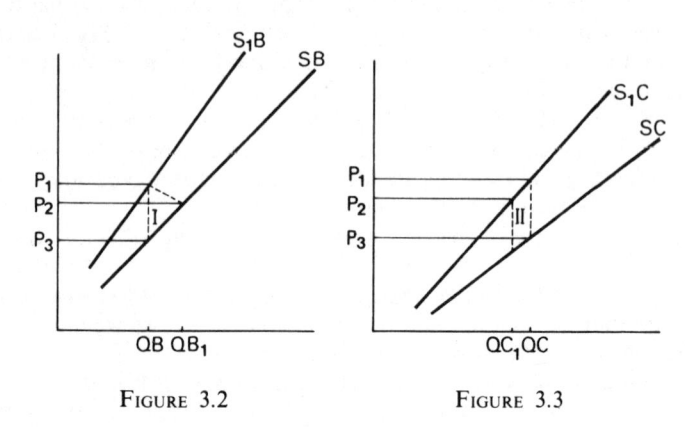

FIGURE 3.2

FIGURE 3.3

The price which equilibrates demand and supply in A equals P_1, at which quantity QB will be bought from B, and a larger quantity QC will be bought from C, C being the more efficient producer. While the producers in B and C sell their products at price P_3, the consumers are paying price P_1; in other words, assuming (1) that price represents marginal value, and (2) the equal marginal utility of money, the producer is selling something, the marginal value of which is worth less to him than to the consumer, and the transfer of an additional unit from seller to buyer would increase total welfare by the amount P_3P_1;[25] in the same way, total welfare will decrease by P_3P_1 if the export is reduced by one unit.

When a customs union is formed between A and B, the supply curve in A is shifted to the right S_2A, since the total supply consists of $SB+S_1C$; as a result, the new equilibrium price, which is lower, is established at P_2, at which the larger quantity QB_1 is being bought from B, while a smaller quantity QC_1 is being bought from C. The triangle I measures the gain in welfare, the area II measures the loss.

This gain and loss in welfare can be computed for each individual product. First, the total gain has to be added up, and then the total loss separately. The two are then compared in order to find out whether the formation of the customs union has brought about an expansion or a reduction in free trade and welfare. Different to the method of computation used by Professor Meade[26] is that used by Professor Scitovsky,[27] whose method takes account of the effect of the increased supply (resulting from the abolition of the duty) on the marginal value of the commodity for the consumer on the one hand, and on the cost of production on the other hand. Assuming that the gap between the marginal value of the commodity to the producer and its marginal value to the consumer is decreasing in a linear manner (see triangle I in the graph), then the gain from the formation of a customs union for one member-country from all products will be approximately equal to: $\frac{1}{2} \Sigma$ *tivi*, where *t* represents the *ad valorem* duty which has been abolished; *v* represents the change in the value of imports; *i* represents the product, and the summation Σ represents the total of the products.

In a similar manner the gain resulting from the trade between all members of the customs union can be obtained by adding together the gains of each individual member. This total will be approximately[28] equal to: $\frac{1}{2} \Sigma \Sigma$ *tivi*.

In order to compare the gain with the loss from the formation of the customs union, the loss has also to be calculated. A loss of benefit, a result of reduced trade between members and non-members of the union, can be measured approximately in a similar manner. Accordingly, the inclusive loss from the reduced rate between members and non-members will be equal to, or less than, $\Sigma (\Sigma$ *tidi* $+ \Sigma$ *tede*), where *ti* are the duties imposed by members upon the import of non-members; *te* are the duties imposed upon the import of members in third countries; *di* and *de* are the respective changes in the import of the countries of the union and the export of such countries to countries outside the union, and the summation Σ relates to all members and all products.

The comparison and weighing of the two effects will give the net gain or loss attributable to the formation of the union[29] according to Scitovsky, who emphasises the differences in the points of view of the world as a whole, and the customs union. He shows that the gains from the diversion of trade into the union belong entirely to the union, while the losses from the diversion are shared between the union and the outside world. It is, therefore, probable that from the union's point of view the gains will outweigh the losses, due to: (*a*) the expansion of trade inside the customs union covering a greater number of commodities than those affected by the reduction in trade with the outside world; (*b*) an increase in volume due to the reduction in price to the consumer as a result of the elimination of the internal tariff, even as regards those commodities in which trade has been diverted into the union.

Furthermore, account has to be taken of the worsening of the terms of trade, which is the result of the formation of the customs union and which brings about a redistribution of the reduced part of the specialisation still existing between the union and the outside world. This redistribution can be assumed to be usually in favour of the union, because on the one hand producers inside the union find less interest in exporting to the outside world and their supply for export will be reduced, which will lead to a rise in price. On the other hand, an outside country may be dependent for its essential imports on the union, and also may have no alternative markets for its exports to the union. It will thus be forced to offer its products at a reduced price, or will be compelled to balance its deficit, which has been created by imports exceeding exports, by a possible devaluation of its currency. The greater the dependence of third countries on the union, the stronger will be the bargaining power of the union during tariff negotiations. For all these reasons it is very possible that a customs union may be beneficial to its members although from a world point of view[30] it may mean a loss. It is argued by Professor Scitovsky that in order for there to be no loss from a world point of view, the newly-created trade in the customs union must compensate not only the loss of the union, but also the loss of the world.

But this interpretation of an increase in world trade, which is based on the compensation of the outside world's loss through the union's gain, is not in accord with the point of view of the GATT. Not only is it contrary to the point of view of the GATT that the outside world as one unit should lose, but it is also contrary to its point of view that any individual country outside the union should be injured (at least, seriously, and without its consent). Membership in the GATT is based on the interests and benefits derived from the organisation, and an increase in world trade at the expense of third parties is contrary to these interests.[31] It should be noted, however, that this comparison of the gain and loss is based on a static analysis.[32] If the rate of economic growth of members accelerates as a result of a customs union, this will probably benefit third countries through an increase in demand for their products.[33]

This analysis raises two questions:

> (a) Is the proposed theoretical solution of weighing gains and losses satisfactory? Can it provide answers at least for the static case in the short run?
>
> (b) Can contentions based on more rapid economic growth justify the formation of the customs union?

With regard to the first question, it can be said that the proposed solution is dubious for several reasons:

> (*a*) Even accepting all the basic assumptions of static general equilibrium analysis, and also the cardinal approach to welfare analysis, the duty cannot constitute a good yardstick of gains or losses, for the reasons already stated (see pages 38–39 above).
>
> (*b*) Moreover, a much more serious deficiency, the changes in the quantities of trade and their value, which arise directly and indirectly in the whole world as a result of the abolition of the duty between the members of the customs union, are not known. Therefore the effects cannot be calculated, even if it were possible

to use the duty as an approximate yardstick of the marginal gain or loss. With present knowledge, no model of 'total equilibrium' can be built that would have the degree of detail necessary for any useful understanding of the problem under discussion.[34]

(c) Thirdly, the basic assumption that the marginal value of money is equal for all income-earners in all countries is questionable. To say that an additional income of one dollar should have the same weight in the calculations, whoever receives it and to whatever country it goes, cannot be justified, for it presupposes an ideal distribution of income between countries. The dollar income lost in a third country may be more important to that country than the gain from the additional dollar of income accruing to the customs union.

(d) The cardinal approach to welfare theory is disputed, and many economists are unwilling to accept this method of analysis as sound.[35]

(e) Furthermore, the model is built on the assumption that technological know-how and the taste of consumers are given, and that the changes are marginal ones capable of being measured. This has been disputed by Richard Lipsey,[36] but since one of the tasks designated for a customs union is to lead to a change in technological knowhow, the introduction of new functions of production, and a change in the taste of consumers by standardisation and harmonisation of consumption habits with those in other countries, the changes will most certainly not be marginal. It seems likely that there would be very marked shifts in the supply and demand curves, so that – as has been indicated by Lipsey – it would not be possible to measure welfare gains and losses.

These contentions do not exhaust the subject, but they are sufficient to show that the suggested solution is not adequate for measuring the results even in the short run.

With regard to the second question, in the long run, there is no theoretical guarantee that the expansion in output and income in the union will lead to a substantial increase in demand from, and gain to, a specific third country or group of third countries, and not to the opposite result. But really the answer has been given above. If there is no possibility of measuring gain and loss in the short run, how can one establish that in the long run the gain will exceed the loss?

The two questions therefore have to be answered in the negative. The problem of how to determine whether a customs union leads to an expansion of world trade and to an increase in world welfare remains unsolved.

PROPOSED SOLUTION

A solution exists which does not require measurement and comparison of effects. But, before considering it, recall Meade's criticism of Viner's procedure, which does not take into account the added imports of a product, resulting from the reduced product price after abolition of the duty on partner products.[37]

In fact, it can be contended that Viner regards this addition as a creation of trade, and refers to trade diversion only with regard to the quantity which was imported originally from country C. He does not disqualify production in a dearer source where the trend is towards liberalisation, even if universal free trade would have diverted production to still cheaper sources, and there is no doubt that the addition is a trend towards the liberalisation of trade: it is new trade, additional to that already existing.

The distinction is important because it defines as a diversion from a cheaper source to a dearer source only that part of the existing trade adversely affected by the formation of the union. The question can be asked whether the trade-diversion effect cannot be isolated from the trade-creation effect. The trade-diversion effect arises only from the new artificial protection of trade which already existed in the past. The creation of trade, on the other hand, is the new addition which results from:

(a) the cheapening of the product to the consumer arising from the elimination of the duty;

(b) the transfer of production from a dearer source to a cheaper source inside the union (specialisation);

(c) the increase in demand as a result of the growth of output and income consequent upon the competition and increase in productivity.

It should be obvious that the theory of customs union which is in accord with the philosophy of free trade should secure the existence of the creation effect without the existence of the diversion effect, and this could be achieved if, by virtue of the MFN principle, third countries could benefit from the same treatment as members of the customs union within the limits of their existing trade with the customs union.

Thus non-discrimination between members and non-members could be ensured within the framework of a comprehensive quota fixed on the basis of the present trade position between the customs union and each one of the third countries.[38] The central idea behind the existence of this comprehensive quota, and the granting of non-discriminatory treatment identical to that extended to the members of the customs union within the limits of existing trade, is that it prevents any diversion of trade in the sense defined above; that is to say, the shift of trade from a cheap source to a dear source as a consequence of new artificial restrictions.

On the other hand, the common external tariff is placed on new trade. Members of the union therefore reap (and rightly so) most of the advantages arising from the formation of a union, since the trade-creation effect (as well as the trade resulting from more efficient manufacture of a product previously imported from outside the union) will accrue to it.

The results of such a solution will be:

(*a*) That inside the union inefficient industries will develop to a much smaller extent and only in so far, as a result of a rise in the real income, as demand exceeds the existing supply provided by third countries within the quota.

(*b*) There will be almost no injury to the exports of third countries and therefore little change in the terms of trade. Such change is liable to lead to unjustified redistribution in income between countries

(*c*) Since only existing imports into the union are involved, it cannot be contended that this trade constitutes a danger to industry inside the union.

(*d*) All the advantages which theoreticians attribute to the formation of a customs union, and for which they justify its existence, remain as they were; that is to say, more efficient division of labour, competition and increase in productivity, cheapening of the products, and a rise in income.

From a theoretical point of view the beauty of this solution is that there will be no diversion. Hence, the need for measuring and comparing the advantages of the union with its disadvantages is removed. It has to be presumed that the existing trade with third countries will continue as in the past,[39] and there will be an increase in total world trade. By definition, this means an increase in world welfare, if the basic assumption is accepted that a situation in which country A has more, and country B no less than previously constitutes an improvement.[40] Even those economists who deny the possibility of measuring and comparing the gain, benefits, happiness, and so on, would have to agree that by the suggested solution the existence of a customs union can be justified as contributing to an increase in world welfare.[41]

This solution is in accord with the spirit of the GATT. It returns, by adjusting the exception through a broader interpretation of the phrase 'raising the barriers to trade', to the GATT's declared purpose and basic principle of the expansion of world trade without injuring third countries. Nevertheless, it is likely to meet with strong opposition on the part of interests likely to benefit from trade diversion. Its use could therefore be limited at least to cases of serious injury,[42] and where the provisions of Article XXIV of the GATT do not facilitate a solution.

It is necessary for the above purpose to formulate criteria which will prove that injury is serious.[43] Where a country conforms to them, it should be entitled automatically to enjoy non-discriminatory treatment as stated above.

NOTES AND REFERENCES

1. Those interested in the history of GATT and the International Trade Organisation (ITO) and the relationship between them should read Clair Wilcox, *op. cit.*, and Williams A. Brown, *op. cit.*
2. See *Basic Instruments and Selected Documents*, 6th Supplement (Geneva: GATT, 1958), pp. 68–109. Also Robert Zinser, 'Das GATT und die Meistbegünstigung', *Handbuch für Europäische Wirtschaft*, Volume 24 (Baden-Baden and Bonn: Verlag Lutzeyer, 1962) pp. 65–7.
3. *Ibid.*, pp. 65–6, and *Basic Instruments and Selected Documents*, 6th Supplement, *op. cit.*, pp. 70–1.
4. Other members of the subcommittee took an intermediate stand, making use of the principles contained in paragraph 4 only when a controversy on the interpretation of paragraph 5–9 had to be resolved. *Basic Instruments and Selected Documents*, 6th Supplement, *op. cit.*, pp. 76–81.
5. G. Jaenicke, 'Das Allgemeine Zoll – und Handelsabkommen: Rechtsgrundlagen und Rechtsprobleme', *Archiv des Völkerrechts*, Tübingen, Volume 7, 1958–59, p. 413.
6. Strangely enough Jaenicke himself does not go so far as to accept this third interpretation but the intermediate one on the legal grounds that paragraph 5 states explicitly that 'the provisions of the Agreement should not prevent the formation of the customs union', and these provisions include, according to him, also paragraph 4; see *ibid.*, p. 401.
7. It should be pointed out that while there is a general legal procedure for submitting a complaint (see Article XXIII), and GATT has the authority to take the necessary action, these provisions are too general and vague. They do not refer specifically to the case of a customs union, and also do not prescribe an automatic procedure for compensation in cases of injury resulting from its formation and not provided for in paragraph 6 of Article XXIV.
8. Seyid Muhammad, *op. cit.*, pp. 253–4.
9. The American approach, rejecting preference and permitting customs unions, is explained by Wilcox, *op. cit.*, pp. 70–1. The approach met with much criticism. See H. A. Henderson, 'A Criticism of the Havana Charter', *American Economic Review*, Manasha, Wisconsin, June 1949; and P. T. Ellsworth, 'The Havana Charter – a Comment', *American Economic Review*, December 1949.
10. *Customs Union* (New York: United Nations, 1947) p. 1.
11. Jacob Viner, 'The Most Favoured Nation Clause' in *International Economics* (Glencoe, Illinois: Free Press, 1951) p. 102.
12. Wilcox, *op. cit.*, p. 71.
13. It is impossible to examine the validity of this fundamental proposition here or the prerequisites necessary and the hypotheses required in order to justify such a proposition. The reader interested in obtaining an introduction to the subject is referred to in R. Sannwald and J. Stohler, *Economic Integration* (Princeton: Princeton University Press, 1959) ch. 1; and also to Gottfried Haberler, *A Survey of International Trade Theory*, revised edition (Princeton: Princeton University Press, 1961) chs. III and VI. Fortunately the examination mentioned earlier is not vital, as the fundamental proposition mentioned serves as the ideological basis for the GATT and has to be accepted, in the case of fully-developed economies, as given. It is, therefore, only necessary to examine how far the concept of the customs union is in accord with the ideal of free trade on which the GATT is based, and whether it leads to the expansion of free trade.

14. Richard G. Lipsey, The Theory of Customs Unions: a General Survey', *Economic Journal*, September 1960, pp. 496–7.
15. Viner, *The Customs Union Issue*, Carnegie Endowment for International Peace (New York and London: Stevens, 1950) pp. 47–8.
16. Haberler, *The Theory of International Trade* (New York: Macmillan, 1950) pp. 384 and 390. It is true that he refers primarily to preferential duties, but as he himself indicates the case should also be extended to customs unions.
17. Viner, *The Customs Union Issue, op. cit.*, p. 43.
18. In the opinion of Viner, *ibid.*, p. 41, the plans of most customs unions known in history were motivated by protectionist and bargaining-power considerations. He endeavoured, however, to formulate some *a priori* generalisations according to which the prospects of customs unions to lead to free trade would be greater, while expressing a warning at the same time against placing too much reliance on these generalisations.
19. James E. Meade, *The Theory of Customs Unions* (Amsterdam: North Holland, 1955) p. 34.
20. *Ibid.*, p. 38.
21. In other words, it is based on the assumption that satisfaction can be measured and added, and it is possible to speak of the happiness of the community as the sum total of the happiness of individuals, and the happiness of individuals as the sum total of their satisfaction. According to the ordinal variety, one can say when one has more or less satisfaction but one cannot say how much. See I. M. D. Little, *A Critique of Welfare Economics*, 2nd ed. (Oxford Paperbacks: Oxford University Press, 1960) p. 13.
22. For the definition according to Meade, and a detailed introductory description of perfect competition and its advantages, see his *Introduction to Economic Analysis and Policy*, American edition edited by C. Y. Hitch (New York: Oxford University Press, 1946) 4th printing, pt. II, chs. I–III.
23. Meade himself admits that these assumptions are unrealistic and that in practice there exist monopolies, indirect taxes, and external economies and diseconomies, and that it is therefore possible that specific cases require more detailed analysis, in order to determine the effect of the formation of a customs union on welfare; but the simple assumption that the gap in marginal value between consumer and producer exists only in external trade, and not in internal trade, serves to emphasise a whole set of relationships existing in practice additionally to any possible ones existing internally.
24. The example is based on Mordechai Kreinen, 'The Outer Seven and European Integration', *American Economic Review*, June 1960, pp. 376–7.
25. It is important to note that the increase in welfare will not be by the full amount $P_3 P_1$ even under the above-mentioned assumptions, since the State's revenues will be reduced as a result of the abolition of duties, and other taxes will have to be imposed instead. However, Meade argues that it is improbable that new taxes will affect welfare to the same degree as the customs duties, since the purpose of imposing customs duties is different and primarily of a protective and commercial nature, and not as the best way of imposing a tax from a welfare point of view; therefore it can be assumed that there will be an increase in welfare. See Meade, *The Theory of Customs Union, op. cit.*, pp. 42–3.
26. The method of computation of gains and losses used by Meade, *ibid.*, p. 66. applies only to the specific case postulated by him, namely, the measurement of marginal changes in welfare as a result of a marginal change in the customs duty somewhere else (see the example given on his p. 59). Furthermore, he assumes a customs union as a final result of successive small reductions in the duty *vis-à-vis* its fellow-members, and vice versa (p. 56), so that he talks about the addition of marginal gains in the case of each product step by step. The same applies to the addition of marginal losses.
27. See Tibor Scitovsky, *Economic Theory and Western European Integration*, rev. ed. (London: Allen & Unwin, 1962) p. 53. His method of computation is based on estimating the total gain and loss in the case of each product, and not step by step as suggested by Meade.

28. It should be obvious that this estimate is exaggerated, since, in addition to what has already been stated, account must be taken of the fact that the shifting of imports from a third country to a member of the customs union (with a higher cost of production and from which the commodities were not imported previously) would mean that the gap in marginal costs will be smaller than the rate of duty ($1:1 + t$), as was the case in the third country from which they were originally bought. The estimate is also exaggerated for other reasons mentioned by Scitovsky, like the assumption of constant marginal productivity in the case of trade creation, as well as the problem of exchange rates. (See *ibid.*, p. 54.)
29. The picture is not really complete because of the absence of a third estimate, which takes account of the changes in the quantities multiplied by the existing customs duties among third countries as between themselves. This third estimate may modify the result, depending upon the degree of substitution in trade, elasticities of demand and supply, geographical distances, *et cetera*. Meade's argument is therefore correct, namely, that the effect of the change on the trade in all commodities between countries in the whole world has, theoretically, to be taken into account. That is to say, that a model of 'total equilibrium' for the whole world needs to be built. Meade, finding such a task beyond his ability, tries to tackle the problem by a cruder method of partial equilibrium and a taxonomic approach; that is to say, 'he attempts to classify a larger number of possible cases, showing the factors which would tend to cause welfare to increase when a union is formed, and to isolate these from the factors which would tend to cause welfare to diminish'. See Lipsey, *op. cit.*, p. 504.
30. Scitovsky does not consider the third estimate. It is unlikely that the changed situation will constitute a gain for all third countries taken together, since if this is the case, what had prevented them from directing their trade in such a way in the first place?
31. That this interpretation is justified can also be seen from the principles suggested by the subcommittee of experts in the League of Nations when discussing the possibility of the European Union in 1931; it was explicitly stated there, *inter alia*, that the creation of the Union must not injure the interests of other countries, but on the contrary tend to encourage economic enterprise with them. In the same connection the report emphasises that it refers to the individual interests of each and every one of the member-States of the League. *Customs Union, op. cit.*, pp. 36–9.
32. See Paul Erdman and Peter Rogge, *Die Europäische Wirtschaftsgemeinschaft und die Drittländer* (Basle: 1960) pp. 28–42.
33. It is argued that as a consequence of the abolition of the restrictions on trade (aside from an increase in specialisation in the various regions in the short run) impersonal competition within the customs union will change the economic climate, eliminate various restrictive business practices, increase standardisation, mass production, efficiency investments, transfer of know-how, elimination of shortages and bottlenecks, all of which will contribute to a faster rate of economic growth, and to a higher real income which will eventually also affect third countries. See Scitovsky, *op. cit.*, pp. 15–52. It is clear, however, that it is difficult to speak of advantages and disadvantages in an abstract manner, and it is necessary to examine in each individual case the specific data in order to determine what will be the effect of the formation of the customs union.
34. An example of the type of simplifying assumption required can be seen in Scitovsky, *op. cit.*, p. 64. Also the more practical method applied by Professor Meade of analysing the principal factors, on the presumption that there would be no change in other factors, is doubtful, since the question can be asked how far account should be taken of the consequences. See, for example, Meade, *The Theory of Customs Unions, op. cit.*, p. 40, where no account is taken of reduced sales on the welfare of Germany.
35. Even if it is not acceptable that there is a possibility of measuring exactly every change in gain quantitatively, this does not mean that case (*c*) cannot be argued, because it can be contended in extreme cases where the distribution of income is most unequal. If in one country imports are vital for the physical existence of the people, while in a

country of the union this is a luxury, it can in fact be seen, on the basis of introspection, that it is clear that the marginal value of the dollar is higher in the third country, although it is difficult to say by how much.
36. See Lipsey, *op. cit.*, p. 506.
37. See Meade, *The Theory of Customs Union, op. cit.*, p. 38.
38. It is impossible to go into detail here. Generally the quota can be based on the percentage of the import of the union from a third country in relation to the total import from third countries, or as a percentage of the import of the union from the whole world, this quota to be increased annually at the rate of increase prevalent before the establishment of the customs union. It may be necessary to include safeguards, in order to prevent serious disruption of the market, in specific industries to the extent that the quota will be less specific. In certain cases it is also possible to fix the percentage of the basis of other considerations. For example, where there is a deficit in the trade balance, in order to ensure the ability to pay in the future for this import, it is conceivably justified to permit a larger comprehensive quota. Such a solution may perhaps also serve for the problems of developing countries and facilitates the securing of a larger market for their new products.
39. To a certain extent, of course, reservations are possible in case trade with a third country is reduced as a result of the more efficient production in the customs union after its formation.
40. See M. W. Reder, *Studies in Theory of Welfare Economics* (New York: Columbia University Press, 1947) pp. 14–15. The definition adopted has had considerable currency in theoretical literature on the subject and has become almost 'the' standard definition: 'welfare increases whenever one or more individuals become more satisfied without any other becoming less satisfied.' (It has been assumed here that a net addition of some commodities obtained by one individual, over and above what he had before, is more satisfying to him.)
41. In fact it is perhaps possible to contest this basic assumption since the actual increase of the gap between A and B and also the 'demonstration effect can bring about a worsening of the welfare of B; it is difficult, however, to say whether and to what extent this factor is of significance between countries, although its influence certainly exists between individuals'. Furthermore, this argument relies on a broader interpretation of welfare than the one used above.
42. In which case, however, the principle of non-discriminatory treatment of past trade should, if necessary, be capable of being extended to future trade.
43. It would go beyond the scope of this chapter to discuss this solution in more detail. To illustrate this point, however, the criteria to be used could include the degree of dependence (percentages to be determined), size of import proportional to total import of the customs union, degree of actual injury, stage of development, balance of payments position and so forth.

PART II
Practice and Theory

CHAPTER 4

Tariff Quotas in the European Community

Several uses of tariff quotas by member countries of the European Community, or by the Community itself, have already been taken to illustrate particular aspects of the application of tariff quotas in commercial trading over recent years. These are only representatives, however, from the much wider range that has developed within the Common Market, and this chapter covers the field in more detail, although their use by the Community to give preferences to developing countries will not be discussed until Chapter 8.

Tariff quotas have been applied in the Community and its member states as a tool of commercial policy for the reasons and purposes discussed in Chapter 1. The national tariff quotas, however, permitted in the Treaty,[1] were primarily to facilitate the harmonisation of conflicting interests of member states with a common external tariff. Under particular circumstances or during the transition period a member state could more easily accept a common external tariff if allowed to apply tariff treatment more in line with its past tariff. Therefore provision was made for the use of this tool in difficult situations.[2]

Some tariff quotas were already in existence in individual member countries before the establishment of the Community. In some cases their existence even provided the reason for their continuation.[3] An example of such tariff quotas, which permitted special treatment by the contracting parties, are those granted to Italy in the case of imports from Libya. The most important example of the use of tariff quotas during a process of integration, is that permitted by the European Coal and Steel Community before the establishment of the European Community.

NATIONAL TARIFF QUOTAS IN THE EUROPEAN
COAL AND STEEL COMMUNITY

Before the establishment of the European Coal and Steel Community, the Benelux countries had much lower tariffs for steel products than the other members of the European Community.[4] The ECSC's harmonisation of tariffs was intended in the long run to be carried out in the direction of the level of the low tariffs of the Benelux countries, who agreed to accept only a maximum increase of two points in their duties, if necessary. This harmonisation programme, however, was to go into effect only after the conclusion of the negotiations taking place between high-duty member countries and third countries which would enable the high-duty member countries to obtain counter-concessions for the planned reductions in their tariff rates of steel products.

In the meantime there were two problems. On the one hand, the Benelux countries wished to continue to enjoy their low tariff in order not to cause disruptions to the processing industry and consumers inside Benelux – as well as to the traditional suppliers from outside the ECSC who enjoyed concessions, granted by Benelux in the GATT. On the other hand, it was necessary to prevent the diversion of trade which would result from the high tariffs in the other member countries when internal barriers to trade between the member countries were eliminated.

The solution in Article XV of the convention[5] – annexed to Article 85 of the Treaty of Paris from 1952 – was that the Benelux countries would maintain tariff quotas for the transition. The quotas were initially based on past imports from third countries in a representative period as well as on the duties in force at the time of signature. They were to be determined yearly for each item of the Benelux Tariff by the Benelux countries, with the agreement of the High Authority of the Coal and Steel Community, but with the possibility of introducing changes every three months. Imports within the tariff quota required an expressed commitment by importers not to re-export the product.

This example illustrates some points worth remembering when discussing the tariff quotas in the Treaty of Rome:

(a) The tariff quotas in this agreement were *explicitly* fixed as a temporary solution during the transition period until the harmonised tariff was determined.

(b) They were very liberal and, more important, their determination was left to the autonomous decision of the member states, although agreement of the High Authority had to be received. The creation of the ECSC attempted to exclude one specific sector, and not the whole economy, from the national boundaries.

Commercial policy had therefore to remain within the realm of the individual member states, since it would be impossible to conduct a commercial policy for one product which was different from the policies followed for the rest. As this could create problems for the Community, the member states were required by the Treaty of Paris, in Articles 71–5, to co-ordinate their commercial policy, with the High Authority being authorised to intervene.

Since the ECSC relates only to one sector, it is relatively easier for member states to forgo sovereign rights than is the case in the European Community, where greater national interests are involved. As a result, the Treaty of Paris shows a much less careful weighing of the checks and balances of institutional decision than does the Treaty of Rome, at any rate as far as tariff quotas are concerned.

BASIS FOR NATIONAL TARIFF QUOTAS

If the legal framework of the European Community is examined with regard to tariff quotas, the different references can be categorised as follows:

(1) specific and explicit references to tariff quotas in the Treaty of Rome itself, and in its Annexes and Protocols;

(2) protocols by the member countries elaborating more specifically points which were left open when the Treaty of Rome was signed;

(3) tariff quotas included in association agreements, as well as in bilateral and multilateral trade agreements; and

(4) tariff quotas determined by regulation of the Common Market institutions themselves.

BASIS FOR APPLICATION OF TARIFF QUOTAS IN THE TREATY

The main Article which explicitly relates to the possibility of applying national tariff quotas, is Article 25 of the Treaty.[6] Sub-article 4 provides that the Commission shall periodically examine tariff quotas which have been granted pursuant to this article, whereas Sub-articles 1 to 3 relate to different specific lists of products for which member states may be granted tariff quotas.

The prescriptions differ from list to list. Regarding the lists covered by Sub-article 1, criteria are established which compel the authorities (the Council) of the Community to grant tariff quotas, especially in those cases where production is insufficient to satisfy the demand of a member state and such supply traditionally depends to a considerable extent on imports from third countries. For products of Sub-article 2 the Commission should grant tariff quotas where a change in the source of supply, or a shortage of supply within the Community, is such as to entail harmful consequences[7] for the processing industry of a member state. No such criteria exist in the Treaty for products covered by Sub-article 3, and the Commission is free to grant tariff quotas at its own discretion.

Why application of tariff quotas is only permitted for certain products
The products included in the lists were either essential raw materials or

semi-finished products, vitally needed in member states for production and processing. Consequently these countries were very sensitive to the possible harmful consequences of the harmonisation of the external tariff. Other lists of products related to agricultural commodities for which no clear-cut common policy had yet been determined. As member states were afraid of the possible harmful effects, they reserved for themselves the right to apply tariff quotas as a kind of safety valve.

Why different sub-articles provide for different treatment
One explanation seems to be the *a priori* negative approach to national tariff quotas.[8] 'Their exclusive purpose is to eliminate, or at least to mitigate, certain adverse effects which could result from a strict application of the process of adjustment of the external common tariff.'[9] But in general, national tariff quotas are really considered to be undesirable and contrary to the customs union.[10]

It therefore seemed desirable for tariff quotas only to be fixed by a qualified majority of the Council on the proposal of the Commission, in order to make it difficult to take advantage of this escape clause. It applied particularly to those products included in Sub-article 1, where the danger of harmful effects of a trade diversion was less as the common external tariff was generally low. On the other hand, in the second sub-article, external tariffs are higher and the danger of shocks and disruptions much greater. This was particularly true for the Benelux countries (and probably also Germany) who had to agree to substantially higher duties than those that were customarily applied in these countries before harmonisation. It seems reasonable to assume that these countries insisted that they should be able to receive national tariff quotas more easily, and when the need arose, directly from the Commission without recourse to a decision of the Council.

Since the nature of the future agricultural policy was unclear, the third sub-article was, without doubt, more in the nature of an outline article.

More precise classification of criteria
The criteria mentioned in Article 25 as pre-conditions for the possible granting of tariff quotas need clarification and elaboration. To a certain extent, additional light is cast on them by the directives included in Article 29[11], but many questions were still left open. Several points were clarified by the Commission itself, when it came to discuss the granting of tariff quotas.[12]

In Article 25(1), for instance, the Commission agreed that 'supplies to the applicant member states are viewed in relation to output in the Community as a whole and it has been agreed that in assessing supplies available to the applicant member state its own production must be taken into account'. Also the condition that supplies to the member state 'must – to a considerable extent – be represented by imports from non-member countries' was interpreted to mean that 'a considerable extent' should not relate just to the imports, but to the total supply of the products available to the applicant member state *including its own production*. Lastly, the term 'traditional dependence on supplies from non-member countries' was interpreted to mean a certain duration and continuity of the imports concerned, without necessarily requiring the tradition to go back earlier than January 1958 when the Treaty entered into force.

With regard to Article 25(2), concerning the shortage of supply within the Community, the criteria which apply are the same as those in Article 25(1). Purchase in the countries of the Community of products previously imported from non-member countries counts as a change in the sources of supply.

Nevertheless, it is not enough to plead a shortage of supplies in the Community; need for imports, must also be shown subject to increased customs duties (following the first moves towards the common customs tariff). This requires proof of harmful consequences for the processing industries concerned, such as the danger of reducing their outlets. It goes without saying that, to the extent that sales of processing industries in non-member countries play a role, the conditions for the application of Article 25(2) are not fulfilled when raw materials used for the manufacture of exported products benefit by the exemption from duty either by virtue of the provisions on processing traffic or by virtue of any analogous tariff provisions.

Also, when Article 25(2) is invoked, it must be shown that the change in the sources of supply increases the costs of the processing industries; that the product affected by the increase of customs duties can only be purchased in the Community at a higher cost price; and that this increase in costs would lead to a reduction of outlets for the processing industries. Furthermore – and this is yet another condition for the grant of a quota – the tariff quota is only allocated to the extent that such an increase of costs cannot be borne by the processing industries concerned.

These elucidations by the Commission do not answer all questions, and further points need to be clarified at a later stage, amongst them decisions about the procedures for applying, discussing and determining a quota, its size, the height of the tariff within the quota, and so on. But despite these unanswered questions, it is evident from the discussion up to now that, firstly, Article 25 is limited to specific lists of products and, secondly, that even for these products, the application of the tariff quota is restricted by a host of criteria and limiting conditions. On the other hand, there are no time limitations imposed on the possibility of applying tariff quotas, contrary to ECSC practice; and they are not restricted to the transition period – at least according to the Treaty.

Other provisions relating to tariff quotas
Among the articles of the Treaty itself there are no other explicit articles relating to tariff quotas. But there are two additional articles which have been used as the legal basis for the application of tariff quotas — among them the second article was the more important provision (although in some cases supporting legal references have been used by Community institutions while granting tariff quotas). The first of these, which has been used only in very rare cases, is Article 15(1).[13] This states that 'irrespective of the provisions of Article 14, any member state may, in the course of the transitional period, suspend in whole or in part the collection of duties imposed by it on products imported from other member states. It shall inform other member states and the Commission thereof.'

It is obvious from the text that the process of accelerating reductions of internal tariffs can also be carried out in the form of a tariff quota, since the wording does not mention rate or duty but only a partial suspension of the collection of duties. This could be done in the form of tariff quotas, although they would have a limited meaning since they apply only to other member states and only during the transition period and, furthermore, can only be applied by an accelerated reduction of the duty towards zero.

The second article which has been used in the past for granting tariff quotas, and which is being used with increasing frequency, is Article 28. In essence this is a general escape clause. It does not specifically mention tariff quotas but is of a more general nature and reads as follows:[14] 'any independent alteration or suspension of duties in the common customs tariff shall be decided by the Council unanimously. After the transitional period has expired, however, the Council may, by a qualified majority on a proposal from the Commission, decide on alterations or suspensions which shall not exceed 20 per cent of the rate in the case of any one duty for a maximum period of six months. Such alterations may only be extended, under the same conditions, for one further period of six months.'

It is obvious that any change in the common external tariff is a serious matter and can therefore be accepted by the member states only if agreed upon by unanimous decision, unless changes are of a limited scope and duration. Article 28 has been used in the past, whenever Article 25 could not apply due to its restrictive conditions.

In 1962, a national tariff quota was granted to Germany[15] on the basis of Article 28 for prefabricated wooden houses from Norway. This was done because Germany was suffering from the consequences of a flood. Article 25 could not be used, despite the tariff quota being a national one, since wooden houses were not included in the list of products for which tariff quotas could be granted. Instead, Article 28 had to be applied.

Other examples of the use of Article 28 as a basis for granting tariff quotas in the earlier stages of the transitional period are those included in the Association Agreements – for example with Greece and Turkey – which will be discussed later on. The need for utilising Article 28 in such cases (as well as in the case of granting concessions or binding tariffs in the GATT) arose from the fact that these agreements and concessions related to all member countries of the Community in relation to third countries. Although, in essence, the quotas were of a national character, the fact that Article 25 referred to all member states, and not to one or a few, made its use for this purpose impossible. This characteristic, in due course, led to Article 28 being used for the application of Community tariff quotas. This Article does not, however, include any guidelines, criteria or conditions and does not even mention tariff quotas specifically.

Protocols which affect tariff quotas
Among the Protocols which were annexed to the Treaty at the time of its signature were two providing explicitly for tariff quotas, and one providing implicitly for their continuation. The first Protocol, which relates to a tariff quota for bananas (Ex.08.01 of the BTN) for the Federal Republic of Germany,[16] has two interesting features, later also used in the generalised system of preferences, the yearly automatic adjustment of the tariff quota, without the need for the renewal of permission from the Community institutions each time, and the division of the quota into two parts: a fixed part, which does not change even when total imports fall below it, and a variable part, computed annually on the basis of the variation in imports.

The second Protocol relates to tariff quotas for imports of unroasted coffee (Ex.09.01 of the BTN) for Italy and the Benelux countries, to be phased out gradually.[17] The third Protocol, which includes tariff quotas implicitly, relates to goods originating from certain countries and enjoying special treatment upon importation into one of the member states. It refers specifically to imports into Italy from Libya and the Trusteeship territory of Somalia and covers, among other items, a list of products for which Italy received a waiver in the GATT[18] in the form of tariff quotas. The Protocol states that the setting up of the Community shall not entail any alteration in the customs treatment applicable when the Treaty comes into force.[19]

THE AGREEMENT OF 1960 REGARDING 'LIST G'

The Conference of representatives of the member states of the Community signed an agreement in 1960 relating to the common external tariff in respect of products of 'List G'. This list refers to those products on the duties of which the member countries were unable to agree during the negotiations of the Treaty, and which had to be deferred for further negotiations after its signature.

To the Agreement are appended seventeen protocols and a final act. Of these seventeen protocols, twelve relate to tariff quotas[20] (Protocols II, V, VI, VII, IX, X, XI, XII, XIII, XIV, XV, and XVII).[21]

Some of these specifically determine, for particular member countries, a tariff quota at a given rate of duty, as is the case with Protocol II, which provides a duty-free quota of 160,000 tons of salt, for the Belgium-Luxemburg union. Others, such as Protocol XI (tariff quotas for certain ferro-alloys to Benelux, Germany and Italy) and Protocol XII (tariff quotas on unwrought aluminium for Benelux and Germany) have a rate of duty within the quota which is fixed, although no specific quantities have been determined. Protocol XV includes tariff quotas for unwrought lead and zinc. In the case of Germany it was fixed at 20 per cent of their processing industries' own requirements; and in the case of Belgium, the same was true only for lead. As far as the Netherlands are concerned specific quantities were fixed for both cases.

Finally, in quite a number of protocols, no specific tariff quotas have been fixed but there are provisions which enable them to be granted should a member state request it. This would require a change in the source of supply, or of inadequate supply within the Community, such as to entail consequences prejudicial to the processing industry in the member states concerned. Such a condition is included in Protocols V, VI, IX, Xb, XI, XIII and XIV. With respect to these quotas not only do the same criteria and interpretation apply that relate to Article 25/2 of the Treaty, but the Commission has declared its intention to base itself on the following principles when granting tariff quotas.

Thus, the following will be treated as 'consequences prejudicial to the processing industries', whether those consequences result directly or indirectly from the incidence of the relevant rates:

(*a*) In the markets of third countries, and in regard to international competition: when there is a case of lowered competitiveness which cannot be remedied by recourse to a finishing trade, drawback, or other system having a similar effect.

(*b*) In the Community market: if an increase in the cost price of products of the processing industries leads to a reduction of their possible sales, whether or not the increase causes the products to be replaced by others; when financial difficulties result from inability to incorporate an increase in costs in the selling prices; when it is impossible to find in the Community market the quantity, or quality of products necessary to the processing industries concerned; and when supplies have to be obtained on terms less favourable than those enjoyed by other Community users and, in particular, combines.

When reviewing the tariff quotas granted, whether at regular intervals or in connection with specific difficulties, or when deciding on requests for their extension, the Commission must take into account the pattern of damage sustained by the processing industries. Some of the protocols, nevertheless, contain special provisions, whose scope depends on the special features of the economic sectors concerned. This is so in the case of protocols granting tariff quotas for certain ferro-alloys, unwrought aluminium, lead and zinc. As stated earlier, they refer either to 'the needs' of the processing industries themselves or to the 'import requirements' of these industries.

The protocol on paper pulp contains the unusual provision that the member states themselves are authorised to open tariff quotas, free of duty or at a reduced rate of duty for certain types of pulp, to cover the whole of their requirements, provided that they so inform the Commission.

It must further be remembered that Sub-articles 1 and 2 of Article 25 of the Treaty lay down limits for tariff quotas, specifically that these 'may not exceed the limits beyond which the transfer of activities to the detriment of other member states is to be feared'. Most of the protocols annexed to the Agreement on List G contain a similar clause, which means that a careful examination must be made at Community level of the economic data relating to the sector under review, especially those concerning trade amongst the member states. Moreover, the clause in paragraph 4 of Article 25, according to which 'the Commission shall periodically examine any tariff quota granted in application of this article' – the protocols annexed to the Agreement on List G contain a similar provision – makes it possible to adjust the volume of the quotas in the light of the economic data, but within the limits of the conditions determined for their being granted. With reference to the agricultural products in List G which are included in Annex II, the Federal Republic of Germany and Italy made known their intentions of requesting tariff quotas for certain agricultural and primary products.[22]

The Commission's declaration relating to these stated that 'in the course of the negotiations certain Ministers made it known that their governments would ask for tariff quotas to be granted under Article 25, paragraph 3, in respect of the agricultural products mentioned below [in footnote 24] appearing in list G.' The Commission declared its readiness to grant such quotas, at nil duty for fish covered by items ex 03.01 B Ia and 1c, and at reduced or nil duties for other products mentioned above (in footnote 24), in favour of consumers and users of industries in member states so requesting within the scope of Article 25, paragraphs 3 and 4:[23]

> – when the market situation within the Community is not such as to afford such industries adequate supplies, quantitatively or

qualitatively, on the same terms as those enjoyed by other users in the Community; or
— when social considerations justify the maintenance of traditional supply channels for the basic foodstuffs (ex 03.01 B, ex 03.02) set out in the list mentioned.

NATIONAL TARIFF QUOTAS IN ASSOCIATION
AND TRADE AGREEMENTS

Explicit references to national tariff quotas are found in some of the Association Agreements and Trade Agreements[24] to which the Community is a contracting party.

Association Agreement with Greece
This Agreement includes national tariff quotas for different purposes. In the Agreement itself, Article 21[25] relates to the possibility of applying the tariff quotas in favour of third countries with which Greece has a bilateral trade agreement, should the trade with these countries prove to be substantially infringed by the establishment of the Agreement with the European Community. Therefore permission is conditionally granted as long as the tariff within these tariff quotas is not lower than the tariff granted to the Community.

Protocol 8 of the Agreement states that such permission will be given by the Community, when the total value of imports within a tariff quota does not exceed 10 per cent of the imports from third countries (based on the last year for which statistical data are available), and in each product the anticipated value imported within the framework of the tariff quota does not exceed a third of the import of that product in the last year for which statistics are available. At the end of the transition period fixed in Article 6 of the Association Agreement, the Council of Ministers is empowered to change this protocol, if it should prove necessary. Use was made of this article with respect to trade with the Soviet Union.[26]

Another important protocol in the Association Agreement with Greece is Protocol 10.[27] This obligates the member states to obtain the prior agreement of the Association Council before the external tariff, which was established on 1 October 1960, can be changed by more than 20 per cent in either direction on the following products: tobacco, dried grapes, olives, collophony and turpentine oil. Furthermore, for these products, one member state, or a few member states, must obtain the permission of the Association Council if they want to reduce, or eliminate, a tariff towards a third country. Similar permission must be obtained if they require a tariff quota of more than 22,000 tons for tobacco and, for the other products, more than 15 per cent of the quantity imported from third countries into the Community, based on the last available statistical data.

For collophony and turpentine oil, tariff quotas higher than the 15 per cent mentioned above may be granted, provided the conditions of Article 25/1 of the Treaty are met.[28] Protocol 14[29] sets specific national tariff quotas for imports from Greece to Germany, one for wine for consumption (65,000 hectolitres), and the second for wine for preparation of vermouth, of vinegar, for distillation and for bottling. Under certain conditions, these may be increased.

If the specific references to tariff quotas in the Greek Association Agreement are summarised it will be seen that they are being used for three entirely different purposes, as follows:

(a) The avoidance of the possible danger of trade diversion between a member of the Association Agreement and a third country with which this member has mutual trade interests;

(b) the assurance of a limited preference during a transition period, while protecting the interest of domestic producers in the Community; and

(c) as an escape clause for autonomous changes, in order to limit in advance the possibility of seriously injuring an agreed situation (as for example, the 15 per cent limit for products of interest to Greece).

Agreement with Turkey

The original agreement between the European Community and Turkey signed on 12 September 1963[30] includes, in Protocol 1 to Article 2, specific references to tariff quotas. Article 2 of the Protocol provides for national tariff quotas for raw tobacco (total quantity 12,500 tons), dried grapes (30,000 tons), dried figs (13,000 tons), and hazelnuts (17,000 tons). Specific quotas are defined, as well as the tariff rates within the quotas, for each of these products in each member country during the transition period. Article 3 of the Protocol states that, with the beginning of the last adjustments to the common external tariff for products included in Article 2 above, the Community will open common tariff quotas for Turkey which will be of the same size as the national quotas granted to it. There are further Articles in the same Protocol relating to tariff quotas, providing for their possible increase (Article 4) for adding new products (Article 6) and so on.[31]

The Council carefully examined, in 1967, a request submitted by the Turkish Government on the basis of Article 6 of the provisional protocol to the Ankara Agreement. On 1 December 1967, they adopted a decision under which additional new annual tariff quotas were to be opened by the Community.[32] During the beginning and middle of 1968, the national tariff quotas for tobacco, dried grapes and dried figs and hazelnuts were transformed, in accordance with Article 3 of Protocol 1, into Community tariff quotas of similar size.[33]

Agreement with Tunisia
The Agreement with Tunisia includes provisions for national tariff quotas in Annex 2 (which relates to Article 2, paragraph 1 of the Agreement), Articles 1 to 5, which mainly relate to various types of fish and their products and for which there was no unified agricultural policy of the Community.[34]

Agreement with Morocco
This includes the same Annex 2 as the Agreement with Tunisia. In this, Articles 2 to 5 all relate to fish and fish products, and individual national tariff quotas have been provided for them.[35]

National tariff quotas with Switzerland
Switzerland had bilateral agreements with Germany, France and Italy, relating to the finishing trade,[36] which have been replaced by an agreement between the Community and Switzerland. It permits imports within a tariff quota to the value of 1.87 million units of account of this trade each way.[37]

Tariff quotas consolidated in the GATT
Examples of national tariff quotas which have been agreed upon in the GATT are those for certain types of cows from Switzerland – then definitely allocated in national quotas[38] – and those for coal into Germany, which were established after agreement of the contracting parties of the GATT had been obtained by the ECSC.[39]

The one basic characteristic which, in general, distinguishes most tariff quotas in trade agreements from autonomous tariff quotas is that there exists a contractual obligation towards another party entitling it to claim full utilisation of the granted quotas. In some of the trade agreements the claim refers to individual member countries; however, to the extent that the tariff quotas are granted by the Community as a whole, the claim refers to the entire Community. This created some difficulties with regard to their allocation and distribution between member countries during the transition period.

The usual procedure during the transition period was for the Community to allocate specific national tariff quotas to individual member countries;[40] in some cases, this allocation was already determined in the agreement, as can be seen in the Association Agreement with Turkey. This was necessarily the case because of the different rates of duty in the individual member countries during the transition period. As progress was made towards the elimination of internal barriers to trade and the establishment of external common rates of duty, the procedures of providing for national fixed allocated tariff quotas become more and more difficult to maintain. On the one hand, there was the danger of trade diversion and, on the other, the contractual

Tariff Quotas in the European Community

obligation was the responsibility of the Community and could not be left to individual member countries. It became essential to develop new guidelines for the treatment of Community tariff quotas by the Community institutions. This subject is discussed more fully in the later pages of this chapter.

TARIFF QUOTAS AND EUROPEAN COMMUNITY INSTITUTIONS

Most tariff quotas are based directly on Articles 25 or 28 of the Treaty itself, or are based on the treaty-making powers of the Treaty (usually in addition to Article 28). But there are a few cases where they are based only on regulations or recommendations[41] which themselves relate to other paragraphs of the Treaty, or are the result of the authority granted to the common institutions by the Treaty. Two such examples are tariff quotas for certain steel products and pig iron in the ECSC, and those which are permitted within the regulation of the common policy for bovine meat.

Tariff quotas for steel and pig iron

In 1963, the trends in world prices of iron and steel products had harmful effects on the production of certain steel and pig iron products in the Community. Prices declined abroad and imports increased substantially. As a result new investments fell off and planned modernisation was hampered. The High Authority made recommendations[42] to limit imports by raising the duty to the minimum duty in force, in Italy, of US$7 per ton.

But since some member countries had granted concessions within the GATT for a few products, there was a need to provide for possible exceptions in these cases. Furthermore, it was also felt desirable to provide exceptions in case it should become necessary to prevent disruption. The recommendations, therefore, made provision for escape clauses, permitting certain quantities of pig iron and steel products to be exempted from the specific duty of US$7. These national tariff quotas were fixed semi-annually and, in 1967 were limited to a more strictly specified category of pig iron, with a drop in the external specific duty to US $5.[43]

Tariff quotas for bovine meat

The Council of Ministers issued, on 5 February 1964, regulation 14/64/EWG[44] which determines the gradual steps for the introduction of a common market organisation for bovine meat. Within these measures, which are based on Articles 42 and 43 of the Treaty, the regulation of the Council refers explicitly to the possibility of applying tariff quotas. In the introduction, the regulation stated that difficulties may arise with respect to the supply of bovine meat for processing purposes, which could be overcome by a tariff quota for frozen meat from third countries. Article 4, when referring to the tariff quota for frozen meat consolidated in the GATT at 20 per cent duty for a quantity of 22,000 tons, permits the importation of additional frozen meat within a tariff quota for processing under supervision of the customs authorities. The Council of Ministers is permitted, by a qualified majority, on the basis of a recommendation from the Commission, to fix within the tariff quota a lower rate of duty than the consolidated 20 per cent.

Finally, Article 18 of this regulation provides a general exception which permits the Council of Ministers – unanimously during the second transition stage and after that by a qualified majority on recommendation from the Commission – to take measures, with respect to products appearing in Annex 1, which may differ from these regulations in order to take account of specific conditions which might arise concerning these products.[45]

NATIONAL TARIFF QUOTAS DURING THE TRANSITION PERIOD

As a result of the decision of 12 May 1960 to speed up the implementation of the Treaty, taken by the representatives of the member states,[46] it became necessary to establish the procedures and methods of application to be used for tariff quotas. Starting in June 1960, the staff of the Commission held meetings with the national administrations of the various countries and their experts, to determine procedures and dates for the submission of requests for tariff quotas. It was agreed that any application for a tariff quota would be submitted by the Commission to the other member states in writing for their consideration and opinion and that these countries could submit an objection during a given period. If necessary, it was also possible to exchange views in meetings called by the staff of the Commission. The experience of these meetings was to show that the representatives of the applying member states did not always know about the possible sources of supply which existed in other member countries of the Community.

When the requests for tariff quotas started to arrive, it became evident that they were not adequately drafted, that they did not include sufficient statistical data and that the arguments advanced were not always in conformity with the provisions invoked. Member states were then asked to supplement or modify them. Moreover, the original requests were submitted late and this delayed their possible enactment, particularly in view of the requirement to consult non-applicant member states on these requests.

Despite all these technical shortcomings, and despite the fact that requests did not include tariff quotas for agricultural products, 159

Tariff Quotas in the European Community   67

applications for tariff quotas were submitted for 1961, and dealt with. Such a large number of requests was actually contrary to the wishes of the institutions of the Community. As the reports of the Community state explicitly time and again,[47] it was felt that the opening of tariff quotas for non-member countries was 'fraught with certain dangers; a break in the unity of the tariff; the creation of divergencies in the cost prices of raw materials and semi-finished products for the Community's processing industries, thus hampering trade liberalisation for processed products'.[48]

It is, therefore, small wonder that the Council of Ministers, when it came to deal with the first requests, discussed the principles according to which these requests should be granted with the intention of reducing their number, lest their sheer volume jeopardise the customs union.[49] The Council suggested, therefore, as one possible solution, reducing or abolishing Community duties, in exchange for a withdrawal of the request for the tariff quota. The experts of member states met several times under the auspices of the Commission and reconsidered the requests submitted, with a view to reducing their number. The efforts made by the Commission and the Council eventually brought about a considerable number of withdrawals by the member states themselves (a total of thirty-six).[50] With regard to forty other applications solutions to the problem had to be found. One solution was the decision to modify one tariff sub-heading, and to suspend, for 1961, the duties of the common custom tariff for twenty-three products or tariff lines, thereby making it possible for thirty-one requests[51] to be withdrawn. Further withdrawals by member states were brought about by the negotiating meetings between producers and consumers in the Community, as a result of which seven requests were withdrawn.

After the withdrawal of various applications and the nullification of others, there were still 83 applications with which the Community had to deal. Of these, the Community turned down twelve, 'most of which were rejected on the ground that they referred to products for which the duties of the national customs tariffs were higher before 1 January 1961 than those which were applied in consequence of the first approximation towards the common customs tariff (Article 25/1 and 2) or because no proof had been established that there was a shortage of supplies in the Community, or not sufficient proof had been given of the harmful consequences for the processing industries of the member states concerned (Article 25/2).'[52]

There are some interesting points to note about the tariff quotas that have been granted, although there are some difficulties in assessing their economic impact. As an indication, the Community stated that the total requests, in volume terms for 1960, did not exceed 0.38 per cent of total imports, and 0.58 per cent of imports from non-member countries. The tariff quotas that were granted, however, reveal, again in volume terms, the sharp differences in individual member country percentages, as Table 4.1[53] demonstrates.

TABLE 4.1
European Community Imports by Volume, 1960

Importing country	Total imports (1)	From non-members (2)	Tariff quotas requested[a]		Tariff quotas granted[a]	
	(million tons)		% of(1)	% of(2)	% of(1)	% of(2)
Germany	127,623	94,261	6.55	8.87	5.83	7.89
France	76,946	53,327	0.22	0.31	0.09	0.01
Belgium/ Luxemburg	63,227	21,870	4.23	12.24	3.25	9.38
Netherlands	62,253	36,550	2.07	3.53	1.21	2.07
Italy	67,182	56,418	1.84	2.19	0.31	0.37
Total	397,232	262,427	0.38	0.58	0.28	0.43

Source: 'Tariff Quotas, 1961', *EEC Bulletin*, No. 9/10; September/October 1961, p. 44.

[a] 73 per cent of the requests (1521m tons) were granted (1121m tons).

TABLE 4.2
European Community Imports by Value, 1960

Importing country	Total imports (1)	From non-members (2)	Tariff quotas requested		Tariff quotas granted[a]	
	(million dollars)		% of(1)	% of(2)	% of(1)	% of(2)
Germany	10,090.0	6,917.6	3.07	4.48	1.91	2.78
France	6,279.5	3,293.0	0.017	0.013	0.003	0.007
Belgium/ Luxemburg	3,957.1	1,783.9	0.47	1.04	0.25	0.54
Netherlands	4,530.7	2,407.9	0.95	1.78	0.34	0.63
Italy	4,715.3	3,322.4	0.49	0.69	0.19	0.21
Total	29,573.5	17,723.8	1.34	2.23	0.76	1.27

Source: 'Tariff Quotas, 1961', *EEC Bulletin*, No. 9/10, September/October 1961, p. 44.

[a] 57 per cent of the requests were granted.

Table 4.1 shows that, for imports from non-member countries, the Belgium and Luxemburg Economic Union had the largest share of requests and grants, followed by Germany. If the situation is examined in terms of value, however, quite a different picture is produced as Table 4.2 shows.[54] Here, the relative share of tariff quotas in imports, both from the rest of the world and from non-member countries of these products, is highest in Germany and second highest in the Netherlands. One other thing can be stated with certainty, namely that the least interested country in this field seems to be France.

In 1961, the number of applications for tariff quotas submitted by member countries was 159, by 1962 the number had reached 278.[55] The increase was partly the result of the first adjustment of national tariffs to the common external tariff in the field of agricultural products and, partly, a reflection of the difficulties experienced in the previous year in organising the submission of applications. The fact that the number of requests for tariff quotas for industrial products which were granted in 1962 was reduced to a figure not exceeding that for 1961 was most important, since by this the 'member states have halted the trend which might have imperilled the Customs Union'.[56] Table 4.3[57] gives a more detailed picture of the requests, submitted under Article 25/1, 2, 3 or list G, in the formative years of the Community.

With the advancement of the adjustment process during the transition period the institutions of the Community became even stricter in granting national tariff quotas. This attitude found its expression not only in the criteria mentioned above, but also, however possible, in attempts to reduce the gap between the duties outside and inside the tariff quota. This was done by eliminating a certain percentage of the preferred duty,[58] and by reducing the quantities permitted under preferred terms.[59] Furthermore, in the Commission's view, national tariff quotas are only justified during the transition period (exactly as was the case in the ECSC), and therefore Article 25 is also not valid beyond that period.

Although the issue has not been resolved in theory, in practice the position of the Commission gains ground. There has been a decline in the number of applications and grants of national tariff quotas.[60] Table 4.4 clearly indicates the trend towards their elimination.[61]

So far this part of this chapter has been discussing the way that national tariff quotas have been used in the transitional period, and mention has been made of the administrative teething troubles that beset their determination and granting when they were first introduced in 1960. The next two sections take a more detailed look at the general procedures and administration. Firstly, those that are involved in the granting of a tariff quota, and, secondly, the administration of the actual imports within its framework.

TABLE 4.3
Tariff Quota Applications by European Community Member States, 1961–66
(under Article 15(1) (2) (3) and List G)

Year: basis for grant	Requests	Withdrawn by member state applying	Withdrawn after a community solution was found	Withdrawn Total	Examined[a] Total	Examined[a] Refused	Examined[a] Granted
1961: para.1	55	13	12	25	30	4	26
" 2	58	21	19	40	18	7	11
" 3	–	–	–	–	–	–	–
List G	46	2	9	11	35	1	34
Total	159	36	40	76	83	12	71
1962: para.1	58	17	13	30	28	–	28
" 2	92	41	32	73	19	9	10
" 3	85	22	5	27	58	28	30
List G	43	1	55	6	37	1	36
Total	278	81	105	186	142	38	104
1963: para.1	29	5	2	7	22	–	22
" 2	29	20	6	26	3	–	3
" 3	47	8	6	14	33	4	29
List G	36	–	–	–	36	–	36
Total	141	33	14	47	94	4	90
1964: para.1	21	3	8	11	10	–	10
" 2	7	2	–	2	5	–	5
" 3	34	3	–	3	31	4	27
List G	37	–	–	–	37	–	37
Total	99	8	8	16	83	4	79
1965: para.1	23	2	11	13	10	–	10
" 2	8	2	1	3	5	–	5
" 3	32	4	1	5	27	4	23
List G	37	3	–	3	34	–	34
Total	100	11	13	24	76	4	72
1966: para.1	11	–	–	–	11	–	11
" 2	4	2	–	2	2	–	2
" 3	39	4	3	7	32	4	28
List G	35	6	–	6	29	2	27
Total	89	12	–	15	74	6	68

Source: *10th Annual Report of EEC Commission*, p. 16.
[a] Examined by the Commission of the European Community.

TABLE 4.4
National Tariff Quotas in the European Community 1961–70
(Article 25 and List G)

Year	Requests	Granted	Withdrawn	Refused
1961	159	71	76	12
1962	278	104	136	38
1963	142	90	43	4
1964	99	79	12	4
1965	100	72	20	4
1966	89	68	21	–
1967	77	61	10	3
1968	68[a]	25	10	2
1969	21	15	4	1
1970	12	9	3	–

Source: Commission of the European Community
[a] Twenty-nine other requests were given a common solution.

PROCEDURE FOR GRANTING TARIFF QUOTAS

There are many problems which are not resolved by the Treaty of Rome and which can only be derived from the experience and actual practices evolved in the Community. These problems prompt such questions as: how is a request submitted; where is it examined; what is the process of examination and what are the various considerations in such examination; what is the process of granting a tariff quota, and is there the possibility of appeal in case of refusal? What types of tariff quota are being granted? Are they by quantity, or by value? Is there a specific duty, an *ad valorem* rate of duty or a mixed one? Is it a relative tariff quota, or an absolute one? What is the depth of cut within the quota in relation to the external duty? What are the considerations for determining the relation between the preference and the regular tariff? The list of potential questions is very long indeed.

The first step towards the granting of a tariff quota is the submission of an application by an interested member state to the appropriate service of the Commission with a reasoned argument. Usually, such a request has to be based on the appropriate paragraphs of the Treaty or the protocols and has to fit the criteria which have been established by the Commission. Generally, it must also include statistical data substantiating its case.

An examination of a specific case will give some insight into the whole procedure. For example, a tariff quota of tens of thousands of tons of a product was requested, at a third of the external tariff rate. The particular product was needed as a raw material for the food industry, and the member state submitted detailed statistics of imports of this particular product from the Community, associated countries and third countries for a period of four to five years, as well as consumption data for the previous eight years. It also submitted details about the duty, which was zero in that member country before the establishment of the Community. Up to the introduction of the Common Market arrangement in 1966 the duty amounted to about 5 per cent, but after that, the external tariff rate was increased to 9 per cent. Most of the imports came from third countries. The written request did not include any economic or legal justification for the application.

This gap was filled orally before the administrative Committee for that product, to whom it was explained that there were difficulties in obtaining the raw material from the associated countries, and that the main supplier among them could not provide the quality needed by the processing industry. Furthermore, the price in that country rose in relation to the preference granted. Finally, the steady increase in the duty imposed on imports from a third country could bring about a rise in the price of the finished product.

A month and a half after this oral explanation by the member state, and half a year after the submission of the original request, the appropriate Directorate-General in the Commission requested the member state to reconsider the submission, since after examination it had come to the conclusion that it could not recommend to the Commission the granting of such a quota. It can be assumed that the Directorate-General's request included the reasons for its position, as well as a summary of the conclusions based on its investigation, without, however, providing all the detailed data on which these conclusions were based.[62]

Usually member states, at this stage, withdraw their applications. But, in the case under discussion, after examining the conclusions of the Directorate-General, the member state argued (i) that the preference had not increased the supply from associated countries and imports had to come from third countries, and that the tariff quota was to be granted only for one year; and (ii) that trade relations with a third country were at stake, and Article 29a should be observed.

The written request of the member state had also been transmitted, according to the accepted procedure for advice, to the other member states. As a result some submitted the objections (i) that a regulation of a common agricultural arrangement had been issued for that product and, in such cases, only exceptions conforming to such a regulation were permitted; and (ii) that the request would affect the preferences granted to the associated member countries.

In the meantime, a final position was taken by the two Directorates-General in the Commission handling this particular request.

Directorate-General for the Industrial Sector
This Directorate stated that before a request by a member state, based on Article 25 in relation to the criteria included therein, is examined, it is necessary to determine whether the request was in accordance with the purpose of that article. This had been formulated very precisely by the European Court, in the case of 24/62, as follows. In order to prevent the disadvantages which might arise in the supplies of individual member countries as a result of the adjustment of the national tariff duties to the common external tariff, it found, after a critical examination of the argument of the member state, that the following main arguments – (i) that the member state was encountering difficulties of supply as a result of the limited ability of the associated members to export the product; and (ii) that there was a danger of a rise in the price of the finished product as the result of the large increase in the external tariff for imports of the raw material from third countries – were such as to justify the submission, if they were found to be substantiated.

To refute the first of these arguments the Directorate-General produced detailed data, including a later year (which proves that the examination took quite a long time), from which it was evident that the supply of raw materials from the associated countries was steadily rising over the previous three years. They also showed that, in fact, there were no difficulties in the supplies encountered by the member states, a fact which was also supported by the production statistics of the finished product, which showed a steady rise.

With respect to the second of the arguments, the Directorate-General indicated, on the basis of statistical data, a trend of falling world prices substantially greater than the increase in tariffs of the third countries (world prices of the raw materials fell to almost half their previous price). Furthermore, the quantity of raw material needed for the production of one ton of the finished product constituted less than a quarter of its weight, and less than 40 per cent of its value. From all this, it followed that the effect of a rise in the tariff would play very little part in the price of the product. They therefore found it incorrect to argue that there was a danger of an increase in price as a result of an increase in the tariff.

As to the higher price of imports from the associated countries, the Directorate-General stated that this was precisely the purpose of the preference. From this evidence it seemed impossible to argue that the processing industry of the member state suffered from disadvantages. Furthermore, the Directorate-General added the consideration that the extension of an exception to one member country would harm other member countries which were operating under similar conditions. It would also severely harm the associated countries for which the product was of primary importance. As to the argument based on Article 29, the

Directorate-General pointed out that this article included additional instructions to the one mentioned by the member state, which they felt had priority in this particular case; reference was made in this connection to Sub-article (c), of Article 29.[63]

Directorate-General for Agriculture
Only one additional argument was produced, namely that even if the rise in tariffs would have had a greater influence than it actually did in the particular case, the request had to be rejected, otherwise discrimination would have followed from the unequal treatment of a member state, something which could not be reconciled with the unified market arrangement for this sector, that had been achieved since July 1967.

The conclusion of both directorates-general was, therefore, that the request for a tariff quota should be rejected for the above mentioned reasons. This opinion, which had been submitted to the Commission, constituted the basis of its reasoned decision as submitted in writing to the member states.[64] It included, with some slight changes of drafting, most of the data and findings mentioned above.

This case was one of a denial of a request. In these circumstances the right of appeal before the Court of the Community is open to the member states. Such an appeal, however, is a lengthy and complicated procedure which both the Commission and usually the member states also try to avoid since it involves substantial manpower and time. All in all, only three cases[65] are known to the author which have been brought before the Court over decisions by Community institutions to reject a request for national tariff quotas.

It should be made clear that there is not always a need for such a lengthy process, for a number of reasons. These could include requests that are not in accordance with the provisions of the article; member states withdrawing their applications as a result of finding supplies within the Community, indicated during the meetings of the experts from the various national administrations; or a decision to reduce the Community tariff, or suspend it, may provide the answer to the problem.

In the cases where a request for a tariff quota has been granted, either by the Commission or by the Council, the decision is announced in the *Official Gazette*. It will include a detailed description of the reasons for the request by the member state, the legal references, an examination of the relevant data by the Commission, taking into account the special interest of the other member states and the associated member, as well as the explanation of the decision itself. A specific example will serve to illustrate this point.

Tariff quota for prunes
One example is Germany's request for a tariff quota of 7500 tons of

prunes at 5 per cent duty, and the decision of the Commission of the 22 December 1964.[66] This request, based on Article 25/3 and Article 29, argued that there was a need to provide the product to the low-income population at a low and stable price, in view of its importance, from a nutritional point of view. As there was no domestic production, and imports came mainly from third countries (95 per cent) the increase in duty had brought about a price rise and consumption had fallen at a steady rate.

The Commission studied current production levels and plans of future production and came to the conclusion that there was still a need to maintain the protective market, to provide an adequate investment climate for the realisation of the programme designed to enable the Community itself to supply the entire consumption of prunes (30,000 tons in 1970). But the unusual drought in 1964 had made it impossible to achieve even the planned targets for that year. The Commission, therefore, was willing to grant a tariff quota to Germany for 1964, especially taking into consideration the fact that such an exception would also contribute positively to the trade relations between the Community and third countries.

Using the level of imports between 1956 to 1963 as a basis for the estimate, it was expected that total imports in 1964 into Germany would amount to 6700 tons of which about 1000 tons could be imported from the Community; therefore, a tariff quota of 5700 tons seemed to the Commission to be justified. The tariff within such a quota had to be based on the following considerations.

(a) The aim of achieving a customs union should be the guiding principle and therefore attention must be given to the degree of present adjustment towards the customs union, in particular the degree of adjustment of the specific duty on this product in the member states.

(b) The special situation of the product for which the tariff quota had been asked must be taken into consideration. The Commission felt that they would be justified in fixing a duty within the quota which would meet the difficulties being raised by the member state without eliminating the desire of the Community to move gradually towards a common external tariff. It therefore seemed to them that it would be appropriate to continue to maintain the existing advantage of 6.4 per cent in favour of member countries, and not to reduce it.

In the light of these considerations, the Commission granted a tariff quota of 5700 tons, at a rate of duty of 7.7 per cent at a time when the external rate of duty toward third countries from Germany – after the adjustment already carried out towards the common external tariff – amounted to 10.4 per cent and the external tariff itself would eventually reach 16 per cent. The condition for granting the quota was that the member states should enjoy a tariff of 1.3 per cent so that an advantage of 6.4 per cent in favour of the member states would exist; furthermore, imports within the tariff quota should be destined only for internal consumption in that member state. This decision was valid from 1 January to 31 December 1965.

Additional information on this subject is included in the *Official Gazette* of 11 April 1969, from which it is evident that the process of decline in the total quantity of prunes imported continued. It can also be seen that the increase in the external duty from 5 to 16 per cent in the period 1961–69 and, within the tariff quota from 7.7 per cent to 11.6 per cent in the period 1964–69, was based on considerations of protection for the Community and not aimed at the interests of consumers in Germany. The Germans asked in 1969 for a quota of 6000 tons, at the original 1961 external duty of 5 per cent, and they received 5000 tons at a duty of 11.6 per cent. This seems to show that the decision is not related to the problem, for the duty within the quota was even higher than the original external tariff outside the original quota being granted by the Germans in 1965.

Tariff quota for tunny
A second interesting example is that of the national tariff quota for tunny for canning, granted to Italy. In this case, too, the member state submitted the request primarily for social considerations, namely, to maintain existing low prices, and to prevent a price rise due to a higher tariff (25 per cent). In addition, the request was designed to continue and secure the proper supply of fresh tunny for the processing industry, for which it depended primarily on third countries.

A tariff quota of 36,000 tons at zero duty was granted, based on the Commission's reasoning that – according to Article 25 – a tariff quota should only be granted in order to prevent disadvantages arising over the supply to a member state through its transition from the national tariff which existed before the first approximation to the external common tariff. In general, a diversion from the progressive stages of approximation is contrary to the interest of the creation of the common tariff.[67] In this particular case, however, the tariff in Italy was zero before the establishment of the Common Market and it served primarily the low-income consumer. This tariff quota has been granted to Italy for many years (see Table 4.5).

This is an example of a tariff quota which has remained duty-free throughout, and where the quota has been increased according to need a number of times, even within one year. The character changed over the transition period from a national to a Community tariff quota, although basically still serving the needs of Italy.

According to the data of the Community itself, imports from third

TABLE 4.5
Tariff Quotas in the European Community for Tunny,[a] 1964–69

Year	Granted on	Granted by	Under Article	Granted to	Quantity (tons)
1964	18/12/63	Commission	25(3)	Italy	25,000
	7/7/63	Commission	25(3)	Italy	incr. of 12,500
1965	22/12/64	Commission	25(3); 29	Italy	36,000
1968[b]	8/11/67	Commission	25(3); 29	Italy	30,000
1969[c]	16/1/69	Council		Common	30,000
			Agreement with GATT	France	976
			28 not specified	Italy	25,928
				Bel.Lux.	96
				Reserve	3,000
	26/6/69	Council	28	Common	incr. of 20,000
	8/12/69	Council	28	Common	incr. of 10,500

Source: *Amtsblatt*, No. 17, 4 February 1965; No. 13, 18 January 1969; No. L.157, 28 June 1969; No. L. 312, 12 December 1969.
[a] Tunny for canning (Ex.03.01.B1). Zero duty throughout.
[b] This tariff quota is probably the one agreed upon in the Kennedy Round signed on 30 July 1967. It consolidated a duty-free tariff quota for 30,000 tons and reduced the MFN duty from 25 to 22 per cent, subject to the reference price being respected.
[c] The total for the year was 60,500 tons: France (2180); Italy (52,000); Belgium/Luxemburg (270); and a reserve of 6050.

countries comprise a substantial share of the total consumption of this product in the Community, as well as in Italy. The question, therefore, arises as to the effect, if any, of the import of tunny within the tariff quota on the price of the final product in the Community generally, and in Italy in particular.

This point is particularly relevant in view of the fact that the primary purpose of this specific tariff quota is to provide cheap food products to Italian consumers. On the other hand, the Community in its considerations does not mention this factor at all. It simply calculates quantitatively the gap between internal production and consumption. But the mere fact that internal production had to be protected behind a tariff of 25 per cent (or 22 per cent since 1 January 1968) means that the particular industry is relatively less efficient. Therefore, total imports might adjust to the higher prices of the domestic industry in the Community. Even if this is not the case, it is possible that exports inside the Community have been subsidised. To some extent a possible answer for the later years can be found in the condition added to the tariff quota consolidated in the GATT, namely that the duty-free tariff quota is subject to the reference price being respected. This, in fact, means that the internal price of the domestic producers will govern the price of the imported product.

It would be useful if a much more elaborate case study of this particular item could be made, in order to see what the economic effects of this tariff quota have really been, and if it has helped the consumer and the producer in Italy, the importer or the exporter (tunny mainly comes from Japan) and what the effect has been on the price structure and on the processing industry in other member countries. At the same time it has to be remembered that the national tariff quota during the transition period was quite liberal and, therefore, the possibility of it being an effective quota was rather slim. Furthermore, during that period, trade was still hampered by internal tariffs between member states. The problem becomes more meaningful within the Community tariff quota, when there continues to be a liberal tariff quota policy; and, at the same time, outside the quota the tariff is relatively high, while internal trade barriers are gradually eliminated.

Summary of national tariff quotas
It is possible to summarise, therefore, the type of tariff quota most frequently in use in the Community. Generally the most common – until recently – related to an autonomous tariff quota for a specific commodity, defined according to quantity in an absolute manner, based on a liberal approach as to size and taking into account past trade, and being granted each time on a one-time basis to be renewed by request. In the course of time the tendency became to grant them only for the transition period, with the intention of their gradual elimination. For this purpose attempts have been made to reduce the quantity granted inside the tariff quota and to increase the rate of duty (which usually was an *ad valorem* duty, inside and outside the tariff quota), so that the gap between the internal tariff and the outside tariff will gradually be reduced, until finally eliminated completely. A tariff quota is generally granted for the use of all third countries (except for those quotas within trade and association agreements).

Usually, the tariff inside the quota is fixed below the MFN common external tariff, although not usually below the original tariff prior to the establishment of the customs union in the member country which obtained the tariff quota. A tariff quota is usually granted for a period of a year.

It should be mentioned, finally, that although this is the most typical type it is by no means the only one, for there are variations and nuances of different combinations. Nevertheless, this is the case most frequently found.

Although this examination of the various elements which go to make up a tariff quota has been made in the context of the discussion on administration, it is equally relevant to the economic analysis of such a quota, as well as to its legality within the GATT. These aspects are discussed in more detail elsewhere in this book.

TARIFF QUOTA ADMINISTRATION

As the imports within the tariff quotas are preferential imports, their administration by the importing country gives rise to various problems. Decisions need to be made as to how they will be allocated and on what principles, who is entitled to receive an allocation and what the size of each allocation should be. The period for which the allocation is valid also needs to be decided on, and measures taken to prevent the blocking of the quota, control re-exports to other member countries and the transfer of the quota benefit elsewhere. Before attempting to resolve these problems it will be useful to mention once again the two basic systems that an importing country can adopt. Both are in use today[68] in the member countries, with some individual differences.

The first is the 'greyhound' system, which is based on the principle of first-come-first-served (with respect to actual imports). According to this principle, imports from any third country enjoy the preferential treatment without discrimination as long as the quota is not filled. The quantities of the product imported are registered at the time of their arrival, in chronological order of their presentation for clearance through customs. If imports can enter the country through various customs stations, usually one of these is charged with overseeing the administration of the quota in the various stations so that the overall tariff quota will not be exceeded. When the quota is approaching completion, the various customs stations are notified by the overseeing station in charge, and further imports within the quota are permitted only after verification by telephone or telex.[69]

According to this particular system no prior licensing is required. Its advantage, apart from being non-discriminatory and in accordance with the GATT (for a detailed discussion see Chapter 2), is that, from an administrative point of view, it prevents the possibility of applications being misused by blocking the quotas. In other words only the actual volumes that are imported enjoy the preference, providing the quota is not already filled. The major disadvantage of the system generally — although in practice no indication has been given anywhere that this difficulty has been encountered — is the uncertainty which faces exporters or importers over the final tariff treatment given to the product on arrival.

Furthermore, experience in non-member countries shows that the desire to enjoy the benefits of the quota leads exporters or importers to try to reach the boundaries as early as possible — as soon as the quota is opened.[70] This leads to an uneven distribution of the supplies over a period of time, and to costly warehousing of imports, as well as to price fluctuations between the early period, when imports are cheap, and the later period, when the quota has been used up. Another disadvantage is that it might favour neighbouring countries, or the financially better-off exporters or importers who can afford the financing of large volumes at one time.

Under the second system, imports within a tariff quota require a prior licence. Applications must be submitted to a central authority which allocates the tariff quota in accordance with certain guiding principles. These are either based on past trade considerations, such as the respective imports of the various importers in a representative reference period,[71] or are based on a first-come-first-served basis in submitting applications.[72] In some cases a combination of these two principles is used with a certain percentage being granted on the basis of past trade whilst the rest is left to be allocated on the basis of first-come-first-served.[73] There are also other criteria of allocation, for instance the particular importance of individual industrial processors.[74]

It is desirable that such an allocation system should allow for a time-limit during which a permit is valid, in order to prevent the blocking of the quota. Secondly, some decision is also necessary about the size of the allocation to be granted to an individual importer so that he may not use up the total quota and resell it at the quota profit. Naturally, this is more true in the case where import permits within the quota are being allocated on the basis of first-come-first-served. The major advantage of this system of allocation is in the certainty provided to the importer and exporter, as well as to the member country, that the quota will not be surpassed. It also permits the central authority to make use of the quota in a way it finds most appropriate, by defining the people who are qualified to apply and the purpose for which the preferential imports are to be used. It is precisely for this reason that in some member countries this type of administrative system has been used so that specific preferential imports of raw materials may be provided for a processing industry, by only permitting certain producers to apply, dividing the imports among them only, according to their past trade.

But such a system is beset with dangers of arbitrary discrimination and misuses. It embodies all the disadvantages attributed to import licensing generally – too much bureaucracy, red tape, inefficiency and excessive interferences of all kinds, which may work to the detriment of the purposes for which the tariff quota was granted.

From this outline of the two basic systems the solutions to the problems outlined earlier begin to emerge. In the greyhound system there is a decentralisation of import allocation between the various customs stations, even though one of them may be charged with the overseeing of the operation of the tariff quota.

In the second system, administration is centred in a central authority in charge of granting licences. The principle of allocation in the greyhound system is first-come-first-served, whereas in the prior-licence system it is usually based on past trade in some reference period, although this need not be the only principle. The size of the import within the quota in the greyhound system is usually based on the actual amount imported, while in the prior licence-system the size may also depend on the allocation criteria in use.

As to who is entitled to enjoy the benefit of the tariff quota – under the greyhound system there is usually a limitation to qualifications; but when the prior-licensing procedure is used special qualifications may be required before it is possible to start importing within the scheme. Suppressing the tariff quota is impossible under the first scheme, whereas in the second the time limit prevents a suppression of the allocation. Usually, provisions are made in both systems to prevent the transfer of the right to a preferential import by a strict code of penalties. The same applies to the re-exportation of the preferred imports.

In the past there were many differences of detail between member countries in the administration of tariff quotas. Some of these were the result of the application of the different basic systems which predominated at that time (either greyhound or prior licensing). Other differences were the result of particular administrative practices customary in individual countries. These differences relate to such questions as:

(a) where can a licence be obtained and which is the authority granting it;[75]

(b) who can obtain a licence and what particular requirements must be met to obtain it;[76]

(c) for how long is a prior licence valid;[77]

(d) can a licence be transferred;[78]

(e) can an imported commodity be re-exported in an unaltered form;[79] and

(f) is an importer bound to a particular customs station.[80]

In addition, many more differences existed in national legislation which affected the treatment of imports within a tariff quota, despite the fact that they did not specifically relate to the administration of tariff quotas themselves. Thus, for instance, there were variations in the requirements for certificates of origin which, in Germany for example, could be even specified differently from case to case.[81] Furthermore, individual requirements for financing imports, as well as other regulations which relate to imports of certain types of commodities, have different national characteristics. Even the definition of an 'importer' varies between countries.

All these differences in detail, as well as others which cannot be discussed here at length, could constitute factors which discriminated between importers of different member countries. In one country, regulations could be more strict, time-consuming or discouraging to a prospective importer, and in another member country they may favour the importer. This problem becomes all the more acute, the more the process of integration advances and the barriers to internal trade in the Community are progressively eliminated.

To the extent that the Community as a whole becomes a contracting party to agreements with outside countries the differences in national administration create difficulties, through the contractual right of the outside party to the agreement to utilise the tariff quota to the full. As however, administrative practices in member countries differ, imports within a total tariff quota may be directed to the member country with the least restrictive administrative procedures. In order to prevent such a situation arising during the transition period, national quotas have been determined for each member state, out of the total tariff quota. This, however, has the disadvantage for the outside party, that if the quota in one particular member country is not fully utilised, it cannot benefit from its contractual right in another member state. Thus harmonisation of the individual administrative practices was called for.[82]

SUMMARY

Before moving on to a discussion of Community tariff quotas it may be helpful to have the rather detailed account of national tariff quotas, which comprises the first part of this chapter, in a more compact form. The main facts that have emerged are:

(1) There were some precedents for national tariff quotas in the member countries before the establishment of the Common Market, for various purposes. These included facilitating the finishing trade, maintaining special relations with dependent territories or taking care of special conditions of industries in particular circumstances, and so on. But these cases were only of marginal importance, as a tool of commercial policy.

(2) The importance of national tariff quotas has only increased within the framework of the Community and, although the purposes here were also varied, the primary reason for their establishment was to facilitate the harmonisation of the common external tariff.

(3) It is for this reason that the possibility of applying national tariff quotas in new member countries played a role in the discussions of the enlargement of the Community.

(4) Initially the national tariff quota was usually of a liberal character, precisely because it served to facilitate harmonisation and not protection. But with the advancement of the process of integration into a full customs union, the protective element started to play a role, in

particular due to the free circulation of goods within the Community at large.

(5) From a legal point of view, the Treaty of Rome, as well as the European Coal and Steel Community, referred explicitly to tariff quotas only with respect to national tariff quotas. This was either by reference to Article 15 of the convention of the ECSC, or by reference to Article 25 of the Treaty of Rome, as well as to the Protocol annexed to the Treaty, or to List G.

(6) National tariff quotas, permitted under the above articles of the Treaty and its protocols, were of a limited nature and could be applied only with regard to specified lists of commodities under very special and strict conditions.

(7) In general, the position of the Community institutions with respect to national tariff quotas is a negative one. They are accepted only as a necessary evil, to be applied as a last resort; furthermore, they are considered to be a measure of a temporary character to be used during the transition period – a position not accepted by the member countries, and without a formal basis in the Treaty, despite its being the situation *de facto*.

(8) From a practical point of view, national tariff quotas never played an important role, if considered in the context of overall imports of the Community and of the individual member countries. That is not to say that, for individual commodities, their importance is trivial; on the contrary, in some of the commodities they play a very important role.

(9) The limited experience with national tariff quotas indicates that from a technical point of view the system operated rather well. It has to be borne in mind, however, that at the peak of the system less than 300 tariff quotas were requested. Thus, conclusions derived from this experience may not be valid for a case when there may be thousands in operation simultaneously, this being a theoretical possibility in the case of preferences for developing countries.

(10) Their history in the European Community shows a continuous process of reduction, with the aim to eliminate them as quickly as possible.

(11) From an administrative point of view, the process of determining a national tariff quota is a time-consuming and complicated process.

(12) There are two prevalent systems of administering imports within the quota, the greyhound and the prior-licensing system. No evidence exists that any of the drawbacks inherent in either of the systems have made themselves felt. Thus, there have been no attempts to block the quota in the prior-licensing system, nor have there been serious overdrafts of quotas in the greyhound system, and no attempt was made to re-export commodities in cases where the prohibition of such action constituted a prior requirement.

(13) The typical national tariff quota was related to a specific

commodity, was defined according to quantity in an absolute manner, was granted on a one-time basis, usually for a year, and could be renewed on request. Starting from a liberal allocation, it became more strict with respect to quantity and the margin of preferences within the quota. The quota was usually a non-discriminatory one, towards all third countries. While this was the usual case, many exceptions existed. Most interesting for future discussions are the examples of greater automation in the determination of a tariff quota, for instance, a case of the protocol relating to the import of bananas by Western Germany.

(14) Experience with national tariff quotas has not been sufficiently studied, either to determine their economic effect or to see to what extent the purposes for which they were originally granted have been achieved. Such an examination would require detailed studies for a specific commodity in order that the precise effects could be understood. Amongst other items it would be necessary to examine the following to obtain an evaluation:

(*a*) whether the purpose is to help the consumer, the producer, the exporter abroad, or the importing manufacturer within the country;

(*b*) whether imports have been carried out within an effective tariff quota or not;

(*c*) the number of importers, exporters and manufacturers;

(*d*) if the intervention of government monopoly is present at any stage;

(*e*) whether the imports enter through various customs stations in the greyhound system, or only one customs station;

(*f*) the number of supplying countries; in relation to the particular commodities; and

(*g*) finally, the structure of the domestic-protected industry and the margin of preference, as this has a bearing on the economic effect of the quota.

(15) With respect to administration, one further distinction is of interest, namely, whether the national tariff quota is autonomous with respect to a member country during a transition period, or whether it is autonomous with respect to other member third countries. Also, if it is contractual to one country or to all third countries.

(16) National tariff quotas had to be granted to *all* member states, in contravention to the specific articles and protocols of the Treaty and contrary to the spirit of the Agreement. This was a result of the absence of unified Community rules and procedures, when the Community institutions had to negotiate trade and association agreements. Such national tariff quotas had to be granted in view of the different external and internal duties prevailing in the member countries. These serious

drawbacks will be discussed more fully when examining the subject of Community tariff quotas in the remainder of this chapter. It is, however, worth noting that if the practice had been permitted to continue, such national tariff quotas could have threatened to undermine the Community character of the external tariff.

COMMUNITY TARIFF QUOTAS

As national tariff quotas could only be applied to specific commodities under special conditions and not in all member states at once, according to Article 25, it was necessary to rely on other articles of the Treaty of Rome, such as Articles 28, 111, 113 and 114, as a basis for them. But these do not actually permit solutions which are contrary to the Community character of the external tariff. The autonomous allocation of national tariff quotas, in the case of trade agreements or association agreements, could constitute under certain circumstances a breach of the Community character of the external tariff.

A preliminary condition of the application of a preferential tariff rate within a tariff quota is its continuity, as long as the quota has not been fully utilised. In other words, within the Community, it is not permitted to apply two different rates of duty to the same commodity at the same time. This could happen if the national quota had already been fully utilised in one country while in another the quota had not yet been completed. Furthermore, this situation could lead to discriminatory treatment for importers in some parts of the Community, who may not enjoy equal access to imports within the overall quota. Such a situation may falsify competitive conditions – in particular in the processing industry – contrary to Article 3 of the Treaty.

There is a danger that the overall tariff quota might not be fully utilised in cases where contractual obligations to a third country, or an associated country, require it. Such a case would be one where a member state had been allocated a national tariff quota which was underutilised, whilst other member states had national tariff quotas which were fully used, but who could have imported more if additional quota quantities were made available. Under these circumstances the overall Community obligation towards third countries may be jeopardised. The problem of national tariff quotas is also directly related to the observance of the re-exportation prohibition.

Thus it becomes more difficult to maintain national tariff quotas where tariff barriers are being eliminated, which is the inevitable result of the process of integration within the Community. These difficulties, together with the fact that an increasing number of tariff quotas had to be negotiated by Community institutions, with third countries or associated countries – which would constitute a breach of the rules of the Treaty and the spirit of the Community if they were turned into national tariff quotas – encouraged the Commission to seek a Community solution, in line with the Community character, which could be immediately applied. At that stage of the process of integration (in the middle of 1966) this meant that compromises had to be made if emphasis was to be put on the immediate application of the scheme.

An ideal solution, but one which would have disregarded actual conditions in the member countries, would have been a Community arrangement in which a central authority would have been in direct contact with the importers, or the customs stations authorised under the scheme. But such a solution could not possibly have been adopted with the existing national legislation in the member countries for, at that time, even the more general objective of harmonising the national laws and regulations that concerned tariff quotas in the member countries was beyond the reach of the central Community institutions. If such a solution could have been adopted it would have transformed the national authorities into executive organs of the central authority. In the conditions prevailing in 1966 neither of these possibilities were realistic enough to be applied immediately.

The Commission, therefore, submitted some guidelines as an 'impulse'[83] to the Council of Ministers for their consideration. These were intended as a temporary solution, to be valid at the most up to the end of the transition period. Their underlying assumption was that each member state would administer for the time being the allocated part of a community quota, in accordance with its own national rules and regulations. Unlike the previous arrangements, under which the overall quota had been allocated in advance, definitely and completely, the guidelines suggested that the quota be split into two blocks. One of these would consist of the major part of the quota, and would also be valid for a substantial part of the period; it should be allocated on the basis of past trade (based on the latest available statistical data as reference period).

According to the suggestions of the Commission the second block would be allocated at the end of the first period on the basis of the percentage of imports, including the utilisation of the imports in the first quota period, up to the latest comparable date for which import figures were available in all member countries. There were, however, some exceptions. In order not to break the continuation of equal treatment within the Community, a member state which had utilised the full allocation granted to it, one month at the latest before the termination of the first block, was entitled to draw the additional quota immediately, notifying the Commission if its action within two weeks. Such an action, however, could only be taken by each member state once. Naturally, this quantity would then be taken into account when allocating the second quota. On the other hand, the overall reserve could be increased above the level originally planned if certain of the member states did not fully utilise their first allocation. In that case, the rest of their first allocation, after the termination of the first block period, would be returned to the overall reserve.

The proposals allowed for the possibility of transferring an unused part of the first allocation to the next period, provided the member state offered proof, based on objective criteria, that this transferred remainder would be fully utilised. It is obvious that their proposal was not intended to be an ideal solution of a permanent nature, but was intended to solve the most urgent problems in the best possible way, bearing in mind prevailing national legislation and the stage that had been reached in the integration of the Community. The most immediate concern of the Commission was the problem that preferred imports in some of the countries had been discontinued, while other countries continued to import at preferred rates. Such a situation was contrary to the nature of the common external tariff, and also discriminated against importers in certain member countries. Furthermore, the allocation into national, finally determined, quotas prevented non-member countries from making full use of their claims upon the Community. This occurred where some member countries might not have been able to use their whole quota whilst, in the other member countries, there existed the opportunity for preferred imports but the quotas had already been used up.

A method had to be found to permit the transfer of quantities allotted from one country to another during the quota period, but such a procedure would have been contrary to the national legislation in the member states. The solution, therefore, seemed to be to allocate the overall quota in blocks for a number of shorter periods, adjusting the internal allocation for subsequent periods on the basis of trade shares in the previous one. Sub-dividing into so many small quotas would be undesirable from an economic point of view due to the uncertainty which would affect importers adversely. The solution, therefore, seemed to be a sub-division into two blocks only, the first block comprising the major share and extending over the longer period, whilst adjustments could be made once within the block period and, finally, during the second period of the quota.

The drawing right was intended to secure the continuity of imports into the Community, without creating a situation whereby a member state which had already utilised its first allocation would be importing at a higher rate of duty than others importing at the same time at a preferred rate of duty. It cannot be denied that this danger could still exist if, within the first period, a particular country utilised not only its first allocation but also its full drawing rights and still needed additional imports; while others, at the same time, had not fully utilised their allocations. It is evident that this danger is considerably less for the period during which the overall allocated share (including the drawing rights) can be utilised is shorter, as it can only be utilised over the first period of the block, instead of the whole period of the quota.

By allocating the remainder in a later period it was intended precisely to ensure that the quota would be as fully utilised as possible. To the extent that there were no other considerations the allocation was based on the experience in that particular year and on the latest returns within the quota period. An additional point which needs emphasis is the fact that the memorandum covering the Commission's suggestions also permitted exceptions and alternatives. For example, whenever forecasts or changing conditions anticipated a change in the import requirement, the member countries' allocations could be affected, sometimes after consultation with other member countries. This meant that the Commission would have to play the role of supervisor, negotiator and arbiter – there was no automatic assurance that allocation would be based on past trade.

This role of the Commission meant that it was desirable that it be given a special mandate as the deciding authority in this field. This mandate was necessary so that the Commission could have the authority to determine alternative ways of managing the administration of the scheme. For instance, a possible alternative mentioned in the memorandum was the prior complete and final allocation of the overall quota into national tariff quotas in those cases where the quotas were likely to be used up quickly, and at more or less the same rate, by the various member countries.

Another important decision which would be the domain of the Commission, was whether national quotas should be administered according to one and the same unified system of administration, or whether their administration could be left to each of the member states to be determined autonomously. As prior licensing was not possible in all the member states – because there was no appropriate law enabling this method of administration in Germany at that time – only a unified system of the greyhound type could be applied, as this existed in all member states. Even so, this system had been applied differently in the various countries and did not ensure a completely identical treatment of importers in all member states. It should also be mentioned that even if countries had been permitted to operate their individual national schemes of administration autonomously and some of them had applied the prior-licensing system, they would still have had to report the utilisation of their quotas on the basis of actual imports cleared through customs – as is the case in the greyhound system – despite the fact that import licences had been issued.

The above memorandum was transmitted for discussion to the group of experts for economic questions, who examined the memorandum during six meetings and came up with a proposal of their own which introduced a number of important changes to the original scheme.

Amongst these was the suggestion that the Council should select the administrative procedures under which a particular Community tariff quota should be administered; this could vary from case to case.

But the most interesting proposal was a suggested method for building a reserve and administering national quotas on the basis of the greyhound procedure. Under this:

(a) Out of the overall quota, the Council would allocate an initial quota to each member state. This would be a substantial percentage of the overall quota and would be at the disposal of the member state over the whole period.

(b) If a member state should utilise 90 per cent of its original allocation it would immediately notify the Commission; it would then be automatically entitled to receive a second allocation, which would normally be set at a certain percentage of its first quota. This percentage would be equal for all the member states and would be determined for each product differently. If there were special conditions which would warrant a different determination of the second allocation, this would be permitted.

(c) If a member state should also utilise up to 90 per cent of a second allocation it would again notify the Commission, and this would entitle it to a third quota, based, as a rule, on a certain percentage of its first allocation. This percentage would usually be lower than the one set for the second allocation, but here too, exceptions would be possible.

(d) The same procedure as mentioned in (c) could be applied time and again, in the case of a remainder.

(e) After utilising its first allocation, each member state would have the right to subdivide its second, or any subsequent allocation, into sub-quotas, and to use one, or more, one after the other, if there is sufficient reason to suppose that the whole allocation might not perhaps be utilised fully. This possibility, however, would not release a member state in any way from its obligation to open an additional sub-quota out of the rest of the quota, should it reach 90 per cent utilisation of the present sub-quota.

(f) Should it happen that the first quota was not fully utilised in some member states, but in other member states the remaining quantities could be utilised, the Council could decide, with respect to the annual tariff quotas, that each member state would have to return those unused quantities which exceeded 20 per cent of its first quota at the end of the ninth month.

(g) The Commission would register the allocated quotas granted to member states, and must be advised, during the operation of the quota, of all notifications from each member state about the allocated quota and the remaining quantities. It would be responsible for ensuring that that the last allocation would only include the remaining quantities.

(h) Each member state would be responsible for introducing the measures needed to compute the imports within the tariff quota until the quota was used up. In order to facilitate the registration of these imports, they would be counted whenever the products were cleared for consumption at the customs.

It seems best to illustrate the scheme with a numerical example.[84] It has been assumed that there is a tariff quota of 40,000 tons, divided into two blocks of which the first consisted of 85 per cent of the overall quota, or 34,000 tons. The second block consists of a reserve of 15 per cent, that is, 6000 tons. The first block has been divided on the basis of past trade among the member countries. On the assumption that Germany's share amounts to 80 per cent of the total imports this would mean a first block of 27,200 tons. If this first block were utilised up to 90 per cent, or 24,480 tons, Germany would then be entitled to draw a second quota of 15 per cent of the first block, or a further 4080 tons. If this quota had in turn been utilised up to 90 per cent, or 3672 tons, Germany would have been entitled to a third block amounting to 7.5 per cent of the original, or 2040 tons; and so on. As long as a remainder was still available it could continue to draw additional blocks of 2040 tons, provided it had utilised 90 per cent of the previous blocks.

This method would obviously enable Germany to utilise a much bigger share — if its rate of utilisation was faster than in other countries — than would have been the case if the quota had been allocated to Germany right from the start according to its relative share in past trade. Instead of obtaining an overall allocation of 32,000 tons, Germany would draw almost 33,320 tons, based on the addition of the following allocations: 27,200+4080+2040 (as long as the original reserve was available). If other countries did not utilise their share, the allocation could have been even larger.

The same would, of course, be true for other member countries who might be in the same position. It would be very important under this system to expedite all procedures connected with imports, and member states with cumbersome administration procedures might not be able to enjoy the benefits of the quota to the same extent. The particular advantage of the scheme, according to the Group, lies in the automatic process of allocation and its continuity. Furthermore, it would reduce the task and position of the Commission — a very important element in the eyes of the member states, who could be reluctant to see a transfer of authority to the Community institutions.

Among other suggestions of the Group were included alternative systems of allocating tariff quotas. One suggestion was the possibility of allocating tariff quotas ahead of time, as well as granting prior licences in the member state. In such a case, if the Council should decide that the tariff quota should be allocated between certain categories of importers, or between all importers generally, this quota would be allocated into final allotments. These would then be granted to each member state who would administer them in their territories. Where the quota was of an annual character, the Council would require each member state to take measures which would permit the adjustment of the quota during the first eight days of the tenth month. The Council at that stage could take the necessary steps to adjust or change the allocation of the quota if the situation should so warrant.

The suggestions were discussed extensively and were also presented to national specialists for comment. The result was a new draft which set out proposals for guidelines for Community tariff quotas, and which emerged in November 1968. The guidelines, in the first place, rearranged and enlarged the number of possible systems of administering Community tariff quotas.

The first of these related to the complete allocation of the tariff quota between member states, at the beginning of the quota period stipulating the same method of administration. This would apply in those cases where it could be anticipated with certainty that the Community tariff quota would be utilised steadily, in which case the entire quota could be allocated among the member states by the Council, without a reserve.

A second system suggested in the guidelines is also one where entire Community tariff quotas are allocated to the member states at the beginning of the quota period, but unlike the previous example, it would enable – in the case of annual tariff quotas – adjustments to be made to the quota for each member state, upwards or downwards, at least two months before the end of the period of the quota. Naturally, this condition would require appropriate legislation in member states to permit the adjustment of a quota during a quota period.

Third was a system which also related to the complete allocation of the Community tariff quotas to member countries at the beginning of the quota period, yet leaving to each member state the choice of the system of administration. If, for instance, there were special considerations – such as different regulations in member states which prevented them from applying the same methods of administration – it would be possible for the Council to decide that the total quota should be completely allocated, without leaving a reserve, and permitting each of the member states to utilise its quota according to its own system of administration.

Finally, there was a fourth system which proposed the partial allocation of the quota at the beginning of the period while building up a reserve; this is the system which has already been fully discussed while dealing with the suggestions of the Group for economic questions. Some additional changes were introduced into the scheme to deal with the case when certain member countries completely used up the available reserve during the first period, before additional quantities could be made available through the return of the unused portions of the quotas of other member countries. If these additional quantities are made available at a later stage, the member state which first completely utilised the reserve would have preference in obtaining an additional allotment up to the customary percentage. Then other member states would proceed in a similar manner, one after the other, in the sequence in which they had applied for additional quotas, on fully utilising their original allocation.

The guidelines did not meet with the approval of the economic group of the Council, though numerous sessions were devoted to discussing this document. The objections had their origin in the authority given to the Commission for the administration of tariff quotas. It appeared during the debate that the experts were always very reluctant to let themselves be persuaded even to the idea of creating a Community reserve for a certain number of quotas. Thus, the abstract approach of how to administer tariff quotas had to be more or less abandoned. From 1968 onwards the Council and Commission could lean on a series of concrete cases of individual Community tariff quotas, in which the principles of the guidelines have been embodied and which were the subject of international arrangements, within the framework of the GATT, association agreements, or commercial agreements.

For 1969, the Commission had already submitted to the Council a series of proposals or rules for opening and administering certain tariff quotas – namely, aluminium and certain ferro-alloys; those which the Community had opened for Turkey, such as figs and hazel nuts; or the tariff quota in favour of Iran, within the framework of a commercial agreement, about raisins. These proposals concerned twenty-four products, and out of these the Council sanctioned thirteen products to become liable to unified administrative measures, according to the greyhound system. It also retained the principle of the Community reserve for the majority of the twenty-four cases mentioned, although it discarded the Commission proposals in three cases.

The Council, in fact, distributed in one allocation the Community tariff quotas in newsprint and magnesium. In the case of ferro-alloys the initial quotas of member states were allocated, not on the basis of percentages of past trade, but on the basis of quotas previously sanctioned by the Commission. Furthermore, it is worth mentioning that in four cases, the Commission had proposed to distribute the tariff quota completely, on the assumption that, in view of their small volume *vis à vis* Community needs, they would be phased out rapidly in an even manner by all member states.

From this it can be seen that, in 1969, the Commission's proposals about the administration of Community tariff quotas were adopted by the Council in the majority of cases without substantial modification. Thus, a practice had been established which engendered respect for the Community character of these quotas.

Since those early discussions the administration of Community tariff quotas has progressed in a number of ways. In the first place the process of harmonisation of national legislation has continued. For example, in Germany a law[85] was passed concerning the method of allocation of tariff quota permits, which specifies the conditions for, and details of, a prior allocation system of permits, and for its management and control. Some changes in the Dutch Administrative Instruction for Community tariff quotas have also been introduced. In the 1968 regulations a telephone procedure was introduced for certain tariff quota products from countries like Turkey and Iran. This was done because speedy utilisation required a change from the prior licensing to the first-come-first-served system of allocation. Similar changes were also introduced in Italy.

There has also been a substantial advance towards the harmonisation of the certificate of origin and the treatment of products originating in a particular country. At the beginning of the transition period, these origin requirements were different in the various member countries, and sometimes even different from case to case.

Secondly, through the introduction of the Generalised System of Preferences,[86] the enlargement of the Community and the agreement with the rest of the European Free Trade Association (EFTA), the role of the Commission in administering tariff quotas has increased little by little. There are, for example, regulations to establish Community supervision of imports of certain products from various sources, such as the rest of the EFTA and Finland.[87] These regulations refer to those products which were contained in lists annexed to protocols of the agreements between the Community and the remaining EFTA countries. It was stipulated that any reduction of duties should be limited to indicative ceilings above which the customs duties applicable to third countries could be reintroduced. The various regulations not only established a system of supervision at the Community level but empowered the Commission, where necessary and after the ceilings were reached, to issue a regulation reimposing the *higher* duty.

TYPES OF COMMUNITY TARIFF QUOTAS

Until now the discussion has referred to Community tariff quotas in general, but they can be divided into important sub-classifications. There are Community tariff quotas which are global in nature, that is, imports within the quota may come from any source. Some of these global quotas are contractual and some of them are autonomous. There are also Community tariff quotas of a preferential character, which can be divided between those granted to one particular country, and those to a group of preferred countries. (This does not refer to quotas within the GSP, which are discussed later.)

An examination of the trend[88] of the development of the Community tariff quotas in the 'original Six' shows that the number of *contractual* Community tariff quotas had fallen from thirteen in 1969 to nine in 1973; their absolute volume remained the same or declined. A comparision of preferential tariff quotas with those established in 1969 shows that, in the main, these original tariff quotas, too, have either been reduced in number, reduced in amounts, or shared by a larger group of countries.

But, in total, the number of tariff quotas has increased, through the additional new agreements made between the Community and various countries.[89] Within this the number of autonomous tariff quotas has increased from one to eight, partly through the reduction of national tariff quotas based on List G which have been transformed into Community tariff quotas.

COMMUNITY TARIFF QUOTAS AND NEW MEMBER STATES

The accession of new member states posed some new problems for the administration of the Community tariff quotas. On the one hand, as has already been explained, the nature of the Community requires that equal and continuous access to the quota should be ensured for all Community importers, and that the rate of levy for the quota should be applied until the quota is used up. In order to put this principle into practice, it was usual for a Community reserve to be instituted. On the other hand, beginning in 1974, new member states had to participate in the Community tariff quota arrangements while they were not fully integrated into the Community, for they were still maintaining internal and external tariffs and rates, which were only partially adjusted.

Thus, according to the Agreement of Accession,[90] by January 1974 these countries had to adjust their external tariff only to the extent of 40 per cent of the difference, wherever their rate of duty differed by more than 15 per cent from the common external tariff (CET). On the same date, they had to reduce the internal duty by 40 per cent. For certain products this applied within the limits of tariff quotas. Therefore there were different duties for the tariff quotas of the Community as originally constituted and for those within the tariff quotas of the new member countries.

To complicate matters even more, there were cases where the new member countries still benefited from previous preferential arrangements – such as those of the EFTA and the British Commonwealth – which enabled the new member countries to import products from these countries either free of duty, or at preferred rates. Furthermore, there were also countries with which the Community had agreements which had not been finalised with respect to the new member states.

The Community solutions seemed to be pragmatic. There were cases where the original Community tariff quota was in fact split into two, with one true Community tariff quota for the Community as originally constituted,[91] and national tariff quotas for the new members.[92] Another solution was found for the case of the products whose tariff quotas represent only a small share of the overall imports into the Community as originally constituted and where imports within the tariff quotas were utilised very quickly. In many of these cases the Community tariff quota was divided into individual national tariff quotas in one single allocation.[92]

Again, there were occasions when a newly agreed tariff duty for the entire Community, both outside and inside the tariff quota, seemed to offer a way around the problem,[93] and there were even Community tariff quotas for the entire Community[94] which disregarded the difficulties. Thus, despite the preferential position which certain countries held with the new member countries, and despite the differential tariffs inside and outside the tariff quotas, only a partial first allocation was made to member countries of the Community tariff quotas, creating a reserve for those who were first to utilise the quantity allotted to them.

Theoretically such an arrangement can create all kinds of unfair situations. For instance, member countries with lower duties inside the tariff quota have the advantage of importing their product cheaper. By using their quota more quickly and drawing on the reserves more heavily they could gain a competitive advantage over producers in other member countries who require the same raw material or semi-finished product. Another theoretical possibility would be the case where a new member country could obtain unlimited quantities of a product at preferential rates, while the member states of the original Community could only use the tariff quota.

In practice, these events have not occurred. The Community officials argue that the reason is that the Community tariff quotas are autonomously established at the request of the member countries, and if the quantities are not sufficient there is no problem in increasing the amounts by granting a supplementary tariff quota. Even when the Community tariff quotas are contractual ones, within the GATT or other bilateral agreements, then the member countries usually are not particularly interested in them, and quotas have been established at the request of the parties to the agreement.

Since the Community tariff quotas for the enlarged Community have only been in operation for a relatively short time, it may still be premature to draw final conclusions. But from enquiries made in the

96 The Role of Tariff Quotas in Commercial Policy

Commission, and in the new member countries,[95] their operation seems to function smoothly and satisfactorily.

NOTES AND REFERENCES

1. This is also evident from the Commissions's Statement in the *EEC Bulletin*, September–October 1961, p. 39.
2. While this case study refers only to the national tariff quotas in the Community as originally established, it is worth while pointing out that national tariff quotas were also used in the enlargement of the Community. See the Treaty of Accession of Denmark, Ireland and the United Kingdom to the European Community; Protocol 8 of the *European Committee's Treaty and Decision of the Council* (London: HM Stationery Office, 1972) Cmnd.4862–1–1 and Miscellaneous 8, Part 1, pp. 88–9. Also see the Agreements between the other EFTA countries and the Community, where national tariff quotas were provided for the new members – Denmark, Norway and the United Kingdom – during the transition period. Also see the Agreement between Switzerland, Leichtenstein and the Community; *GATT* L/3758, Addenda, protocol 1, Annex A and B; and the Agreement with Austria, *GATT* L/378, Addenda 1, Protocol 1, Article 1(4), p. 11.
3. See Horst Lauberan, 'Der Gemeinsame Zolltarift und seine Handhabung', *Zeitschrift für Europarecht*, Vol. 2, p. 196.
4. For examples, see James E. Meade, Hans Leisner and Sidney Wells, *Case Studies in the European Economic Community* (London: Oxford University Press, for the Royal Institute of International Affairs, 1962) p. 407.
5. *European Yearbook*, Vol. II, published under the auspices of the Council of Europe (The Hague: Martinus Nijhoff, 1956) pp. 549–51.
6. *Treaty Setting up the European Economic Community* (London: HM Stationery Office, 1967) pp. 11–12.
7. With respect to the meaning of 'harmful consequences' see the discussion on List G which follows.
8. National tariff quotas, as opposed to Community tariff quotas are those granted to one or a few member states only, and not to all member states uniformly.
9. See *EEC Bulletin*, September–October 1961, p. 39.
10. This is the position in many of the Commission's Reports as well as stated in the name of the European Parliament and the Council of the European Community. See, for instance, *Tenth General Report on the Activities of the Community* (Brussels: European Community, June 1967) Commission Sec. II.
11. *Treaty Setting up the European Economic Community, op. cit.*, p. 12; which states that in carrying out the tasks entrusted to it under this section (including Article 25) the Commission will be guided by:
    (*a*) The need to promote trade between member states and third countries;
    (*b*) Developments in conditions of competition within the Community in so far as they lead to an improvement in the competitive capacity of commercial concerns;
    (*c*) The Community's requirements as regards the supply of raw materials and semi-finished goods; in this respect the Commission will take care to avoid distorting, as between member states, conditions of competition in respect of finished goods; and
    (*d*) The need to avoid serious disturbances in the economies of member states and for ensuring rational development of production and an expansion of consumption within the Community.
12. *EEC Bulletin*, September–October, 1961, p. 39.
13. *Treaty Setting up the European Economic Community, op. cit.*, p. 8.
14. *Ibid.*, p. 12.

15. *EEC Bulletin*, No. 5, 1962, p. 35.
16. According to the Treaty, the Federal Republic of Germany enjoys an annual duty-free tariff quota based, from the first approximation of external duties and until the end of the second stage, on 90 per cent of the quantities imported in 1967, less the quantities coming from the countries and territories referred to in Article 131 of the Treaty. From the end of the second stage until the third stage ends, the quota will be based on 80 per cent of the quantity defined above. This quota would be increased by 50 per cent of the difference between the total quantities imported during each preceding year and those quantities which were imported in 1956. If imports should be lower by comparison with 1956, the quota would not be smaller than the quota determined initially for each of the respective periods. As soon as the common custom tariff applies in its entirety, the quota should be based on 75 per cent of the import of 1956 and again be increased by 50 per cent as above. After deduction of the imports from countries and territories referred to in Article 131 of the Treaty, the figure of imports for the year 1956, serving as a basis for calculating the quota, was 290,000 tons. A final provision of this protocol was the agreement of the member states that, if the countries and territories are unable to supply the quantities required by West Germany in full, the member states would declare their readiness to agree to a corresponding increase in the German tariff quota. It should be mentioned in this respect that the Yaoundé Agreement in Protocol XI includes a declaration of member states with regard to tariff quotas for bananas, which makes it conditional upon the member states to consult the associated members exporting bananas as to whether under certain conditions they are able to supply parts or the total amount required (see *Das Abkommen von Yaoundé*, published by EWG, Annex 1). As far as the actual experience with the quota is concerned, the point needs to be made that, in fact, the associated countries were unable to supply the quantities required by Germany and thus the tariff quota for bananas during the transition period was much higher than the one determined beforehand. In 1967, for example, instead of a tariff quota of 380,000 tons, Germany had a tariff quota of 613,000 tons. See *Fruit: A Review by the Commonwealth Secretariat*, No. 17 (London: Commonwealth Secretariat, 1968) p. 136.
17. In Italy, the tariff quotas consisted, initially, of the total import of 1956 and within these limits the duty applicable was that which existed on the date the Treaty came into force. This quantity would be reduced by 20 per cent, starting from the sixth year and up to the end of the second stage, and in the third stage the annual quota would consist of only 50 per cent of the initial quota. For four years after the completion of the transition period, imports from third countries could continue to enjoy preferential treatment within a tariff quota which would be 20 per cent of the original quota. As far as Belgium is concerned, tariff quotas have been fixed, which are completely duty-free up to an amount which is equivalent to 85 per cent of the quantity imported during the last year for which statistics are available. These annual quotas would be granted from the beginning of the period of transition till the beginning of the third stage. With the start of the third stage, the quota will consist of 50 per cent of the original tariff quota.
18. *Basic Instruments and Selected Documents*, 1st Supplement, *op. cit.*, pp. 14–17.
19. *Treaty Setting up the European Economic Community*, *op. cit.*, p. 132.
20. *EEC Bulletin*, No. 3, 1960, p. 34, states 'the resort to the use of tariff quotas, a solution which was undesirable in itself [but which] provided the only means of reconciling the essential economic and social needs of this or that member state.'
21. See Protocols in the *Treaty Setting up the European Economic Community*, *op. cit.*, pp. 207–25.
22. The list for Germany included herring and sprats, fresh cod, hake, haddock and rockfish, certain types of wine and natural cork.
    For Italy it included tunny fish and sardines, cod (including stockfish and klipfish), fillets of cod (including those of stockfish and klipfish), denatured ethyl alcohol of any strength for chemical use.
23. *Ibid.*, pp. 228–9.

24. A tariff quota extended by the Community as a whole to one particular country is not considered here a national tariff quota.
25. See — *Abkommen zur Grundung einer Assoziation zwischen der Europäischen Wirtschaftsgemeinschaft und Greichenland, op. cit.*, p. 29.
26. For more detailed discussion, see *GATT*. L/3384, L/3387, L/3406 (5 pec. (70) 104) and L3447.
27. *Ibid.*, p. 106.
28. Protocol 10 was used when the Community established a temporary tariff quota for Balsam turpentine oil, as well as collophony, which, though called a Community tariff quota, was in effect pre-allocated into national tariff quotas by the Council's Decision 65/68/EWG of 2.2.65. See *Amtsblatt der Europäischen Gemeinschaften, Amtsblatt*, 9 February 1965.
29. *Ibid.*, p. 114.
30. See 'Gesetz zu dem Assozierungsabkommen vom 12 Sept. 1963 zwischen der EWG und der Türkei sowie zu den mit diesem Abkommen in Zusammenhang stehenden Abkommen', *Bundesgestzblatt*, Vol. 1, II, Bonn, 21 May 1964 No. 20 (Z 1998 A), pp. 530–8.
31. *Ibid.*, p. 550.
32. *First General Report on the Activities of the Communities, 1967* (Brussels: European Community, February 1968) pp. 355–6.
33. Decisions of the Council from 21 December 1967, *Amtsblatt*, No. 4 L7, as decision of the Council from 24 June 1968, *Amtsblatt*, No. L144, 26 June 1968.
34. *GATT* L/3226, Addenda 1, p. 9.
35. See *GATT* L/3227, Addenda 1.
36. The three bilateral agreements were with Italy (additional protocol from 20 June 1936 and Article 6 of the Trade Agreement between the two countries from 22 January 1923), with France (agreement based on exchange of letters from 1 May 1946), with Germany (additional agreement from 25 April 1952, in the form of the Additional Agreement from 1 November 1957, to the Tariff Treaty between Switzerland and West Germany (20 December 1951). See *Amtsblatt*, 24 September 1969.
37. See *Amtsblatt*, 24 September 1963 (for agreement) and 31 December 1969 (for detailed order).
38. See *Amtsblatt*, 5 February 1965 and Jahrgang No. 19–254/65, where a tariff quota for 20,000 units of cows, consolidated in GATT was allocated between Germany, France and Italy by a decision of the EEC Council on 26 January 1965 (65/52/EWG).
39. See *General Report* (Luxemburg: High Authority of European Coal and Steel Community 1960) pp. 51–2 and 60.
40. See Protocol 1(2) of the Association Agreement with Turkey, as well as the example of turpentine mentioned in *Amtsblatt*, 9 February 1965.
41. For a distinction between a recommendation and a regulation see Articles 189 and 190 of the *Treaty Setting up the European Economic Community, op. cit.*, p. 61.
42. See *Amtsblatt*, No. 8, 22 January 1964.
43. See 'Dritter Gesamtbericht über die Tätigkeit der Gemeinschaften 1969', p. 416. For the specific tariff quotas which have been determined for pig iron as well as for the various steel products, see, for example, Ambl.1964, Ns. 26, 42, 49, 70, 86, 141, 211, 219, as well as the *Annual Reports* of the ECSC.
44. See *Amtsblatt*, No. 34, 27 February 1964, pp. 562–70.
45. Article 18 of this Regulation 14/64/EWG, as well as Article 28 of the Treaty, has been made use of, for instance, in Regulation 6/65/EWG of the Council by permitting Germany a national tariff quota of 6000 tons of frozen bovine meat for a period of five months in 1965. See *Amtsblatt*, No. 16, 1 February 1965, p. 198/65, article 4.
46. Which meant that the approximation of the national tariff to the common external tariff was brought forward one year to 1 January 1961, instead of 1962.
47. See Vierter Gesamtbericht über die Tätigkeit der Gemeinschaft (1.5.60–30.4.61) EWG May 1961, page 38, and 16, last two paragraphs as well as *EEC Bulletin*, 1961,

p. 49. Also *Tenth Annual Report of the EEC* (Brussels: 1967) p.17.
48. *EEC Bulletin*, No. 1, 1961, p. 48.
49. *EEC Bulletin*, September–October 1961, p. 42.
50. See *Tenth Annual Report of EEC*, *op. cit.*, p. 16.
51. *EEC Bulletin*, September–October 1961, p. 43.
52. *Ibid.*, p. 43.
53. *Ibid.*, p. 44.
54. *Ibid.*, p. 44.
55. Based on the data of a table in the *Tenth Annual Report*, *op. cit.*, p. 16.
56. *EEC Bulletin*, September–October 1961, p. 48.
57. *Tenth Annual Report of the EEC*, *op. cit.*, p. 16.
58. *Ibid.*, p. 17.
59. An interesting example is the case of prunes in Germany which will be discussed later in more detail.
60. An Article by Jean Louise Giraudy, 'Les contingents tarifaires: une anomalie qui devrait disparâitre', *Revue du Marché Commune*, 14 February 1968, pp. 127–9, argues that at that time there was no longer a real problem which justified national tariff quotas, except in lead. In the others either the evolution of the economic situation made them obsolete or experience proved that little use was made of them by the beneficiary. Therefore, these should be eliminated in order to prevent a proliferation of such exceptions being demanded during discussions of the enlargement of the Community.
61 Source: Commission of the European Community.
62. Though the author has no information about this specific case, the assumptions have been based on similar examples of replies.
63. See note 11.
64. Most of the answers of the Commission are in a letter, and the answer is submitted in detail only if the subject is particularly delicate.
65. Case 24/62: Klage der BRD vom 24 July 1962. Urteil vom 4 July 1963. Case 25/62: Klage der BRD vom 27 July 1962. Urteil vom 15.7.1963. Case 34/62: Klage der BRD vom 19 October 1962. Urteil vom 15 July 1963.
66. *Amtsblatt*, (65/38/EWG) No. 17, 4 February 1965.
67. *Ibid.*, (65/37/EWG) 22 February 1965.
68. It should, however, be mentioned that in the early days of the transition period, only one or other system was predominantly applied in each member state. Thus Germany and Belgium/Luxemburg predominantly applied the greyhound system, whereas Holland and France applied the prior-licensing system. Italy occupied an in-between position.
69. In Germany, under the greyhound system, detailed instructions are given as to the treatment of the imported quantities arriving when the quota is about to be filled. Usually, tariff quota benefits are determined by the hour of arrival of the imported goods, and the request for clearance through customs which is submitted during workdays as specified in the regulation. The treatment of a request arriving after working hours is also specified. If a case occurs that at the same hour at different custom stations requests for quota benefits are submitted (together with customs clearance of the imported commodity), the benefits are allocated according to a more or less relative share of the total import in relation to the open remainder of the quota. As an illustration, if 978 tons remains of a certain tariff quota which can be distributed between importers A and B, and importer A has imported 1300 tons and importer B has imported 216 tons with the request for quota treatment, then only 978 tons of his 1300 will be allowed to importer A when calculating his share, as this is the total quota that remains to be shared. Thus, importer A will receive $\frac{978}{1194}$, and importer B a share of $\frac{216}{1194}$, of 978 tons.
70. See Chapter 2.
71. This is, for instance, the exceptional case in Belgium/Luxemburg with respect to seed

potatoes as well as raw lead, where allocation is based in accordance with past trade.
72. In France and Holland the granting is usually automatic according to the date of arrival of the request, as long as the amount open is not exhausted.
73. In Holland, in the case of raw lead and zinc, authorisations initially only total 80 per cent of the quota and these are distributed with reference to the traditional imports from third countries. Only at the end of the year is the remainder of the quota allocated according to the chronological order of applications. This system, in the case of raw lead and zinc, is the result of an agreement between the interested economic circles which suggested that everybody should receive at least 80 per cent of their traditional imports.
74. This criterion has been used for some of the products for processing in Italy, where the quota is distributed on the basis of data given by the Ministry of Trade and Industry.
75. For instance, in France, unlike other member countries, a 'favourable opinion' has to be obtained from the ministry in charge of the resources before the customs administration can grant an allocation, whereas usually the customs administration is the only authority.
76. With respect to certain products in most countries, only the processors or certain qualified persons are entitled to obtain permits.
77. In Holland, one month, in France, three months, in Italy up to the end of the quota period.
78. In Belgium and Germany, where prior licences are given only in exceptional cases, they cannot be transferred. In France, Holland, as well as in Italy, this is also the rule for industrial products. But in the case of products for direct consumption, imports may be transferred from one importer to another in all member states.
79. Although in Germany, Italy, Holland and Belgium/Luxemburg, the importer has to sign a declaration not to re-export the product in unaltered form, this is not the case in France.
80. In Holland, France and Italy, the authorisation may be used only in the one customs office for which it has been given (in France, however, the importer may change the customs office once in exceptional circumstances). In Holland an authorisation is valid only for one importation, whereas in France and Italy it is valid for several importations.
81. See for instance, Deutscher Gebrauchs–Zolltariff 1961, pt V (c), Zollkontingente, p. 3.
82. To what extent these differences continued to exist, even after the transition period and the constant efforts to bring about harmonisation through adjustment in the national instruction, can be seen from a comparison of the national instructions of the member countries during 1968–1970. See, for instance, for comparison: *Netherland* order of the 1968 tariff quota–2–020 Tariff Contingent beschikking 1968 Regulation, 2–025 Voorschrift Tariff Contingent 1968. *Italy*–cinc: astampa n.576/Div. XIII del 13 December 1968–Contingenti Tariffari Eo Nazionali: systemio; Gestone, *Belgium*: Instruction sur les Contingents Tariffaires C. D. 625 1970 D. T. 10,000–Ministère des Finance, Administration, les Douanes et Accises. *Germany*: Deutscher Gebrauchs–Zolltariff 1969–pt V–Anweisungen des Bundesminister der Finanzen Zum Deutschen Zolltariff. (c)–Verfahren bei Zollkontingenten–as well as earlier annual editions of part V of the German Customs Tariff.
83. These suggestions of the Commission have been called 'impulses' in order to avoid any strict formal implication.
84. This is based on the case which constituted the background for a draft decision of the Council in the specific case of a Community tariff quota for ferro-silicum manganese (T.No. 73.02), which was consolidated in GATT and which was deliberated at an additional group meeting.
85. Passed on the 20 December 1968. See *Bundesgesetzblatt Jahrgang 1968*, Vol. I, No. 95, 23 December 1968, pp. 1389–99.
86. See Chapter 7.

Tariff Quotas in the European Community

87. *Journal of the European Communities Legislation,* 27 December 1973, pp. 29–66 and 87–8.
88. For a detailed comparison of 1969 and 1973, see *Amtsblatt*:

For 1969

27 Nov 1966	Vol. 11	No. L287
23 Dec 1968	Vol. 11	No. L308
27 Dec 1968	Vol. 11	No. L310
28 Dec 1968	Vol. 11	No. L311
18 Jan 1969	Vol. 12	No. L13
24 Jan 1969	Vol. 12	No. L18
27 Jan 1969	Vol. 12	No. L153
28 Jan 1969	Vol. 12	No. L157
31 Jan 1969	Vol. 12	No. L187
24 Sept 1969	Vol. 12	No. L240
21 Nov 1969	Vol. 12	No. L240
31 Nov 1969	Vol. 12	No. L274
7 Dec 1969	Vol. 12	No. L307
12 Dec 1969	Vol. 12	No. L312
20 Dec 1969	Vol. 12	No. L320
27 Dec 1969	Vol. 12	No. L324
30 Dec 1969	Vol. 12	No. L328

For 1973

28 Dec 1972	Vol. 15	No. L291
31 Dec 1972	Vol. 15	No. L302
21 May 1973	Vol. 16	No. L133

89. In practice, most of the agreements of the Community with other countries or areas include some tariff quotas, or indicative ceilings, which may be invoked
90. See *Amtsblatt,* Vol. 15, No. 73, 27 March 1972, Articles 32, 39, 41.
91. See, for instance, *Official Journal of the European Communities* Vol. 17, No. 48, pp. 71–86 (in agreements with Cyprus and Egypt) or page 5 (tariff quota for certain textile products from Turkey).
92. *Ibid.,* Vol. 16, No. L365, pp. 29–30 and 34–8.
93. *Amtsblatt,* No. L73, 27 March 1972, Protocols 14 and 15.
94. See *Official Journal of the European Communities,* Vol. 16, L.365, pp. 39–108 and 176–87.
95. The interested reader is referred to *Her Majesty's Customs and Excise Notice No. 771* (London: HM Stationery Office, March 1973) which provides all the basic information on the nature and administration of the tariff quotas in the United Kingdom.

Further announcements and details are published from time to time by the Department of Trade and Industry in their Journal, *Trade and Industry*; and in the case of quotas covering foodstuffs or agricultural products by the Ministry of Agriculture.

CHAPTER 5

Tariff Quotas in the United States

Tariff quotas in the United States occupy only a very marginal place in its commercial policy at the present time. In fact, a recent four-volume study of the Tariff Commission[1] dealing with trade barriers in the United States, and comparing them with those in other countries, hardly refers to this tool of commercial policy.[2] Nevertheless, the accumulated experience in this field in the United States is of interest and is valuable since it adds to knowledge of the topic in general, and may prove instructive when considering the application of this tool.

The intention of this chapter is to concentrate mainly on an examination of the specific experience of two tariff quotas. One relates to the woollens and worsted fabrics tariff quota which, after four and a half years of operation, was terminated at the request of all parties concerned; the second is that of stainless steel table flatware, which is still in operation today, after having been withdrawn for a number of years and then renewed. Nevertheless it seems proper to give, in an introduction to this part, a somewhat broader survey of the subject as a whole in the United States on the basis of the data available.

In 1973 the number of tariff quotas in operation was about fourteen.[3] Seven of these, relating to the import of cattle, fish, dairy products and potatoes, were tariff quotas which were granted by the United States as a result of trade agreement concessions. Two others, relating to brooms and brushes, were created by the Tariff Schedule Technical Amendments Act of 1965. A tariff quota for stainless steel table flatware was established originally in 1959 by Proclamation No. 3323, following an escape clause investigation under Section 7 of the Trade Agreement Extension Act of 1951. Lastly, there are four tariff quotas granted to the Philippines alone and covering cigars, tobacco, coconut oil and pearl buttons, which were established on the basis of the revised trade agreement of Laurel and Langley, from 6 September 1955. Their purpose was to bring about a gradual phasing-out of the mutual preferential agreements which had been in force between the United States and the Philippines in one form or another since 1899.[4]

CHARACTER OF UNITED STATES QUOTAS

There are substantial differences in the character of the United States tariff quotas. First, as already mentioned, some tariff quotas were introduced following concessions granted in trade negotiations, and as such were unallocated global quotas designed to liberalise trade rather than restrict it. There were also tariff quotas which were granted for other reasons, for example protective purposes. Instances of this are the tariff quotas for whisker brooms and brushes, where the bulk of the import came from non-GATT nations (at the time), such as Mexico, Hungary and Poland.[5] The original single rate of 25 per cent *ad valorem* for all these items was broken into sub-items and, while the *ad valorem* duty was reduced to 20 per cent for limited quantities of specific items, over-quota rates were established which were approaching twice the within-quota rate.[6]

Another example of a protective tariff quota is the one for stainless steel table flatware, which is discussed more fully later in this chapter, and which was based on the escape clause procedure. While the tariff quotas for whisker brooms and brushes are unallocated quotas, the stainless steel table flatware quota today is allocated into country quotas.

Variations exist in the levels of tariff rates inside and outside the different tariff quotas. In some, the over-quota rate of duty is substantially higher than the rate within the tariff quota, while in others the margin is relatively unimportant. The size of the margin may play a role in explaining the protective effect of some quotas. It is interesting to note that none of the tariff quotas in the United States at present in force are based on value terms. They are usually fixed in terms of quantitative units of measurement, weight, or size, or else as percentages of consumption or production on the above units of measurement. Some of the annual tariff quotas are broken down into sub-quotas for shorter periods, whereas in other cases the total annual quantity can be utilised in full at will.

While it is not strictly a tariff quota in the commercial use of the term this would seem to be the appropriate place to make a brief mention of the system,[7] introduced in the spring of 1973, by which the United States authorities are effecting the change from one method of control of oil imports to another.

From the beginning of the 1960s the quantity of imported oil into the United States had been strictly limited to prevent excessive quantities of cheaper foreign oil entering the country to the detriment of indigenous producers — annual quotas being allocated to individual importers/refiners. Only imports of residual fuel in later years were unlimited, though licences had to be obtained for them. In the early years of this decade the supply and demand situation was changing; local producers were now unable to meet the growing demands of the consumers and imported oil was needed to fill the gap. A change in the import control system was therefore necessary.

The new system set quantitative limits on the imports of crude oil and refined products. Initially these were at the levels established prior to the introduction of the change, with existing quota holders retaining their quantities, but these are being reduced progressively and will be finally eliminated by 1978. A licence fee has to be paid for any quantities above the quota, with one fee for crude oil and two different fees for refined products, depending on the quality. These licence fees are also being introduced progressively, being lower in the earlier years.

These are the main, tariff quota-like, characteristics of the scheme – for there is only a small distinction between paying a licence fee or a duty above a certain level – though there are certain concessions for imports of crude oil to newly-established processing plants. Since the introduction of the scheme, demand has been depressed by the increase in oil prices and an additional $2 per barrel imposed by the President on oil imports, so fee-paid imports have not reached very high levels. If the scheme remains unchanged, however, such quantities will inevitably grow. But it should provide for a smooth transition from one control system to another, with the additional social advantage of transferring the financial benefits previously enjoyed by a limited number of refining companies to the national exchequer.

EXPERIENCE WITH TARIFF QUOTAS

Not only does the character of the various United States tariff quotas differ, but experience with the operation of these quotas is also varied. There are those which have not been utilised fully or at all, either because of lack of interest or because of some non-tariff restriction. An example of a tariff quota that is not utilised through lack of interest seems to be that for cigars from the Philippines. Despite the substantial preference granted to these cigars from the Philippines, imports have been far short of the applicable tariff quota.[8] Another possible example is perhaps the tariff quota for tuna fish.[9]

There are several examples of tariff quotas not being utilised through some non-tariff barriers. The tariff quota for cattle has not been utilised to the full as imports can come only from Canada and Mexico, not only because of the cost of transport but also because the permission of the health authorities is only granted to these countries for reasons of disease control. Nevertheless the tariff quotas are in force at their original level, and have not been changed since the agreement of the GATT of 1948.[10]

Another example of non-utilisation of tariff quotas (at any rate during the first half of 1971[11]) is the tariff quota for whole milk, fresh or sour, of 3m gallons. This rate has been in effect since January 1948, but has evidently not been utilised, due to the Federal Import Milk Act of 1927, as amended, to which this item is subject. The Act is administered by the Food and Drug Administration (FDA) of the United States Department of Health, Education and Welfare (HEW), and prohibits the import into the United States of milk and cream unless the person by whom such milk or cream is shipped or transported into the United States has a valid permit from the Secretary of HEW. This Act was passed 'to regulate the importation of milk and cream into the United States for the purpose of promoting the dairy industry of the United States and protecting the public health'. According to the Tariff Commission, the import permits do not impose quantitative restrictions on imports of milk and cream, but are issued in accordance with the objectives of the Act. It should be stated however, that the policy of granting permits has been extremely restrictive.[12]

There are, on the other hand, tariff quotas which have not only been fully utilised, but where imports at over quota rates have far exceeded the tariff quota. For instance, in the case of fish – fresh, frozen or filleted cod, haddock, hake, pollock, cusk and rosefish – imports for many years exceeded the quota by two or three times. The main explanation for this substantial import beyond the quota seems to be the growing gap between increasing demand and declining domestic production, while the margin of the difference between tariffs inside and outside the quota is relatively unimportant.[13]

One last point needs to be made about the character of United States tariff quotas. Some which existed in former years, like that on fluid milk and cream, fresh or sour, containing over 5.5 per cent but not over 45 per cent of butterfat, became effective and over-quota imports started to come in. They were then transformed into absolute quotas by Presidential Proclamation No. 3790 of 30 June 1967, which made the tariff quota subject to quantitative restrictions under Section 22 of the Agricultural Adjustment Act as amended (see item 950.00 of the Appendix to the Tariff Schedule of the United States [TSUS]), and the annual quota of 1.5 million gallons was allocated entirely to New Zealand.[14] A similar case in point seems to be that of butter.[15]

ADMINISTRATION OF TARIFF QUOTAS

Most of the tariff quotas are administered by the quota section of the Bureau of Customs in the Department of the Treasury. To the extent that the principle of first-come-first-served is the ruling allocative principle of the benefits from the tariff quota, elaborate arrangements have been made to monitor imports exactly and accurately – with the help of computers and a whole system of clocks showing the different hours in particular ports of entry – in order to determine which will enjoy the tariff quota advantage and which will have to pay the higher duty.

The opening of the tariff quota is set at a standard time, usually noon Eastern time, translated to the specific time then prevailing at the various ports of entry. This takes into account the geographical difference of such a vast area as the United States with so many ports of entry for imports from all over the world, all entitled to benefit from the quota on a first-come-first-served basis.

There are some cases, however, where the allocative principle of the quota benefits is somewhat different from the first-come-first-served within the quota. A case in point is the quota for fish, where imports within the quota constitute only a quarter of total imports, and practically all the quota is filled immediately after opening, since importers are allowed to bring in the produce on account of the quota prior to its being opened. In each port imports may be substantially higher than the quota and the quota is allocated proportionately to total imports after it has closed. This means that United States fish importers calculate cost and price calculations on the full rate of duty (which incidentally is not very high) and then receive a refund on some portion of it, which appears to them as a windfall gain.

In some tariff quotas additional administrative tasks have to be performed, for instance, when country allocations have to be observed or when tariff quotas are broken down into sub-quotas. Nevertheless it can be stated that on the whole the administration of tariff quotas in the United States causes no undue difficulty and the handling of the few tariff quotas in operation by the Bureau of Customs can be carried out quite smoothly. This statement needs to be qualified in two ways: first, it does not mean that a tariff quota as such creates no difficulties, since indeed it may, as will become abundantly clear from the case study of woollen and worsted fabrics discussed in the next section. Secondly, it must be obvious that the statement refers to the administration of a very limited number of tariff quotas.

It is questionable whether it would be true if a more substantial part of the trade were covered by tariff quotas.[16] In such a case serious problems could arise over their administration since a wider application of this technique would require the customs authorities to keep track of shipments in numerous ports and other points of entry as the quota becomes filled. Additionally, with many quotas to watch, each quota would be supplied by many producers and importers from many countries, each of whom would need to be notified of the breaking point so that they would know when it became necessary to pay the higher tariff.

Some of the difficulties encountered in the operation of the tariff quota may become clearer from the more detailed examination of the

Tariff Quotas in the United States

woollen and worsted fabrics tariff quota which follows. This was in operation in the United States for four years, from 1956 to 1960.[17]

WOOLLEN AND WORSTED FABRICS

The legal basis for this tariff quota was a Note of Reservation included in the United States tariff schedules agreed upon during the negotiations in the GATT in 1947, as has been discussed early in Chapter 2. This note limited the concessions which were granted in items 1108 and 1109(a) of the Tariff Act of 1930 to the United Kingdom during these negotiations.[18] The United States had, in 1947, a highly developed textile woollen and worsted industry and the general conditions of that industry were rather prosperous. But domestic producers, as well as the trade unions, feared that the concessions granted to the United Kingdom, which reduced the *ad valorem* part of the duty by 50 per cent or more[19] to 20–25 per cent, depending on the nature of the product, could create in the future possible severe competition from British imports. They therefore demanded, and secured in the concession, a quantitative limitation to which these reduced rates applied, and beyond which the tariff might be raised to 45 per cent.

During the years 1953–54 producers and trade unions felt that the development of imports in relation to domestic production justified the application of the tariff quota on the basis of the aforementioned Note, and asked the Government to take appropriate action.[20] But it became evident that the Note of Reservation as formulated[21] in the Agreement raised a number of difficulties and problems, and lacked clarity with respect to its interpretation. The Note's exact wording stipulates that 'the United States reserves the right to increase the *ad valorem* part of the rate applicable to any of the fabrics provided for in item 1108 or 1109(a) of this part to 45 per cent *ad valorem* on any of such fabrics which are entered in any calendar year in excess of an aggregate quantity by weight of five per cent of the average annual production of similar fabrics in the United States during the three immediately preceding calendar years'.

DIFFICULTIES IN INTERPRETING THE NOTE

A first difficulty was to determine whether the 5 per cent referred to the total imports of the products included in tariff item 1108 or 1109(a), or to various specific types of categories in that tariff item. The producers pointed out that items 1108 and 1109(a) 'cover fabrics for numerous markets in a wide variety of weights, constructions, finishes, and quality. No one familiar with the trade would consider all these fabrics to be similar, like or directly competitive. They include fabrics for summer suits weighing about nine ounces per linear yard, and fabrics for overcoats weighing about thirty-two ounces per linear yard, and fabrics for overcoats that might cost no more than $2 a yard and fabrics that might sell for $50 or more per yard. Practical recognition of this diversity with some semblance to reality can be made in the import statistics on apparel cloths by cross-classification of weight brackets and quality brackets.'[22]

In the light of this they claimed that the 5 per cent limit should apply to each classification rather than to the total imports under 1108 and 1109(a), if the Geneva reservation was to have any meaning as a protective device to domestic producers. The representatives of the producers indicated that the reservation refers to *any* of such fabrics which are entered in excess of 5 per cent of production of similar fabrics. They interpreted the term 'similar' to mean like products or directly competitive in the meaning of Article XIX of the GATT.

This position was contrary to the Government's interpretation, which stated 'the reservation would be construed to relate to *total* production of goods encompassed within para. 1108 and 1109(a) rather than similar fabrics or like or directly competitive fabrics'.[23] Furthermore, during the hearings in 1956 the representatives of the Government presented additional interesting arguments to strengthen their interpretation.

It seemed to them that an approach based on 5 per cent for each individual category was unreasonable since it would permit increased preferred imports in those products in which domestic production was the largest. Protection of domestic industry would dictate precisely the opposite course, namely to permit larger imports in those product ranges of categories which were not produced domestically at all, or only sparsely, thus being of a supplementary and not a competitive nature.

They felt that the problem of fixing categories raised the question of how to sub-divide them, and by what criteria, since there were various possibilities of classification — such as by value, weight, destination, composition of blends and so on — and the question was where to stop. Furthermore, from the administrative point of view such a classification of categories may become difficult to handle. Any classification by categories might enable importers to shift from one category to another so as to avoid the application of the trigger point, and the overall injury would then be that much greater since no application of a quota would exist.[24]

To these arguments of Government representatives,[25] the importers[26] added some of their own. They pointed out that, even in 1947, there were probably items for which imports amounted to more than 5 per cent of domestic production. If the arguments of the producers were correct, why had no tariff quotas been applied to these items in 1947? Further, in view of the difficulty of establishing the data and facts even for the overall determination of the percentage, how did the producers expect to determine the data and facts in sub-categories where the information available was even less reliable? If the implication of the words 'aggregate quantity of similar fabrics' was to be taken to mean like products or directly competitive products, should it not also include fabrics made of synthetic or other man-made fibres, which were sufficiently similar to woven woollen fabrics to displace them to a large extent in the manufacture of clothing?

The second major difficulty which arose related to the fact that the Note stipulated that the comparison between imports and domestic production should be on a weight basis. Yet while import statistics were compiled by weight as well as by the square yard, domestic production was compiled on a linear basis,[27] with the linear yards also classified into weight brackets (of ounces to each linear yard). These comparable compilations of data caused great difficulties when estimating the percentage of imports in relation to domestic production, the formulae for converting one measure into another resting on specific assumptions about the relationship between weight and yardage of specific fabrics, as well as the relationship between linear and square yards. According to the testimony of experts during the hearings of 1956 it was argued that the possible range of error could be 1 per cent either way.[28] Variations of this magnitude in the estimate could be rather crucial in view of the fact that imports in 1952–55 averaged more or less 5 per cent of total domestic production, and only a small variation either way could determine the need for applying the quota or not.

Two additional aspects complicated the factual determination of the ratio of imports to domestic production. The definition of fabrics which are wholly or mainly made of wool was different for imports – by value – and for domestic production – by weight. Therefore it could happen that a fabric, defined in imports as made of wool, would not be so defined in domestic production, and *vice versa*. This differentiation could also have some impact on the comparison and the determination of the percentage. It is however important to state that the differentiation relates only to marginal sub-items (at least in the period up to 1956) since most of the imports were wholly or mainly of wool, both by value and by weight.[29]

The other complication related to certain fabrics which, though not imported, are by definition included within paragraphs 1108 and 1109(a), such as the fabrics produced for government agencies as well as certain non-apparel fabrics included in 1109(a). While the producers demanded the exclusion of these items from the calculations determining the 5 per cent, the importers insisted on their inclusion. The government's position was that 'United States production was to include woollen and worsted fabrics for government agencies as well as fabrics for civilian use even though these agencies do not buy goods from foreign manufacturers'.[30]

Some idea of the difficulties in establishing the apparently simple fact as to whether the 5 per cent had been reached or not can be obtained by comparing, over time, figures provided by the importers' representative (Mr Bronz) and the producers' representative (Mr Yardley). Annual average domestic production of woollen and worsted fabrics for the years 1952 to 1954 was 293.4m lb. according to the importers, or 257.6m lb. if the producers' figures are accepted. Details of the yearly fluctuations are given in Table 5.1. As a consequence imports, which in 1955 amounted to 14.3m lb., either represented as annual average of 4.87 per cent, calculated on the importers' figures, or 5.55 per cent on the producers'.

TABLE 5.1
Estimated United States Production and Imports of Woollen and Worsted Fabrics, 1952–56

	1952	1953	1954	1955	1956
Production (million lbs)					
Bronz, Trade Union Testimony(1)	324.1	302.8	253.2	285.7	291.3
Yardley, Producers' Testimony (2)	291.5	257.3	223.9	...	...
Imports (million lbs)					
Bronz	12.5	12.1	9.3	14.3	17.3
as % (1), 3 preceding years				4.87	
as % (2), 3 preceding years				5.55	
Production (million linear yds)[a]					
Bronz (3)	244	271	261	293	310
Producers; broadweave. (4)	352	336	284	318	375
Producers; apparel (5)	308	291	262	298	313
Imports (million linear yds)					
Bronz	16	16	13	20	23
as % (3), 3 preceding years				7.65	
as % (4), 3 preceding years				6.01	
as % (5), 3 preceding years				6.95	

Source: Mr Yardley, Producers' Testimony, Hearings of the Tariff Commission and Committee on Reciprocity Information, 1956 (CRI Hearings, 1956). Estimates, from Mr Bronz, Trade Union Testimony, 30 November 1959; and producers of broad woven woollen and worsted fabrics, and producers of these cloths for apparel.
[a] Average 54 inches.

Table 5.2 will help to explain these difficulties, for it shows roughly the relative importance of the various items under dispute, by giving a more detailed breakdown of the components of 1108 and 1109(a), computed in pounds, for the various years.

TABLE 5.2
Wool Cloth Production in the United States, 1947–58
(million lb)

Classification	1947	1950	1952	1953	1954	1956	1958
Apparel fabrics							
50% and over, wool by weight							
Government	11	11	63	17	1	2	5
Men and boys	199	156	97	116	99	126	92
Women and children	137	133	104	107	116	131	122
25–49.9%[a] wool by weight	n.a.	15	12	10	9	14	6
Unclassified apparel fabrics	26	–	–	–	–	–	–
Non-apparel fabrics							
25% and over, wool by weight							
Blanketing:	n.a.	n.a.	12	12	2	1	1
Government	1	1	1	1	–	–	–
Crib blankets							
Other blanketing:							
100% wool reprocessed	23	18	13	20	10	6	3
re-used wool:							
100%	2	3	2	2	3	1	3
50–90.9%	7	6	7	7	3	4	3
25–49.9%	8	6	6	6	2	2	1
Woven wool felts (not paper-makers)	n.a.	1	1	1	1	1	1
Other non-apparel fabrics[b]	5	6	2	2	5	3	2
Total	419	356	320	301	251	291	239

Source: Compiled for the hearings of the Committee of Reciprocity Information (CRI) by the representatives of the United Kingdom's exporters.
[a] 1947 total included in 50 per cent and over figure, probably overstating totals by about 6m. The 1950 figures are probably incomplete.
[b] Understated slightly after 1950.

In view of the unclear factual situation, the importers claimed 'that the United States Government, enjoying the discretionary right under the Treaty to increase the *ad valorem* rate on woollens and worsteds when 5 per cent of imports by weight is more than the average annual domestic production of the three previous years, must exercise such discretion in keeping with the precise terms of the Treaty. It must determine weight by facts and not by guesses.[31] And, furthermore, should not attempt to implement the reservation of a solemn Treaty by merely basing it on conjecture.'

Another example of the lack of clarity of the Note was whether the quota should be automatically implemented once the ratio of 5 per cent had been established, or whether implementation by the Government was optional. The representatives of the manufacturers demanded an automatic implementation, but the representatives of the Government felt that the application of the reservation was not mandatory, and that the United States Government had complete freedom in the matter. The importers were of the opinion that as the formulation of the reservation left the option open, there must be a reason for invoking the reservation. They could think of only one reason, namely the serious injury, or threat thereof, to the domestic producers, which might justify the application of the quota. They denied the existence of this situation in the case under discussion.[32]

Despite their demand for the automatic invocation of the reservation, the producers nevertheless enlarged on the injury which imports were causing the domestic producers. For that purpose they, and the trade unions, presented various indicators, such as the continued decline in the number of employees, in working hours, in the number of looms and spindles and so on, and the increased number of mills closed and employees put out of work. The major argument was that while production of the woollen and worsteds industry in the United States had been reduced almost to half between 1947 and 1955 (57 per cent), imports in the same period increased more than seven times. This severe situation was particularly hard for specific areas in New England, where, as a result of the closing of plants, thousands of people were made redundant who could not easily be absorbed into other industries because of age, difficulty of retraining, the need for very substantial investments, and so forth.

The producers and trade unions readily admitted that imports were not exclusively to blame for this state of affairs, and that other factors played an important role. Amongst these were the transition to the use of synthetics, man-made fibres and blends of various kinds, the transfer of production from the north to the south of the United States, and the establishment of modern and more efficient multi-fibre plants competing effectively with the old established one-fibre industry in New England. Nevertheless there was no doubt in the producers' opinion that imports were a contributing factor to the distress of the woollen and worsted industry and one which added the final blow. In particular the new industries, which had developed in countries like Japan, could compete at any price as wage rates there were substantially below those of New England. This cheap labour put pressure on the prices and cost structure of these products in the United States.

In their view the seriousness of the situation could best be indicated by the low profitability of the industry in the United States, and the lack of desire to invest in it. Since there was a need to preserve the production potential for reasons of defence, and since a reasonable amount of prosperity was needed in the textile industry of the United States in specific areas, it seemed logical to expect the Government to invoke the reservation in order to prevent any further deterioration of the industry.

In answer to these arguments the importers maintained that there was an underlying fallacy in the whole approach of the hearings, as there was no longer a woollen industry in the United States, but rather a multi-fibre one as the same enterprises which once produced only woollens were currently producing blends of various types, and fabrics of synthetic and man-made fibres. Americans were buying the same quantity of clothes, except that they were not mainly those defined as woollen and worsteds.

Some importers even argued that the whole reservation was obsolete as it had been agreed at a time when nobody anticipated the appearance of man-made fibres, and that under these new unforeseen conditions the reservation should be abondoned. Furthermore the reservation, if applied to 5 per cent of domestic production in 1948, would have amounted to a much higher quantity, namely something like 20.8m pounds.[33]

They contended that it was ridiculous to argue that imports were responsible for the bad situation of the woollen and worsteds industry (particularly in the New England area). Total annual imports were about 14m pounds, while the output of the woollen and worsted industry had been reduced by almost a third between 1947 and 1955, from 418m to 286m pounds.

No correlation existed between imports and the reduction in domestic production of woollens and worsteds. As the figures showed, there were years when production as well as imports declined, and others where both increased, and there were cases where imports increased and production declined. Imports were not related to the conditions of domestic production, but to the general prosperity of the United States. When the income of the population of the United States increased, there was a rise in demand for distinctive fabrics from foreign countries.[34] These fabrics were of a non-competitive nature, as it did not pay American mills to compete in this type of fabric for, in general, their equipment was not geared to produce small lots of diversified fabrics, but rather fabrics for mass consumption.

The major injury to the woollen and worsteds industry in New England came from the competition of the newly-established efficient plants in the South. The reason that these enterprises, which in the past had been concentrated to the extent of 80–85 per cent in the New England area, had moved partially to the South was the non-existence of strong, well-entrenched trade unions which prevented the establishment of a modern multi-fibre industry[35] in New England. It was this competition, and not imports, which injured the New England industry.

A further point made by the importers related to the fact that during the whole discussion of the hearings it had not been proved that imports were cheaper than local products, and very few examples had been given which showed that cheap competition really existed. The truth of the matter was, according to them, that imports were more expensive, and that competition consisted mainly of style and quality. Furthermore, the whole debate centred around 5 per cent of domestic production, and it was obvious that a mere 5 per cent could not constitute a serious injury. After all, the purpose of the concession was to provide for an increase of imports. The contribution which imports made should not be underestimated for they provided the stimulation and diversity of style which the domestic industry copied, a year after their appearance, in mass-produced quantities. It was necessary to remember that there were various parties who were interested in the continuation of imports, not only the importers themselves, but also the manufacturers and tailors of high quality dresses, the various channels of distribution such as department stores, and finally the consumers, interested in purchasing high quality clothes made up in imported fabrics.[36]

CONCEPT OF THE TARIFF QUOTA

Interestingly enough, the concept of the tariff quota itself was originally suggested by the members of the trade unions. They felt that 'the value of the tariff quota is, that it is probably more in harmony with the fundamental philosophies of a free-moving market than the absolute quota systems'.[37]

Furthermore, they recognised 'that the problems of the woollen and worsted industry are in some respects different from those found in any other industry affected by imports, and these imports are not only a source of competition but a source of ideas and stimulation. We acknowledged and recognised that wool and worsted manufacturers the world over share alike in a common fund of knowledge in design, style and quality, and the differences in products, and that the importing into our domestic market of a modest amount of such material would be stimulating and would keep our American industry on its toes in so far as design and style are concerned.'[38] But like the domestic producers, they preferred the percentage of the quota to be somewhat smaller, around 2 per cent of domestic production.

The producers' position was originally less favourable to the tariff quota concept, but during the hearings of 1956 the Chairman of the National Association of the Woollen Manufacturers made the following statement: 'As mentioned to this Committee in October 1954, we were not the architects of this Geneva reservation, but we think it has a lot to recommend it. I would point out that it is not a quota and there have been some dispositions or some tendencies to refer to quota. We didn't write it, but it is a pretty good concept. It says in effect that the larger the domestic pie, the greater share we make available to the foreign producer at these bargain rates, but when they exceed that limitation then the bargain sale is over. But it does not put any absolute limit on the quantity of goods that the foreigners can send to this market, and just as they were able to overcome the 45 per cent duty in the past, there is every reason to believe that if the American market is a healthy, prosperous one, they will have their fair share of that too, whether the duty is 25 per cent or 45 per cent.'[39]

On the other hand, the importers were much less enthusiastic and drew attention to the difficulties which they would encounter if a tariff quota were to be invoked. In the first place the imports in this industry have a seasonal character – for instance, on 15 December an American importer could receive from a mill abroad samples of cloth designed for the following autumn. These samples would be shown to the trade in the United States, with the importer receiving orders on the basis of these samples. Only then would these fabrics be manufactured according to the orders. The mills abroad would not start production before orders were received. Thus the goods ordered would not arrive before April–June, and would then be supplied to the trade for use for the production of clothes for the autumn.[40] Stocks, especially of highly fashioned goods, could not be maintained. It would therefore be very difficult for these producers or importers to compete within a tariff quota where a deadline had to be met. The quota would probably be utilised by importers of standard products, which could more easily be produced for stock, maintaining the product in bonded warehouses until the tariff quota was opened.[41]

INVOCATION OF TARIFF QUOTA

Despite the strong arguments of the importers, developments during 1956 in the field of imports were such that President Eisenhower issued a Proclamation (No. 3160) on 28 September 1956, invoking the so-called Geneva Wool Fabric Reservation upon the recommendation of the Interdepartmental Committee on Trade Agreements. The President's action was to be effective from 1 October to 31 December 1956. The President specified that the higher *ad valorem* duty (45 per cent) would apply only after, and if, 3.5m pounds of imports entered the country, and only until the new calendar year began. The breakpoint of 3.5m pounds for the rest of 1956 was equal to one-quarter of a quantity (14m pounds) determined by the President to be not less than 5 per cent of the average annual United States production of similar fabrics for the calendar years 1953–55. In 1957, and subsequent years, the President would notify the Secretary of the Treasury of the amount of imports above which the higher duty would apply in that year.[42]

Such notifications were issued for subsequent years. On 24 May 1957, a tariff quota of 14m pounds was established for 1957; and, on 7 March 1958, a new tariff quota was established for 1958 of 14.2m pounds, while the import of certain hand-woven fabrics for religious purposes was permitted at 30 per cent *ad valorem* after the breakpoint. On 21 April 1959, a quota for 1959 of 13.5m pounds was established. At the same time the President further amended the proclamation of 8 September 1956 by establishing an over-quota rate of duty of 30 per cent *ad valorem* for a maximum of 350,000 pounds of over-quota, for imports of certain high-price, high-quality fabrics.[43]

On 8 February 1960, the President informed the Secretary of the Treasury that, for the calendar year 1960, the tariff quota on woollen and worsted fabrics dutiable under tariff paragraphs 1108 and 1109(a) would be 13.5m pounds, the same as for 1959. In the press release announcing the wool fabric quota for 1960, the President noted that many problems had arisen during the operation of the quota and stated that in an effort to find a more satisfactory solution to those problems, the United States issued notice of its intention to renegotiate the tariff concessions involved.[44]

On 9 November 1960, the Department of State issued a press release which announced that new tariff rates on certain woollen and worsted woven fabrics would go into effect on 1 January 1961, replacing the existing tariff quota system. The elimination of the tariff quota and its replacement by the new tariff schedule was the result of the unsuccessful experience and criticism voiced by all parties concerned. The Tariff Commission and Interdepartmental Committee for Reciprocity Information conducted a number of hearings in which the actual experience with the woollen and worsted tariff quota was carefully scrutinised. Testimony by the various parties concerned, and cross-examination of the witnesses, produced voluminous evidence which gave quite a good picture of what had occurred. Some of this is discussed below, but it first seems desirable to present a factual picture of imports, both inside and outside the quota, from the main sources as they developed over the four years for which the quota was in operation on a full annual basis. This is given in Table 5.3, which is divided into three parts, according to (*a*) value, (*b*) weight, and (*c*) size. They include unit prices.

This table makes it clear that the tariff quotas, and more so the tariff beyond the trigger point, only curbed total imports during the first two years of their full operation, compared with 1956 imports, which then reached 17.3m pounds (See Table 5.1, p. 110). In the two later years imports rose beyond the 1956 level. It is obvious that if the domestic industry had hoped to prevent a substantial inflow of imports from competing on the domestic market, then the tariff quota as a tool of protection had not proved to be an adequate commercial policy device.

Furthermore, the evidence indicates that total imports, even during

TABLE 5.3
United States Imports of Woollen and Worsted Fabrics, 1957–60
(a) by value

	1957	1958	1959	1960
		(£'000)		
From all sources				
(1) Total	59,014	58,905	64,314	79,185
(2) Within tariff quota	52,073	52,121	40,074	39,737
(2) as percentage of (1)	88.2	88.5	62.3	50.2
(3) Outside quota of 45% duty	6,939	6,593	21,688	35,083
(4) " " " 30% "	—	192	2,553	4,264
From Britain				
(5) Total	29,922	25,076	25,532	26,919
(5) as percentage of (1)	50.7	42.6	39.7	34.0
(6) Within tariff quota	26,622	22,491	16,597	13,267
(6) as percentage of (2)	51.1	43.2	41.4	33.4
(7) Outside quota of 45% duty	3,300	2,443	6,938	10,088
(8) " " " 30% "	—	141	1,997	3,585
From Japan				
(9) Total	13,571	19,141	18,096	24,943
(9) as percentage of (1)	23.0	32.5	28.1	31.5
(10) Within tariff quota	12,371	17,770	11,637	14,807
(10) as percentage of (2)	23.8	34.1	29.0	37.3
(11) Outside quota of 45% duty	1,200	1,368	6,457	9,969
(12) " " " 30% "	—	3	1	167
From Italy				
(13) Total	6,983	7,066	13,016	19,965
(13) as percentage of (1)	11.8	12.0	20.2	25.2
(14) Within tariff quota	6,113	5,580	7,443	8,733
(14) as percentage of (2)	11.7	10.7	18.6	22.0
(15) Outside quota of 45% duty	870	1,485	5,344	10,475
(16) " " " 30% "	—	—	229	237

Source: derived from United States Tariff Commission compilation taken from the official statistics of the United States Department of Commerce.

118 The Role of Tariff Quotas in Commercial Policy

(b) by weight

	1957	1958	1959	1960	1957	1958	1959	1960
		(000 lb.)				($ per lb.)		
From all sources								
(1) Total	15,897	16,373	22,489	29,334	3.71	3.60	2.86	2.70
(2) Within tariff quota	14,208	14,248	13,694	13,010	3.71	3.66	2.93	3.05
(2) as percentage of (1)	89.4	87.0	60.9	44.1				
(3) Outside quota of 45% duty	1,688	2,063	8,248	15,142	4.11	3.20	2.63	2.32
(4) " " 30% "	—	61	547	1,101	—	3.14	4.67	3.88
From Britain								
(5) Total	8,018	6,233	6,897	6,768	3.73	4.02	3.70	3.98
(5) as percentage of (1)	50.4	38.1	30.7	23.1				
(6) Within tariff quota	7,321	5,599	4,504	3,400	3.63	4.02	3.68	3.90
(6) as percentage of (2)	51.5	39.3	32.9	26.0				
(7) Outside quota of 45% duty	776	584	1,927	2,411	4.25	4.18	3.60	4.18
(8) " " 30% "	—	51	456	877	—	2.76	4.38	4.09
From Japan								
(9) Total	3,772	5,176	5,046	6,758	3.60	3.70	3.59	3.69
(9) as percentage of (1)	23.7	31.6	25.1	23.0				
(10) Within tariff quota	3,447	4,818	3,241	4,135	3.59	3.69	3.59	3.58
(10) as percentage of (2)	24.3	33.8	23.7	31.6				
(11) Outside quota of 45% duty	325	356	1,805	2,581	3.69	3.84	3.58	3.86
(12) " " 30% "	—	—	—	42	—	—	—	3.98
From Italy								
(13) Total	1,716	2,882	8,246	13,728	4.07	2.45	1.58	1.45
(13) as percentage of (1)	10.8	17.6	36.7	46.8				
(14) Within tariff quota	1,478	2,083	4,580	4,777	4.17	2.68	1.63	1.83
(14) as percentage of (2)	10.4	14.6	33.4	36.5				
(15) Outside quota of 45% duty	237	799	3,637	8,835	3.67	1.86	1.47	1.19
(16) " " 30% "	—	—	29	115	—	—	7.90	2.06

Source: derived from United States Tariff Commission compilation taken from the official statistics of the United States Department of Commerce.

Tariff Quotas in the United States

(c) by area

	1957	1958	1959	1960	1957	1958	1959	1960
	('000 sq.yds)				($ per sq.yd)			
From all sources								
(1) Total	32,235	34,328	46,433	62,020	1.83	1.71	1.39	1.28
(2) Within tariff quota	28,635	29,881	8,381	28,428	1.82	1.74	1.41	1.40
(2) as percentage of (1)	88.5	87.1	61.1	45.8				
(3) Outside quota of 45% duty	3,599	4,350	16,975	31,518	1.92	1.52	1.28	1.11
(4) " " 30% "	—	97	1,076	2,074	—	1.98	2.37	2.01
From Britain								
(5) Total	15,748	12,918	14,059	14,264	1.90	1.94	1.82	1.89
(5) as percentage of (1)	48.9	37.6	30.3	23.0				
(6) Within tariff quota	14,148	11,590	9,382	7,420	1.88	1.94	1.77	1.79
(6) as percentage of (2)	47.3	38.8	33.1	26.1				
(7) Outside quota of 45% duty	1,600	1,261	3,829	5,365	2.06	1.94	1.77	1.88
(8) " " 30% "	—	67	849	1,499	—	2.10	2.35	2.39
From Japan								
(9) Total	7,783	11,437	11,128	15,440	1.72	1.67	1.63	1.61
(9) as percentage of (1)	24.4	33.3	24.0	24.9				
(10) Within tariff quota	7,133	10,582	7,082	9,175	1.73	1.68	1.64	1.61
(10) as percentage of (2)	24.9	35.4	25.0	32.3				
(11) Outside quota of 45% duty	740	853	4,046	6,154	1.62	1.60	1.60	1.62
(12) " " 30% "	—	—	—	111	—	—	—	1.50
From Italy								
(13) Total	4,017	5,860	17,130	28,294	1.74	1.31	0.76	0.70
(13) as percentage of (1)	12.5	17.1	36.9	45.6				
(14) Within tariff quota	3,429	4,250	9,530	10,284	1.78	1.31	0.78	0.84
(14) as percentage of (2)	12.0	14.2	33.6	36.2				
(15) Outside quota of 45% duty	587	1,610	7,531	17,770	1.48	0.92	0.71	0.62
(16) " " 30% "	—	—	72	231	—	—	3.18	1.29

Source: derived from the United States Tariff Commission compilation taken from the official statistics of the United States Department of Commerce.

the first two years of the operation of the tariff quota, as well as during the later years, exceeded the tariff quota itself, and that the excess of imports beyond the quota limits was increasing at an accelerated pace. Thus imports during 1960 were approximately nine times in excess of imports in the first year by weight, eight times by size, and five times by value. A number of reasons can be given by way of explanation.

(a) The uncertainty as to the exact date of applying the trigger point beyond which a higher duty had to be paid was a major disadvantage. Coupled with this were doubts as to the size of the quota, defined as a percentage of the annual domestic production in the previous three years. As this could not be calculated until a few months after the end of the year, importers brought in woollen and worsted cloth in the hope that they would enjoy the quota rates, but when these imports arrived, they were charged the full over-quota rate. The situation became more severe as the time span until the quota was filled continued to shorten as is shown by Table 5.4.

In 1959, the estimated imports charged against the unannounced quota were slightly over 6.1m pounds on 28 March, as compared to 7.1m pounds the previous March. Through 2 May 1959, the figure was 9.85m pounds, charged against the tariff quota of 1959, leaving a balance of 3.66m pounds still open. This information became available on 12/13 May and, by 19 May, the quota was filled, less than a month after it was announced. Such speed was unexpected, and was mainly due to the sharp increase in the import of Italian wool fabrics which amounted to 1.99m pounds in May alone, against 400,000 pounds in May 1958. During April and May Italian imports were 2.3m pounds above those in April and May 1958, and at substantially lower prices.

Exporters in the United Kingdom did not expect the quota to be filled before 1 July; even after the reduced quota had been announced, they had no reason to expect that the quota would be filled six weeks before that date.[45] They were, therefore, caught with a substantial part of their orders either on the way or still in the process of production.

The process of producing relatively high-priced British wool fabrics, which takes between four and six months, forced importers to make their decision before the size of the quota had been announced. They had to gamble on these orders being able to enter within the quota, and had no choice but to receive the imported fabrics, despite the higher rates of duties which had in the meantime come into force. That this was the case generally is best indicated by the monthly import figures after the break-point given in Table 5.5.[46]

TABLE 5.4
Utilisation of United States Woollen and Worsted Fabrics Tariff Quota, 1957-59

Year	Tariff quota opened	Tariff quota closed	Imports in operation	Amount	Imports	Excess above quota
					(million lbs)	
1957	24 March	25 July	17 weeks + 4 days	14.0	15.9	1.9
1958	7 March	1 July	16 weeks	14.2	16.4	2.2
1959	21 April	19 May	4 weeks + 3 days	13.5	19.7[b]	6.2[b]
					(million sq.yds)	
1957				28.5[a]	32.2	3.7[a]
1958				29.9[a]	34.3	4.4[a]
1959				28.0[a]	40.3[b]	12.3[b]

Source: CRI 1959, p. 19
[a] Estimate.
[b] Through September 1959.

TABLE 5.5
United States Imports of Woollen and Worsted Fabrics after Break-point 1959 ('000 lb.)

Country	June	July	August	Total
United Kingdom	888	491	261	1,640
Italy	936	488	519	1,943
Japan	630	460	169	1,259
Other	301	261	101	663
Total	2,755	1,700	1,050	5,505

Source: see note 46.

The table indicates that the main excess import arrived in June and decreased during the two subsequent months. Since the total excess import in 1959 amounted to 8.8m pounds, it is obvious that within the last four months of the year the average monthly imports were even lower. This supports the argument that the main cause of the excess import was that importers were caught in the middle of the process when the break-point was unexpectedly announced at an earlier date, and not because the higher tariff was insufficient. While such imports are unprofitable, and may cause severe financial losses they nevertheless contribute to the excess imports beyond the tariff quota.

(b) There were also importers who took a calculated risk by hedging against a possible rise of the tariff through the charge of higher prices[47] from the start. In some cases, as evidence indicated, the suppliers were willing to guarantee 50–100 per cent of the risk of a duty increase beyond the quota, the guarantee depending on the size of the order. In other cases arrangements were made between the producers, exporters and buyers to split the excess tariff three ways.[48] Naturally this enabled importers to disregard the curbing effect of the steep tariff rate of the over-quota.

(c) A third reason for the excess imports could have been that part of the woollen and worsted trade is highly fashioned, expensive cloth, which is not in competition with domestic production. This has a relatively inelastic demand, so that despite the higher tariff a certain, albeit smaller, quantity continued to be imported.

(d) The cheaper the price of the fabrics, the lower the duty to be paid on them, and this allowed them to compete with domestic products even beyond the quota limits. This seemed to be the main explanation for the substantial imports from Italy outside the quota.

While total imports increased during the four full quota years, whichever of the three criteria of weight, size and value was used, the quota itself – which was fixed for each of the four years – not only did not increase, but when judged by weight and value in fact decreased, although, according to size in square yards, it remained more or less the same. The reduction in the global quota, which was fixed in terms of weight, can be explained by the fact that the woollen industry was in the process of contraction in the United States, and the 5 per cent of imports had to be adjusted accordingly. Less understandable was the reason for the reduction in value terms of imports within the quota. It would seem *a priori* that a tariff quota defined in terms of weight would lead the foreign exporters to try to utilise such a quota by exporting light, expensive fabrics to the maximum extent, for these would enable them to import more units at higher prices, and thus earn the maximum foreign exchange without paying higher duty. A noticeable tendency towards lighter fabrics in fact took place inside the quota over the years, but this was not the case with respect to value, for prices generally fell within the tariff quota, although less than outside it. This is perhaps a sweeping generalisation for it is based on the overall figures in the tables above, which only represent general averages; contradictory trends between different countries, and between the different categories of products within the export countries, are hidden and are not explicitly clear.

Figures for the United Kingdom, for instance, indicate a much smaller price reduction per square yard[49] inside and outside the quota than all other main suppliers, as well as in comparison to average price for total imports to the United States, inside and outside the quota. In fact, the fall in price is relatively so small that it could be that the absolute figures are misleading, in view of the price movements in raw wool which fluctuated rather substantially during that period. The wholesale index for prices in the United Kingdom, for instance, based on the best quality of raw wool, was 105.3 in 1956; 114.2 in 1957; 83.1 in 1958; 81.1 in 1959; and 80.1 in 1960 (base year 1955).[50]

It would be too difficult to calculate the exact influence of the changing price index on the price of the finished product, in view of the lack of data on the exact raw material content of an average square yard of cloth. This is particularly true if account is taken of the changing quantity of yards per pound in the various types of cloth.

Nevertheless, some allowance has to be made for such a fall in the raw material price, and the raw material is assumed to constitute around one third of the price of the finished cloth. The fall in price of raw material, between 1957 and 1960 for instance, was around 29.9 per cent, so about 9.9 per cent of the reduction in price could be explained by the fall in the raw material. Yet the price reduction in the final product between 1957 and 1960 was only, within the quota, 11 cents per square yard, or 5.85 per cent, so that in fact prices per square yard for the processing industry increased. This is all the more evident in the averages for the total exports for the United Kingdom where the price fall was even smaller.

On the face of it, exports from the United Kingdom seemed to behave according to expectations, but this is a questionable deduction since nothing is known about a concerted, deliberate policy of the United Kingdom's exporters only to export within the quota the better, higher-priced, lighter fabrics. It is more likely that the competitive advantages of the United Kingdom in the highly styled, fully-fashioned fabrics enabled it to increase its exports in the lighter weight, high-priced fabrics, as shown in Table 5.6, despite its overall reduction of total exports and the fall of its relative share inside and outside the quota.

The table shows in particular that Japanese exports increased in all weight categories, although the biggest increase was in the six to eight ounce at the price range of $2 to $4 per pound. Japan managed to achieve high prices through the introduction in 1958 of a deliberate export licensing control system for the quota-type products to the United States. This enabled them to limit exports of cheap products, thus trying to earn a higher income from the exports within the quota.

There were countries where this trend was not noticeable. Furthermore, within the quota limits not only do different countries compete, but also different types of products, all of which are included within the tariff items 1108 and 1109(a). Some of these are easier to produce and require a shorter time for their production. The tariff quota introduced an additional element of competition, namely that of time. The quicker a product arrived when the quota was in operation, the more chance it had to enter at a lower tariff. With a quick and standardised production process it was possible to prepare the fabrics in a shorter time or ahead of time, keeping them in bond for the opening of the quota. This resulted in the major part of the quota being filled by imports of the standard products which were produced cheaply and quickly, whereas the highly styled, fully fashioned goods, usually produced to order, had a much smaller chance of being included in the quota. Imports of highly fashioned, high-quality and styled goods, which had been traditionally imported into the United States for many years, decreased. This explains the decrease of imports from France and the United Kingdom.

Thus the non-competitive goods, which were desirable imports, were replaced by the substantial increase of the cheap standardised goods, mainly from Italy which managed in terms of quantity to capture, over the four-year period, a share of 36.5 per cent of the tariff quota by weight as compared with 10.4 per cent of the tariff quota in 1957, and a total share of 47.9 per cent in comparison with 10.8 per cent in 1957. Yet, by value, the share inside the quota increased only from 11.7 per cent to 22

TABLE 5.6
A Comparison of Woven Cloth Imports into the United States in 1955 and 1958, from Main Suppliers, by Weight and Price ('000sq.yds)

	Total 1955	Total 1958	Italy 1955	Italy 1958	Japan 1955	Japan 1958	United Kingdom 1955	United Kingdom 1958
Not over 4 oz per sq.yd	806	1510+	35	144+	26	486	321	462
Over 4 – not over 6 oz per sq.yd								
1. Not over – $1.25 per pound	N	83+	N	78+	N	N	N	N
2. Over – $1.25 – not over 2.00	5	41+	1	26+	N	N	N	11+
3. Over – $2.00 – not over 4.00	1599	2277+	188	974+	332	554+	456	338–
4. Over – $4.00 per pound	4137	5808+	621	963–	62	984+	2240	3897+
Over 6 – not over 8 oz per sq.yd								
1. Not over – $1.25 per pound	4	470+	N	455+	N	N	3	15+
2. Over – $1.25 – not over 2.00	91	789+	19	583+	N	27+	65	21–
3. Over – $2.00 – not over 4.00	6280	8097+	386	312–	1884	5475+	3186	1319–
4. Over – $4.00 per pound	6739	5229–	1369	519–	137	2174+	4218	2318–
Over 8 – not over 10 oz								
1. Not over – $1.25 per pound	6	727+	5	724+	N	N	1	N
2. Over $1.25 not over 2.00	222	429+	92	238+	3	1–	109	74–
3. Over – $2.00 – not over 3.00	2896	1934–	33	82+	167	627+	2439	1116–
4. Over – $4.00 per pound	890	736–	185	142–	1	109+	444	378–
Over 10 – not over 12 oz								
1.	16	193+	N	159+	N	N	14	33+
2. (as above)	802	481–	123	23–	8	14+	626	425–
3.	1754	1612–	18	33+	96	424+	1260	791–
4.	393	584+	132	97–	60	218+	113	133+
Over 12 – not over 18 oz.								
1.	25	384+	1	364+	11	8–	11	8–
2. (as above)	289	480+	21	149+	11	96+	210	171–
3.	1854	1968+	21	141+	48	172+	1554	1282–
4.	198	215+	25	31+	24	4–	61	80+
Over 18 oz per sq.yd								
1.	9	23+	1	19+	N	2+	N	N
2. (as above)	40	26–	30	3–	N	13+	6	3–
3.	79	128+	4	2–	5	46+	42	39–
4.	45	16–	9	1–	1	2+	2	5+

Source: Derived from Tables 12–15 of the Northern Textile Association Statement of 20 November 1959.
Notes: N = none or negligible.
+ = increase between 1955 and 1958
– = decrease between 1955 and 1958.

per cent, and total from 11.8 per cent to 25.2 per cent. This development was contrary to the purpose for which the trade unions introduced the tariff quota concept, namely to stimulate local production as far as new ideas, designs and fashion quality were concerned.

The United Kingdom, with whom the original concessions were negotiated, was disappointed, and finally requested a renegotiation of the concessions. But not only Britain was dissatisfied with the existing form of the tariff quota. All parties concerned eventually reached the conclusion that this form of import protection served no useful purpose. It had become clear that the tariff quota caused disruption and chaos in the marketing of the products in the United States, and it threatened the existence of the thousands of custom tailors who relied mainly on imported fabrics. It affected the income of the clothing manufacturers and the various channels of distribution, which were faced with the choice of ordering the products far ahead of actual use. They had to tie up money for a long period, pay interest and storage fees, and take the risk of losses due to fashion changes, all of which increased the cost and risks of the imports; or else they had to face the danger that the products would be imported at a duty which was 80 per cent above the quota duty, and had either to absorb the extra cost or shift it to the buyer. Very frequently successful fashion lines which entered at the lower duty rate could not be reordered in view of the higher price which would have to be paid beyond the quota limits, when the importers were unwilling to absorb the extra cost. Thus consumers had to do without the fabrics, or had to be willing to pay a higher price. Retail shops, which could not absorb the extra cost and who had to shift it on to the consumer, were affected in the ability to compete with the larger channels of distribution which were in a better position to maintain a unified price throughout the entire year.

It also became evident that the tariff quota did not protect the domestic manufacturers of woollen and worsted fabrics, and that it did not encourage the desired imports but rather those which were undesirable. Similarly, it did not enable the United States to ensure the exports of those countries for which the concession had originally been granted.

SUGGESTIONS FOR CHANGE

The trends, discussed in the preceding paragraphs, had already become evident during the period of operation of the quota. In the various hearings mentioned above, various contradictory proposals to improve and perfect the tariff quota systems – not to speak of proposals to eliminate them entirely – were made. The domestic manufacturers and the trade unions were on the whole in favour of the tariff quota. They felt that tariff quotas should be sub-divided by category as well as by country. This would eliminate the heavy pressure of foreign competition on one category of fabrics, and ensure a market to all foreign countries. They also suggested that the quotas be fixed on a monthly or quarterly basis, thus alleviating the pressure of concentrated imports on the price structure of domestic industry.

At the same time the producers requested a higher duty inside the quota. They suggested the over-quota duty as the quota duty, with a new over-quota duty to be raised by 50 per cent, or the maximum permissible under the 1939 agreement. Furthermore they demanded that the computation base of domestic production be reduced by eliminating government purchases, as well as blankets, blanketing and products of 25 to 49.5 per cent wool from the calculations. They also demanded that the quota should be determined on the basis of a smaller percentage than 5 per cent.

Foreign exporters and the United States importers were on the whole hostile to the idea of the tariff quota and considered it as a form of economic punishment serving no useful purpose.[51] They also suggested possible improvements in the scheme. They first proposed to broaden the base of production by the inclusion of the various blends with wool produced in the United States, as well as retention of all the items currently included, which the manufacturers had demanded should be excluded. They suggested that the quota be increased to 7 per cent of domestic production and proposed that the over-quota duty should either be limited to 35 per cent, or be based on the original pre-1947 trade agreement rates.

It was also requested that the date for the tariff increase should be a fixed date in the calendar year, preferably 7 July, and that goods in transit on that date should enter at the lower tariff. Another suggestion was that 20 per cent of the total quota should be put aside for the small clothing manufacturers and that the expensive fabrics quota should include a different weight category structure, with the overall quota of these to be increased beyond the 350,000 pounds. Another request was that cheap reprocessed woollens should not be considered within the quota, this being reserved for the new virgin wools.

Naturally many of the suggestions of the producers, importers and exporting groups were opposed by other representatives of the same or different groups. For instance, the idea of allocating country quotas was opposed by the countries which had managed to increase their exports substantially over the years. They claimed that a country quota would freeze past trade trends, and would not permit any account to be taken of innovations and improvements in qualitative and price-competitive advantages. By the same token a quota by category could freeze design and style innovations, and a quarterly or monthly tariff quota would only multiply the rush periods and the scramble with imports which ensued.

The exporters of cheap woollens argued against the exclusion of their goods, claiming that these products were not in competition with the woollen industry, but rather with the cheap synthetics or artificial fibres. They maintained that they contributed towards the welfare of those American consumers who could not afford to pay the regular prices of woollen and worsted goods.

For their part the manufacturers argued that price differentials between different producing countries were such that no tariff could be devised which on its own could do justice to all foreign exporters. If a tariff were too high for the United Kingdom, the low-wage countries would still be able to compete, whereas if the tariff took account of production conditions in the United Kingdom, a tremendous inflow from low-wage countries would flood the United States. Therefore, their solution was for the allocation of imports by country quotas (preferably absolute quotas, but if not absolute, then tariff quotas), or else some form of voluntary export restrictions.

Importers objected to the idea of the high tariff inside and outside the quota. They argued that the differential of 25 per cent *ad valorem* was more than sufficient to give protection to domestic industry in view of the fact that this nominal rate of protection of the final fabric was intended effectively to protect only the mills, as the raw wool was protected by the specific additional duty. Therefore the effective rate of protection was substantially higher than the cost differential between foreign and domestic production costs of the woollen and worsted fibres. This was all the more so since the wage differentials were really not a sufficient indicator of the cost of production, for productivity and efficiency of production also needed to be taken into account. What counted, in the final analysis, was not the hourly wage rate but the cost of producing a square yard of cloth.

DEVELOPMENTS AFTER THE TERMINATION OF THE TARIFF QUOTA

After consultations and negotiations with interested suppliers, the United States finally announced the new tariff on 9 November 1960, for the year beginning January 1961. The main changes that were introduced were the elimination of the tariff quota, and the fixing of the *ad valorem* part of the rate of duty at 38 per cent for fabrics valued at over $2 per pound (instead of 25 per cent within the quota and 45 per cent outside it). For fabrics valued at less than $2 per pound the new duty was an additional 76 cents, but with a maximum *ad valorem* limit of 60 per cent. Certain fabrics for religious purposes, which enjoyed on the *ad valorem* part a lower over-quota rate of 30 per cent, could now be imported the whole year around with an *ad valorem* part of duty fixed at 25 per cent.[52] The change in the rates of duty resulted in a definite decline in imports[53] in the years following their introduction, measured by weight and (with the exception of 1965) on the square yard basis. But in value terms, imports since 1965 are shown to have increased over those of 1960, and this can only be explained by the rise in price of the finished imported product.

The overall change in total imports can be explained by the drastic reduction in cheap Italian imports which the high new rates of duty apparently prevented, at least within the framework of the woollen fabrics category. Between 1960 and 1967 the Italian imports were reduced to about one-tenth of their former quantity by size and weight, and to about one-fifth of their former value. The new rate of duty did not, as was hoped, improve the position of the United Kingdom, in comparison with either 1960 or 1955, whether the imports were judged by value, size or weight.

Japan was the one country which seemed really to profit from the elimination of the quota and the introduction of the new tariff rates, and managed to increase its export by almost two and a half times by weight, size and value. To a certain extent the increase resulted from the lower price of exports per square yard in comparison to that of Britain and France while price and quality were maintained steadily throughout the period. To some extent price developments strengthened the argument of the domestic producers who claimed that a unified tariff could not be applied to countries with such divergent wage structures as Japan and England, and that, to ensure a limited import from different countries, country quotas were justified. This seems to be corroborated by the development of new cheap sources of exports, namely the Republic of Korea and Uruguay, whose prices per square yard were below those of Japan, although above those of the cheap products from Italy in 1960/61.

Another interesting point which becomes clear from the data is the continuation of the trend towards more square yards per pound despite the elimination of the quota. This trend was shown during the quota years and cannot be attributed to the desire to utilise larger quantities within a fixed quota in terms of pounds, but is rather a change in consumer habits.

An important question that remains to be answered is whether the reduction in total imports affected the domestic industry and in particular whether it was helpful. An examination of the statistics[54] shows that despite the new higher tariff and the elimination of the tariff quota, and consequent reduced import, the woollen industry continued to decline. Output did not drop steadily, but the trend was a declining one. The same trend can be seen from the figures given in the census of 1967,[55] when they are put against those of 1958.

This comparison shows that while in 1958 there were 411 companies with 469 establishments, in 1963 there were 304 companies with 361 establishments. By 1967, the number of establishments had fallen to 310 and from then on a further reduction in the number of establishments took place. During the same period the number of employees fell by 13,400. It seems, therefore, that importers were right when they claimed that imports were not the cause of the hardships of the woollen industry. This seems particularly true in view of the evidence presented by the Tariff Commission which stated that import prices were generally above domestic production prices.

It may appear strange that imports during the tariff quota period, unified with an above-quota rate of 45 per cent, had encouraged imports more than the imports at the lower tariff rate of 38 per cent. But it would seem that the major reason was the cheap imports from Italy, encouraged by the low duty and the ease of production which enabled them to seize the major share of the quota. In addition, there were excessive imports, sometimes even at a loss, due to ignorance about the size of the quota and the date of the break-point to the higher duty. The possibility of balancing the high tariff cost with the cheap tariff within the quota enabled importers to bring fabrics into the United States at a lower tariff rate than 38 per cent.

The experience of the woollen and worsted tariff quota was a complete failure. It did not work as a protective device for domestic production. It failed to serve as a stimulant for the development of new designs, fashions, innovations and ideas as envisaged by the trade unions. It did not permit controlled imports of desired fabrics, as hoped by the contracting parties of the original reservation, and from the point of view of the importers and channels of distribution, as well as the consumers themselves, it brought a complete disruption of the market, chaos and losses.

In view of this experience, it might be argued that this device of commercial policy should be totally disqualified. But even in the United States, there have been other, and different, experiences, one being the case of stainless steel plate tableware, which have been rather successful. This particular example, therefore, deserves to be discussed before final conclusions are drawn.

STAINLESS STEEL TABLE FLATWARE

The tariff quota for stainless steel table flatware was introduced in November 1959 and was in operation, with some modifications, until the end of the quota in October 1967. It was abandoned at the end of that quota year, yet renewed in 1971. Since the information with respect to this particular case is readily available,[56] it would go beyond the scope of this book to present a detailed description of the quota, and only a brief sketch is given here.

The role of stainless steel table flatware in the United States has been increasing in importance[57] over the years. The introduction of this kind of table flatware had many advantages in view of cheapness and easy maintenance. The production process is very simple, as the metal is stamped, formed, graded and polished, all of which requires hand labour. It can be produced easily all over the world, due to the availability of the necessary machinery and the fact that labour input is high. As cheap labour is a comparative advantage, countries with low wages are able to compete successfully with domestic producers in the United States market.

Imports in 1953, the first year for which figures were available. amounted to 883,000 dozen, and reached 10.6m dozen in 1957, or 44.7 per cent of total consumption in the United States. The industry in the United States therefore demanded an investigation of the injury inflicted on it by this increased import. It should be mentioned that the total industry in the United States consisted of around twenty enterprises and that, of these, seven small concerns produced stainless steel flatware exclusively, while twelve others made other products, such as sterling silver, plated, and miscellaneous types of flatware, hollow-ware, cutlery, kitchen utensils, or a combination of several of these articles.

The total number of employees in the above establishments during the period 1959–66 averaged about 9000, and somewhat more than two-fifths of the total man-hours of some 15m per year were devoted to the production of stainless steel flatware. Output ranged from 11m dozen in 1953, to 30.3m dozen in 1966. It should be mentioned that 85 per cent of the production was concentrated in nine firms, and that the total value of output ranged from an f.o.b. value in 1953 of $10.8m to $69.2m in 1966.

The Tariff Commission examined the request on the basis of Section 7 of the Trade Agreement Act of 1951 (as amended) and unanimously agreed, in 1958, that there was serious injury to the industry. In October 1959, President Eisenhower invoked a tariff quota of 5.75m dozen pieces (which did not exceed the price of $3 per dozen, and were not larger than 10.2 inches). The introduction of the tariff quota really limited imports to between a quarter and a third of United States production which was a substantial improvement over the years before the introduction of the quota, when the ratio of imports to production reached over 80 per cent (in 1957). The tariff quota itself was maintained at the concessional rates, yet the over-quota rates were three to four times the tariff rate inside the quota. This severe over-quota rate limited the import of quota-type ware in excess of the quota to not more than 250,000 dozen pieces in any calendar year.

On 7 January 1966 the President enlarged the quota from 5.75 to 7m dozen pieces, and made it retroactive to 1 November 1965. Imports which entered in excess of the enlarged tariff quota were subject to over-quota duties which were lower than the previous rates, but which were, however, still twice as high as the tariff inside the tariff quota. Nevertheless they brought in 671,738 dozen pieces of quota-type flatware in excess of the enlarged quota in the calendar year 1966.

The tariff quota expired on 11 October 1967, after the escape clause restriction based on the Trade Expansion Act of 1962 had not been renewed by the President. This course was taken after an investigation by the United States Tariff Commission stated that two-thirds of the domestic industry had modernised its production capacity sufficiently to be able to compete with foreign imports. It was also considered that protection of the inefficient third would be futile since such protection could only prevent imports but not internal competition from the efficient plants. Account was also taken of the general forecast of increasing consumption in the United States. Despite a vague recommendation of a majority of two commissioners to continue with the tariff quota, the minority recommendation was followed to let the tariff quota terminate, to continue with a surveillance of the effects of this elimination in order to see whether help might be needed at a later date.

Experience during the quota years had indicated that the over-quota tariff was rather prohibitive, and the reduction during the last year of operation before its elimination in 1967 reflected the price sensitivity of this commodity, together with the income elasticity which evidently also played a part in the determination of total imports. During the whole period of the operation of the quota, Japan was the major supplier of quota-type stainless steel table flatware; nevertheless the relative share of Japan's export fell from over 90 per cent at the beginning of the period to 77 per cent at the end. This was mainly the result of the Japanese policy of export licensing which was introduced in 1957 and maintained throughout the period, keeping exports from Japan to the United States in the quota-type products at a smaller volume than the overall tariff quota of the United States or, in the last year, equal to it. Since Japan tried to control prices and quality, as well as to regulate the flow of the stainless steel table flatware over the whole period by subdividing the overall quota into sub-quotas, they lost a portion of the United States market for the low-end ware to new competitors in other Far Eastern countries, namely Taiwan, Korea and Hong Kong, which together accounted in 1966 for 10 per cent of total imports.

The immediate result of the elimination of the tariff quota was a substantial increase in imports, which jumped from 7.8m dozen pieces in 1967 to 14.9m dozen in 1968, 25.9m in 1969, and 34.4m in 1970. This meant an increase of the ratio of imports to production from 30 per cent in 1966 to more than 128.6 per cent in 1970.[58]

The industry[59] once again asked the Government to examine the situation, in particular the injury inflicted upon it, and to renegotiate the concessional rates of duty. The Government informed member governments of the GATT on 30 September 1969, on the basis of Article XXVIII of the GATT, that the United States reserved the right to amend the concessional rates. This reservation was extended to 30 June 1970, and then renewed, but it was not until 1971 that the United States informed the GATT of the renewed application of a tariff quota for stainless steel table flatware, which included a number of interesting changes based on past experience.

At the same time a number of Tariff Commission investigations[60] were conducted, which determined that the articles imported were directly competitive with the stainless steel table flatware produced in the United States, and that, largely as a result of the concession granted under the trade agreement, these were being imported in such increased quantities as to cause, or threaten to cause, serious injury to that industry. These findings were mostly determined unanimously as to the industry in general and specific firms within it. The Government therefore negotiated with contracting members of the GATT, under Article XXVIII, the revision of the concessions granted, and on 21 August 1971 the President of the United States signed a Proclamation (No. 4076),[61] establishing a tariff rate quota on certain stainless steel table flatware, beginning on 1 October 1971. The quota was established for an overall quantity of 48.6m units for each quarter of the calendar year, and unlike the earlier quota, was allocated to sources of import (on the basis of the average imports in 1968 and 1969) as follows: Japan (33m); China (6.3m); Korea (4.8m); Hong Kong (1.5m); European Community (1.5m); United Kingdom (0.6m); and others (0.9m).

According to the Proclamation, beginning in 1972 the Tariff Commission should determine the apparent United States consumption of stainless steel table flatware in the preceding period, and should inform the President. In its first report it should also inform the President of the consumption in the calendar year 1970.

The administration of the quota could be increased for each calendar quarter in any calendar year, commencing with 1972, by an increase in the quarterly allocations over the allocations for the last quarter of the immediately preceding calendar year. This would be by a percentage (not in excess of 6 per cent) which the President would determine was the percentage increase in United States consumption of stainless steel table flatware during the preceding calendar year – unless economic conditions in the United States industry indicated that a smaller growth rate, or no growth rate, was warranted. The quota was also to be administered in such a manner that a country which had not utilised fully its allocated share in a given quarter could utilise the difference of 10 per cent of the allocation, in the immediately following quarter, without setting it against that quarterly allocation.

The tariff quota invoked in 1971, therefore, immediately tried to reduce imports to an annual quantity of 16.2m dozen instead of the 34.4m which were imported in 1970, the shares were allocated to individual member countries, and these shares were broken down to quarterly quotas. These new elements of the scheme are relevant in view of earlier experience when Japan lost its share in the market because, through its export control, it prevented its exporters from competing for the full quota, while Korea, Taiwan and Hong Kong expanded their output.

Furthermore the division into sub-quotas prevented the concentration of the imports at the beginning of the quota year. Stainless steel table flatware is a standard commodity which can be stored in bond and which can be imported when the quota opens in order to benefit from the low tariff rate. In fact experience during the period 1960–66 indicated that, despite the Japanese regulations of exports, the quota was very rapidly filled, as can be seen from Table 5.7.

TABLE 5.7
Utilisation of United States Stainless Steel Table Flatware Tariff Quota, 1960–66

Quota period beginning	Flatware entered under quota in first quota month (million dozen pieces)	Month in which quota was filled
1 November 1960	4.9	December 1960
1 November 1961	3.5	April 1962
1 November 1962	2.2	June 1963
1 November 1963	2.0	April 1964
1 November 1964	2.6	February 1965
1 November 1965	5.75	November 1965
1 November 1966	6.7	January 1967

Since the tariff quota introduced in August 1971 is valid until 1976, and no detailed figures have been presented by the Tariff Commission, except the determination of the apparent consumption (see, for instance, the Report to the President by the United States Tariff Commission on 1 May 1974), it is difficult to give an evaluation of the actual operation of the tariff quota since its renewal. There seems to have been no request in the GATT from the exporting countries, or the United States, asking for modification or renegotiation, and it therefore seems safe to assume that the quota operates to the satisfaction of all parties concerned. This is despite the fact that evidently some part of the imports comes in at overquota rates, paying the higher rate of duty.

COMPARISION OF THE CASES

There are several different and distinctive characteristics which help to explain the different fates of the two tariff quotas which have been discussed here.

First is the difference in the product coverage. While the products covered by the woollen and worsted fabrics quota were varied in character, purpose, price, design, quality and so on, the stainless steel tariff quota refers to a more standardised specific type of product, easily defined and classified. It is suggested that the more complex the product group, the less is the chance of applying the tariff-quota successfully.

Secondly, the size of the tariff quota for stainless steel table flatware was fixed for most years and known ahead of time, while late arrivals could be easily stored in bond until the opening of the following year's quota, whereas many of the exports of woollen and worsted fabrics were highly fashionable and could not be sold after the change of the season, or only at an extreme loss. Furthermore, the size of the quota was determined only after calculation of the past three years average production in the United States, so the size of the quota was not known in advance. It is evident that the more standardised and storable the product, and the more certain the terms of the tariff quota, the better are the chances of eliminating unprofitable excess imports beyond the quota limits.

Thirdly, the size of the tariff quota in relation to total consumption reached 25 per cent in the case of stainless steel table flatware, whereas the tariff quota for woollens and worsteds was at the most only 5 per cent of total consumption. At the same time the over-quota rate of duty in the case of stainless steel table flatware was three to four times (and later twice) the rate of duty inside the quota, whereas the rate of duty of the woollen and worsted imports at the over-quota level was never more than twice, and sometimes even less than twice, the rate of duty within the quota. It can safely be assumed that a larger tariff quota and a higher duty are contributing factors in avoiding excess imports, and these played the desired role in the case of stainless steel table flatware.

Fourth, the number of enterprises producing stainless steel table flatware in the United States was never more than twenty-two, whereas the number of woollen and worsted mills ran into a few hundreds. Furthermore, competition between countries, as well as producers in those countries and importers from them, was fierce in view of the many participants in the woollen and worsteds fabrics tariff quota. On the other hand, imports of stainless steel table flatware were mostly regulated by the main supplier, who was responsible for between 77 and 90 per cent of all imports and maintained export control over this product. It should also be stated that the stainless steel table flatware tariff quota is today being allocated on a country basis, and broken down into sub-quotas which permit a more orderly import of this product than was the case in the woollen and worsted fabrics quota.

These characteristics – the structure of an industry, the number of competitors and the limitations on competition – have wide ramifications affecting the internal price structure and marketing conditions. Another difference is that the stainless steel table flatware industry was expanding, with consumption rising, while the woollens and worsteds industry in the United States was a declining one.

To what extent the individual features were responsible for the success or failure of each of the two tariff quotas is hard to determine. But it stands to reason that each feature of the above contributed its share. It would require a much more elaborate examination of various tariff quotas with different combinations of the above features (and possibly others too) in order to determine the role each played in bringing about the total effect.

Finally, it is important not to lose sight of the purpose for which both tariff quotas were invoked. However different their legal basis, their invocation was of a protective nature, and while within-quota imports were even desired, this was not the case with over-quota imports. Any evaluation of the features contributing to success or failure has therefore to be judged with this purpose being made explicitly clear, because some of the features may be judged differently when other objectives are being sought.

NOTES AND REFERENCES

1. United States Tariff Commission, *Trade Barriers Report to the Committee on Finance of the United States Senate and its Subcommittee on International Trade* (Washington: US Government Printing Office, 1974).
2. *Ibid.*, Vol. 3, p. 10, contained the only reference to tariff quotas found by the author.
3. Appendix II gives the details for these, other than for the tariff quota for stainless steel flat tableware, which is the subject of detailed description in the last part of this chapter.
4. As to the details of developments in these trade agreements, see George C. Reeves, *Tariff Preferences for Developing Countries, Existing and Proposed Arrangements*, Staff Research Studies, United States Tariff Commission (Washington: US Government Printing Office, 1971) pp. 124–32. Of particular interest is the form of reduction, which is based on the principle that the quantity of the duty-free tariff quota becomes smaller by the same percentage by which the duty is increased towards the final lowest rate of duties applicable by the United States to imports from foreign countries. Thus if, for instance, the proportion of duties applicable to imports into the United States from the Philippines should rise from 0 per cent to 5 per cent of these lowest duties, then each quota will be reduced by 5 per cent of their quantity. When the rate rises to 10 per cent of the lowest duty applicable, the quota is reduced to 90 per cent of the quantity and so on.
5. For details see, for example, United States Tariff Commission, *Summaries of Trade and Tariff Information*, Schedule 7, Specified Products, Miscellaneous and Nonenumerated Products (Washington: US Government Printing Office, 1968) Vol. 5, pp. 61–70.
6. The over-quota rates were established in specified rates of duty for imports, each valued at not more than a given price. The exact *ad valorem* equivalent therefore depends on the actual value of each unit imported.
7. 'New United States Energy Policy', *Petroleum Press Service*, May 1973, pp. 164–6.
8. See *Summaries of Trade and Tariff Information*, 1967, Schedule 1, Vol. 2, Tobacco and Tobacco Products (TSUS Item 170.72,) p. 73.
9. *Summaries of Trade and Tariff Information*, 1969, Schedule 1, Vol. 3, Fish Products, Shellfish and Shellfish Products (TSUS Item 112.30).
10. *Summaries of Trade and Tariff Information*, 1968, Schedule 1, Vol. 1, Cattle, pp. 59–73.

Tariff Quotas in the United States

11. As is evident from the leaflet TAC of 12 August 1971 in the *Department of Treasury News*, Bureau of Customs, Washington.
12. *Summaries of Trade and Tariff Information*, 1968, Schedule 1, Vol. 1, Dairy Products and Birds' Eggs, Fluid Milk and Cream, p. 8.
13. *Summaries of Trade and Tariff Information*, Schedule 1, Vol. 2, Fish Fresh, Chilled, Frozen or Cured.
14. *Summaries of Trade and Tariff Information*, 1968, Schedule 1, Vol. 4, Dairy Products and Birds' Eggs, pp. 7 and 17.
15. *Ibid.*, Butter and Cream containing over 45 per cent of Butterfat, pp. 46–7 and 51.
16. As is the case in the GSP of the European Community and Japan.
17. Only the last quarter of the year.
18. It should be mentioned that, in 1947, Britain was the primary supplier to the United States of products in these paragraphs (about 80 per cent of the total imports according to testimony given in the Hearings of the Tariff Commission and Committee on Reciprocity Information, *CRI Hearings*, 1959, p. 5, whereas many countries which (later) became major suppliers did not at that time have any woollen and worsted industry capable of exporting, or were still in the stage of reconstructing their industry after World War II.
19. Prior to the 1947 trade agreement the United States *ad valorem* part of the duty on woollens was based on the dollar value per pound, and ranged from 35 per cent on the goods valued at more than 32 cents per pound to 45 per cent on goods valued at not more than 80 cents per pound (see *CRI Hearings*, 1959, p. 196).
20. See *Memorandum of the National Association of Wool Manufacturers*, submitted by Edwin Wilkinson on 20 October 1954 to the CRI.
21. From the testimony in the *CRI Hearings*, 1956, p. 138, it becomes clear that at least some appeals made before 1956 were turned down partly because of submission in terms which were contrary to the wording of the Note.
22. *Memorandum, op. cit.*, p. 2.
23. *Ibid.*, p. 3; and *CRI Hearings*, 1956, pp. 2–3.
24. See *CRI Hearings*, 1956, pp. 70–7.
25. It should be mentioned that in the light of some of these arguments of the Government, some of the producers' representatives retracted their position on categorisation, and agreed to the application of the tariff quota to all of the imports in these paragraphs. See *ibid.*, p. 76.
26. *Ibid.*, pp. 279–80.
27. *Ibid.*, p. 137. A producers' representative explains that factories which do not use common carriers for shipment do not need to know the weight. Due to this – and the lack of official requirements for such data about weight – domestic producers did not collect them.
28. *Ibid.*, p. 186.
29. According to the evidence presented in *ibid.*, p. 164, the Tariff Commission estimated that the fabrics produced domestically which contained 25 to 50 per cent pure wool were not more than 5 per cent of total domestic production in 1954 and 1955. According to importers, the percentage increased in those years because of the increase in blends of 40–50 per cent wool and 55–60 per cent dacron, where the price of dacron was substantially lower than that of wool – $1.35 per pound against $1.70–1.90 per pound for wool.
30. See *Memorandum, op. cit.*, pp. 2–3, as well as the opening statement of the Chairman in *CRI Hearings*, 1956, p. 3.
31. *CRI Hearings* 1956, p. 168.
32. *Ibid.*, p. 276.
33. *Ibid.*, p. 174.
34. *Ibid.*, p. 179.
35. *Ibid.*, p. 179.
36. *Ibid.*, pp. 253–83.

37. *CRI Hearings*, 1959, p. 331.
38. *CRI Hearings*, 1956, p. 85.
39. *Ibid.*, p. 83.
40. A similar process takes place with the fabrics for the winter, spring and summer seasons, the dates being respectively September, November, December (for fashions from France, for instance, see the CRI statement of Mr Bronz of the French Woollen Importers Committee, 19 January 1959).
41. *CRI Hearings*, 1956, pp. 269–70.
42. From the press release of 28 September 1956, issued from the White House as an attachment to the text of the President's Proclamation: also see the further supplementing Proclamation 2761A of 16 December 1957.
43. Proclamation 3317 of 24 September 1959, which also amended the Proclamation of 28 September 1956, made certain technical clarifications of that Proclamation.
44. Department of State, *Trade Agreement Program*, 13th Report, (Washington: US Government Printing Office, 1960).
45. Based on the statement of Bernard B. Smith from the American Trade Association for British Woollens Incorporated to the Committee on Reciprocity Information on 14 July 1959.
46. Based on the statement of Roger M. Grimwold, Chairman of the Wool Manufacturers' Council, and William F. Sullivan, President of the Northern Textile Association, CRI Hearings, 1959.
47. *CRI Hearings*, 1959, p. 573.
48. *Ibid.*, pp. 190–1.
49. The price per pound inside the quota (as well as outside it) in fact increased. This however was able to happen not through a rise in the price of a square yard, but owing to the increased quantity of square yards included in one pound, which is the result of lighter cloth being produced.
50. The figures are based on FAO data taken from the *FAO Annual, 1971* (Geneva: United Nations, 1972) p. 587.
51. 'We believe that the tariff quota, whatever its purpose may have been, has served primarily to give birth to a spurious, new and novel type of American protectionism – protection not by tariff, *but by chaos*; protection by undermining the economy of American small business, protection by precipitating domestic unemployment without providing correlative advantage to the larger and more powerful industry that the tariff quota was designed to protect.

    The tariff quota results in a fluctuating duty, a kind of duty that cannot be applied to a fashion industry, without threatening the economy of that industry.' From the **Statement of Bernard B. Smith on behalf of the American Trade Association for** British Woollens, Inc., presented before the Committee for Reciprocity Information on 9 December 1957.
52. These new notes were in force up to the end of 1967 although in August 1963 a change in their TSUS classification took place; see *Summaries of Trade and Tariff Information* Schedule 3, Textile Fibers and Textile Products, Vol. 3 (of 6 vols) – Fabrics, Woven, Knit, Pile, Tufted and Narrow (Washington: US Government Printing Office, 1970) Tariff Commission Publication 345, pp. 51–2.
53. The following discussion of the results is based on data appearing in the *Summaries of Trade and Tariff Information*, Schedule 3, Vol. 3. *Ibid.*, Table 2, p. 60.
54. *Ibid.*, Table 1, p. 59.
55. *1967 Census of Manufactures, Vol. II, Industry Statistics*, Part 1, Major Groups 20–24 (Washington: US Government Printing Office for the US Department of Commerce, 1971) pp. 22A–6, Table 1A, Industry 2231.
56. The following publications were issued by the United States Tariff Commission (Washington: US Government Printing Office). Tariff Commission publication numbers are shown wherever possible in brackets at the end of each item:

    10 January 1958. Escape Clause Investigation under Section 7 of the 1951 Trade

Agreement Act, as amended.
31 January 1958. Memorandum to the President on the above Investigation.
24 July 1959. Supplementary report on the above Investigation.
1 November 1961. Report to the President under Executive Order 10401 [38].
1 November 1962. Report to the President under Executive Order 10401 and Section 351(d)(1) of the 1962 Trade Expansion Act [73].
1 November 1963. Report to the President (No. TEA–IR–I; 63) under Section 351(d)(1) of the 1962 Trade Expansion Act [223].
14 April 1965. Report under Section 351(d)(1) and Section 351(d)(2).
November 1966. Report to the President (No. TEA–IR–I–66) under Section 351(d)(1) of the 1962 Trade Expansion Act [189].
September 1967. Report to the President on Investigation No. TEA–I–EX3 under Section 351(d)(3) of the 1967 Trade Expansion Act [217].
December 1970. Report on Investigation No. 332–63 under Section 332 of the 1930 Tariff Act [305].
December 1970. Report on Investigation No. TEA–W–30 under Section 301(c)(2) of the 1962 Trade Expansion Act [347].
May 1971. Report to the President No. TEA–F–21 under Section 301(c)(1) of the 1962 Trade Expansion Act [393].
August 1971. Report to the President on Investigation No. TEA–F–25 under Section 301(c) of the 1962 Trade Expansion Act [414].
December 1971. Report to the President on Investigation No. TEA–W–120 under Section 301(c)(2) of the 1962 Trade Expansion Act [442].

57. *Ibid.*, September 1967, p. 14.
58. *Ibid.*, December 1971, p. A23.
59. Statement of Stuart C. Hemmingway, L. B. Martin and E. A. Allan, on behalf of the United States Manufacturers Association; *Tariff and Trade proposals Hearings before the Committee on Ways and Means*, House of Representatives, 91st Congress, 2nd session on Trade and Tariff proposals, part 6 of 16 parts, 22 May and 1 June 1970, p. 1809.
60. See for instance TC Publications 305, 347, 393, 414 and 442, *op. cit.*
61. All the above data are taken from *GATT* L 3582.

CHAPTER 6

Tariff Quotas: a Partial Equilibrium Analysis

The previous two chapters gave many examples of different uses of tariff quotas in practice, in the European Community and the United States, and have shown how varied have been the consequences of their application. In view of their increasing importance, not only within the framework of the Community but also as a result of the GSP for developing countries, a closer examination from an analytical point of view seems justified, particularly as very little has appeared in the literature[1] on this subject.

In this chapter, however, only a start is made, with the hope of stimulating further work on the subject. At the same time the discussion here elucidates certain aspects of the tariff quota which either have not been discussed at all or have merely been touched upon in other chapters of the book. For example, the comparison of qualitative and quantitative tariff quotas with *ad valorem* or specific duties, their effect on consumers, importers and exporters or the comparison of the tariff quota with the tariff and the guillotine quota.

Since tariff quotas generally have a rather limited impact on the whole economy, it seems appropriate to examine the effects of tariff quotas in partial equilibrium terms. The first example is a comparison of tariff quotas with a guillotine quota or a tariff of equivalent size.

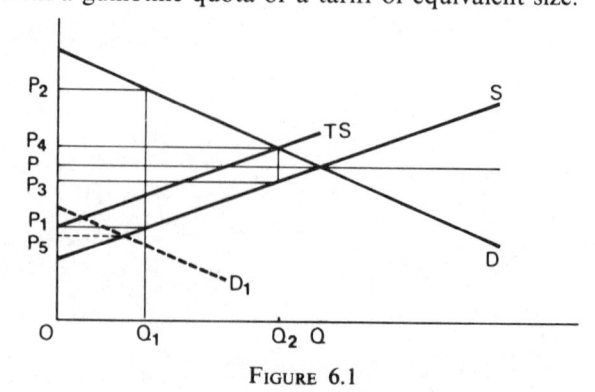

FIGURE 6.1

140

Figure 6.1 shows the domestic demand and the supply of imports[2] for a particular product under various conditions of trade control, assuming competitive conditions among producers and consumers and increasing costs. This indicates that, under conditions of free trade, OQ will be imported at the price OP. If, however, a quota is fixed of OQ_1 then, in the importing country, the export supply price under competitive conditions in the exporting country will fall to OP_1 and the import demand price will rise to OP_2. The owners of the import licences, allocated to them by the government, will pocket a quota profit of $P_1P_2 \times OQ_1$. The case of a specific tariff can be illustrated by drawing a line parallel to the supply schedule and to its left, thus representing at each point the additional cost of the tariff for each unit of the export supply (TS).

Under the assumption of a specific tariff the total quantity demanded and supplied will be reduced from OQ to OQ_2 while the price to the exporters will be P_3 and to the importers P_4. The difference between these two prices multiplied by the quantity imported ($P_4P_3 \times OQ_2$) will be the government revenue from the tariff. If a tariff-free quota of OQ is allowed, after which the specific tariff TS is applied, the only difference is that part of the revenue ($P_3P_4 \times OQ_1$) instead of accruing to the government will accrue to the licence holders.

The discussion so far has, however, left out some important characteristics of both the tariff and the guillotine quota.

If the import demand at a given price is much greater than the quota, then a quantitative restriction will raise the price above the price under a tariff since, in the latter case, the price mechanism is permitted to work, unless a tariff is prohibitive. Demand for imports under a tariff can be satisfied provided the duty is paid. Yet if import demand is shifted to a range which is below the quota limit, making the quota ineffective (to D_1 in Figure 6.1), then the import price within the quota (P_5) would be below the import price plus the tariff TS, and the quantity imported larger.

A comparison of the effects of tariffs and quotas, in this wider sense of the reaction to shifts in the demand schedule[3] is of particular importance in demonstrating the specific characteristics of tariff quotas, for it indicates their relatively liberal character. *The tariff quota behaves like an ordinary quota as long as the tariff quota is ineffective and then starts to behave like a tariff once the quota has become effective* and demand substantially exceeds the quota limits. It thus has the advantages of both, if a less restrictive measure is considered an advantage.

The next example examines with more precision some different types of tariff quota and their effects. The customary two-country model has been used where, in both countries, production takes place under competitive conditions and increasing costs. The number of consumers is also large and demand relatively elastic.

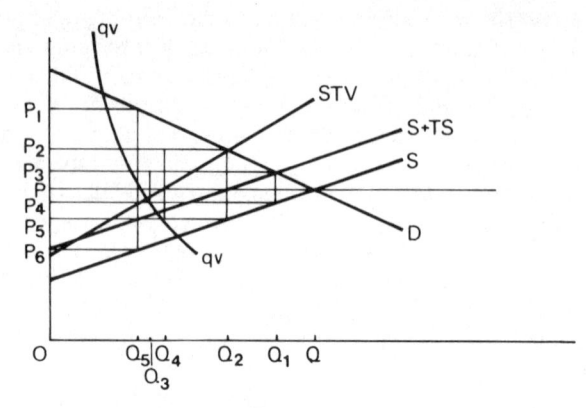

FIGURE 6.2

Under these assumptions, the derived demand in the importing country and the supply of the exporting country are shown in Figure 6.2 by the lines D and S respectively. OP depicts the free-trade equilibrium price and OQ the quantity imported at that price. The parallel line $S+TS$ represents the specific tariff per unit to be paid in addition to the export price, while STV represents an *ad valorem* tariff on the same supply schedule. The quantitative quota is represented by OQ_5 – while $qv\,qv$ represents a qualitative quota[4] (drawn in such a way as to equal the quantitative tariff quota at OP).

Comparison is first made between the specific tariff and the *ad valorem* tariff shown in Figure 6.2, where the specific rate is lower than the *ad valorem* one. Consequently the quantity imported with an *ad valorem* tariff is smaller (OQ_2) than under the specific tariff (OQ_1). Furthermore, not only is the import price higher than under a specific tariff but the export price is also lower, due to the increasing cost nature of the supply. The implication of this for the tariff quota of a quantitative type like OQ_5 is that importers receive in the case of an *ad valorem* tariff a bigger margin of gain from each unit within the tariff quota, since the import price is determined by P_2 (higher than P_3) and the export price is P_5 (lower than P_4). Thus while the total number of units to be imported within the tariff quota remains the same, importers will gain more under an *ad valorem* duty (beyond a certain range)[5] than under a specific tariff.

Looking next at the qualitative tariff quota with both alternative tariff rates, and starting with equal quotas (qualitative and quantitative) at free trade prices, it is clear that under tariff protection (in an increasing cost model which affects export supply prices) the qualitative quota will permit a larger quantity of imports within the tariff quota than the quantitative quota, in all price ranges below the free trade equilibrium price. Since the specific tariff in Figure 6.2 is lower than the *ad valorem* tariff, it becomes obvious that the largest quantity of imports at the lowest export price and the highest import price is attained by combining a qualitative quota with an *ad valorem* duty ($P_2P_5 \times OQ_4$).

Such a tariff quota may be the most advantageous to importers. It is, however, much less advantageous to all other parties concerned.

(*a*) The export price per unit, as well as the total quantity exported, are the same as under a quantitative quota with an *ad valorem* tariff. Thus from the point of view of the exporting country it is a less desirable form of quota than the one with specific tariff[6] (under the particular conditions stipulated in this two country model – to be altered later on).

(*b*) From the point of view of the consumers in the importing country the *ad valorem* duty raises the price of the unit imported and brings about a more severe restriction of the quantity imported than with a specific tariff.

(*c*) From the point of view of the government in the importing country – the loss of customs revenue is the highest.

All the above is true only if the demand of the importing country cuts the supply curve at the level where the specific tariff is lower than the *ad valorem* tariff, otherwise the opposite is true. But irrespective of the individual differences of the tariff quota discussed above, the pessimistic conclusion might be drawn that there is no gain to be obtained from a tariff quota, apart from the importers pocketing an excess profit. It would appear that a specific tariff, imposed on the total import, would permit the attainment of both a low import price and high export price, the only difference being that instead of the tariff quota gain going to the importer it would be absorbed as revenue by the government. Such a pessimistic conclusion would, however, be premature, as the tariff quotas so far discussed have been presented for illustrative purposes under some very specific assumptions. These now need to be relaxed before a more balanced evaluation can be made.

Firstly, very little reference has been made to the *size* of the quota in relation to the time period for which it is given. If the tariff quota is larger than demand for some time, and imports come in not under the allocation system of licences but rather under the 'greyhound' system of 'first come, first served', then the competitive price may rule, since in fact for such time the quota is ineffective.[7] Only when the total quota is filled – after a period of months – does the tariff quota become effective and the price of imports rise. Secondly, the discussion until now has assumed, among other things, the existence of two countries of more or less equal size, the absence of the exporting country's power to influence its export price; increasing costs of supply, the existence of exports despite the tariff; a single product rather than a group of products; and so on.

Certain changes, therefore, need to be made to the original assumptions so that their effect can be illustrated, for example in the assumed case of a *small country* enjoying a preferred tariff quota. First it will now be assumed that this country is a very small supplier of the product to the importing country (for instance, a small country in relation to a large importing area).[8] Under such circumstances the exporting country has no influence over the price of the product demanded – and has to adjust its output to the given price in the market. On the other hand the assumption of increasing supply cost from the exporting country is maintained, representing a familiar situation where the exporting country's supply consists of output from a number of firms with different cost structures. A second assumption is that the exporting country benefits from a bilateral preferred tariff quota which no other country enjoys.[9] The effects of different types of tariff quotas are examined for those cases when no individual producer, consumer or trader can influence the prices, and, also, where the export licence authorities in the exporting country can influence the price.

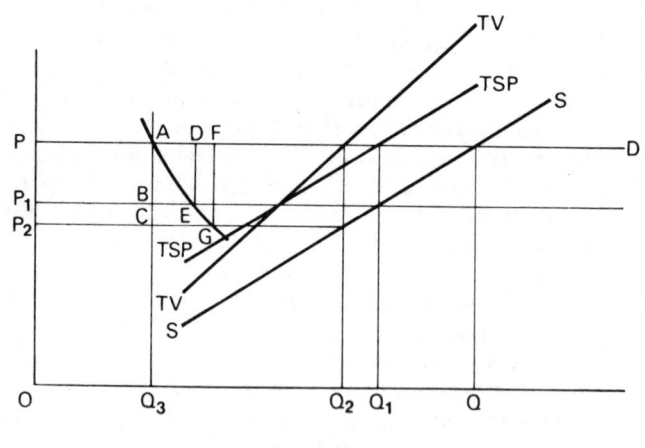

FIGURE 6.3

In Figure 6.3 the derived demand for imports in the importing country is represented by the horizontal line *PD*, indicating a completely elastic demand, while the supply available from the particular small country increases with price, as the line *SS* shows.

A specific tariff (*TSP*) parallel to *SS* cuts demand to the left of Q at Q_1 and the *ad valorem* tariff *TV* cuts demand at Q_2.

With the specific tariff, the export supply price in the exporting country will be P_1 (absorbing the cost of the specific tariff imposed by the importing country), while, with the *ad valorem* tariff the export supply price will be P_2 (which is below P_1, the tariff cost being similarly absorbed).

If a quantitative tariff quota OQ_3 is applied to imports, the gains of the importers (under the assumption of an effective quota) would be $PABP_1$, in the case of a specific tariff, and $PACP_2$ if used in conjunction with an *ad valorem* tariff. The quantity sold within the quota would be the same in each case.

If, instead of the quantitative quota, a qualitative quota is introduced, equal to the quantitative quota at free market prices, then the quantity to be imported within it will be larger in the case of an *ad valorem* duty than under a specific tariff, as long as the specific rate is below the *ad valorem* rate.

This means again that the profit for importers is the largest when the tariff quota is a qualitative quota and the tariff is an *ad valorem* tariff (the gain for importers under such circumstances is the area $PFGP_2$). But, contrary to the case presented in Figure 6.2, the total difference between export and import prices has to be absorbed by the exporting country.

While from the exporter's point of view the specific tariff is more desirable than the *ad valorem* tariff, it also makes no difference to him in this case whether there is a tariff quota or not, or of what kind.

Finally, the least desirable tariff quota from the point of view of the importer is the quantitative tariff quota with a specific duty since the gain there is the smallest (assuming a specific tariff which is below the *ad valorem* duty).

If the exporting authorities can influence prices within the quota through licensing, thus permitting exporting firms to obtain most if not all of the quota gain, then no one type of quota can *a priori* be considered to be the most advantageous, since various contradictory forces are at play.

The tariff itself determines the output and supply price. Since it is assumed that the *ad valorem* tariff is higher than the specific tariff, the supply price and quantity are *larger* under a *specific* than an *ad valorem* rate of duty. Assuming there is a possibility for exporters to reap the quota profit, there nevertheless remains the question of which represents the greater gain for the exporting country: (a) the total gain $PACP_2$ + the revenue $OQ_2 \times OP_2$ or (b) the total gain $PABP_1$ + the revenue $P_1O \times OQ_1$. This depends on the elasticity of supply, the difference between the two tariffs and the size of the tariff quota. What is, however, obvious is the fact that the exporting authority trying to raise prices within a qualitative quota eliminates the advantage of such a quota over a quantitative quota, since at price OP the qualitative and quantitative quotas are the same (by assumption).

An important point with respect to the tariff quota of the preferred country is the question of price fluctuation.

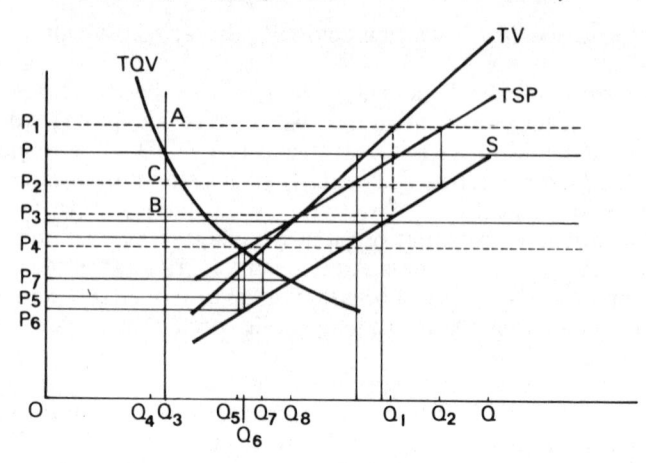

FIGURE 6.4

In Figure 6.4 if the world price rises from P to P_1, and the preferred exporting country can influence the preferred export price within the limits of the quota, the quantitative quota becomes even more valuable than the qualitative quota (which at each higher price permits under a quota a smaller and smaller quantity of imports than the quantitative quota).[10] Yet as far as the *ad valorem* versus the specific tariff rate is concerned the situation is dependent on the specific elasticities of the supply, the difference between the two tariffs and *size of the quantitative quota*. For though P_1ABP_3 is bigger than P_1ACP_2 there has to be added to the first the smaller normal export revenue $OP_3 \times OQ_1$ as compared with $OP_2 \times OQ_2$ for the second.

Under the situation where there is a fall in price, to P_4, opposite conclusions can be drawn.

(a) With a quantitative quota the specific tariff becomes higher than the *ad valorem* tariff and therefore a smaller quantity can be sold under the specific tariff than under the *ad valorem* one (the difference is between OQ_6 and OQ_7); and

(b) the export price is lower under the specific tariff (P_6) than under the *ad valorem* tariff (P_5).

The most interesting point, however, is that the qualitative quota also under export control may permit a much higher export quantity (OQ_5) within the quota at the price P_4 than under the quantitative tariff quota (specific or *ad valorem*) at this price. (A possible extreme is that all imports will be within the qualitative tariff quota.) If the qualitative tariff quota is effective, and the specific duty paid is higher than the *ad valorem*, the additional amount exported under specific duty is smaller,

Tariff Quotas: a Partial Equilibrium Analysis 147

and the total export price lower ($P_6 \times Q_5Q_6$), than in the case of the *ad valorem* rate of duty ($P_5 \times Q_5Q_7$).

In this particular graph, if no control were exerted and world prices fell to P_4, actual exports would all take place at Q_8 within the tariff quota, where the export price per unit is higher (P_7) and the quantity larger than any other situation except for free trade.

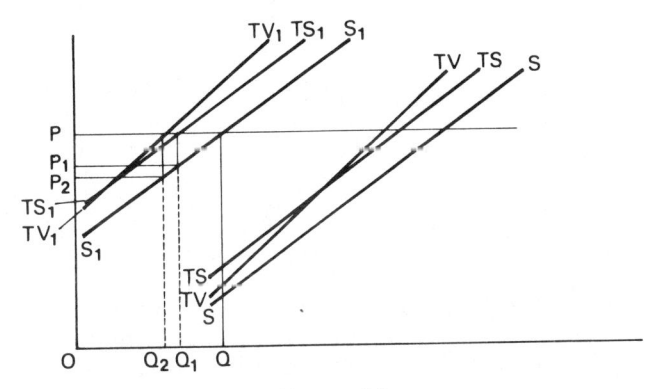

FIGURE 6.5

Figure 6.5 illustrates the case where supply is radically curtailed, the supply schedule SS being shifted upwards to where the supply line cuts the quota limit, to a position S_1S_1.

In such a case total exports at the specific rate of duty would be OQ_1 at price P_1, while with an *ad valorem* duty they would be OQ_2 at price P_2. Under a tariff quota, however, the whole quota will be disposed of by the exporters at world market prices.

This is precisely the case where a preferential tariff quota is of benefit to a country, since otherwise its exports would be few or nil.[11]

A different situation arises where a tariff quota of a global nature is extended to a large number of countries, while the quota itself constitutes a very small share of actual imports coming from all over the world. The tariff quota granted by Australia to all developing countries, who are therefore competing one against the other, is a good example. In cases such as these individual exporting countries have no power of influence on their export price. The tariff quota as seen from the point of view of the importing country is set out in Figure 6.6.

The supply is completely elastic and the derived demand of the importing country cuts world supply (S) at OQ_1 where the price $OP+T$ is the import price (assuming a world price of WP, developing country price of LDP, and a tariff of $P+T$).

Under such circumstances the price ruling in the market will encourage importers to import the product from developing countries as

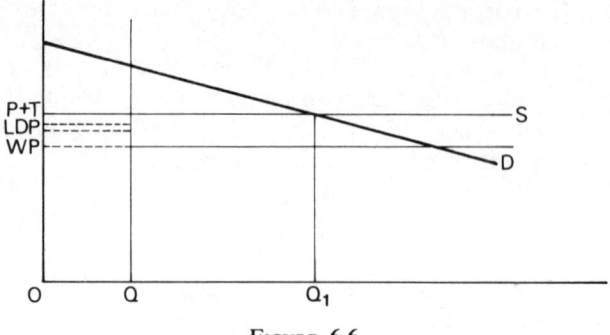

FIGURE 6.6

long as the quota is ineffective, despite their higher price (due to higher production costs), provided they will receive an extra gain in addition to the normal profit of importing.

The higher the degree of tariff protection against the rest of the world, the better the chances of exporting the product from the developing countries as a whole, since the margin of preference is higher.

The final case to be discussed in detail in this chapter is one in which the total global quota is large enough to have an effect *in toto* on the supply price and export distribution between the developed and developing countries. This is shown graphically in Figure 6.7, where it has been assumed that the importing country applies a quantitative tariff quota in favour of developing countries.

In order that the effect of any changes can be shown as clearly as possible, it has seemed desirable to separate the importing country (A) from the developed exporting countries (B) and from the develop-

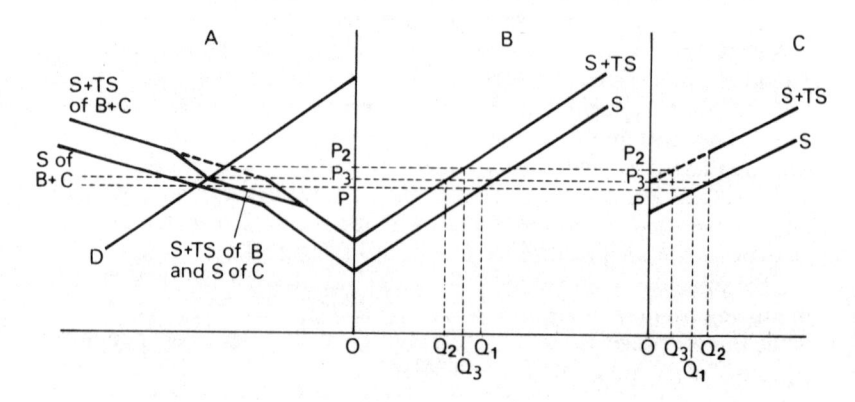

FIGURE 6.7

ing exporting countries (C). The former have the major share of the trade and the latter the smaller share, due to their relative inefficiency. A derived demand for imports, and supply for exports, can be drawn by deducting domestic supply in the importing country, and domestic demand in the exporting countries.

If OP is the free trade import price, then OQ_1 will be imported from B, with the smaller value of OQ_1 from the less important C group of supplying countries. If the same tariff were imposed on imports from both sets of countries, the exports from both sets would be reduced, in both cases to OQ_3, and the price would rise, although not by the full amount (to P_2). If the duty were imposed only on B, while from C the imports were free within a tariff quota as long as the tariff quota was not fully utilised, there would be a shift to C in the quantity previously bought from B, less being purchased in B (OQ_2) and more in C (OQ_2).

If demand cuts the aggregate supply at the inflection points, where the quota is effective, but no duty-bearing exports from C are forthcoming, the quota margin in C rises yet only B increases its exports If the demand cuts the aggregate supply | TS beyond the inflection point, not only does C fill its quota but it will be able to continue exporting in excess of the tariff quota, despite the tariff wall.

A similar set of graphs has been drawn in Figure 6.8 to depict the effect of a qualitative tariff quota. Here the combined supply curve at each price (so long as exports within the quota in C are not surpassed) would have to take into account the two opposing tendencies of an increasing supply in B with duty and a decreasing supply in C without the duty.

The analysis permits more than just the comparison of the reactions of derived demand and supply to changing conditions of free trade, tariff or tariff quotas. The prices derived from this exercise, if referred back

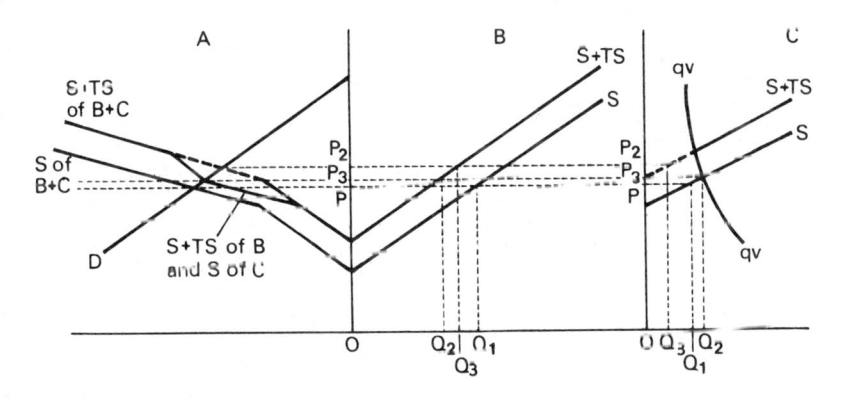

FIGURE 6.8

and superimposed on the original demand and supply curves in the various countries, would reveal the reaction of domestic consumption and production to changing trade control measures. It would be shown, for instance, that the existence of a tariff quota in favour of one exporting country not only shifts the export trade in its favour but that, in total, such a tariff quota has a positive effect on demand in the importing country. There the reduced import prices will increase consumption while at the same time the relatively costly domestic supply will decrease. Thus the tariff quota permits consumption at lower prices than with full duty. In addition more will also be consumed domestically in the exporting countries through the lower price.

While several other cases of tariff quotas could be presented in the graphical form that has been used in this chapter, it is hoped that enough has been done to stimulate analytical interest in the many facets of the subject. From the limited discussion here that has accompanied the diagrams it is evident that:

(*a*) tariff quotas are a more liberal tool of trade restriction than either quotas or fixed tariffs;

(*b*) there are only a few general clear-cut answers as to the effects of a tariff quota since much depends on the specific case;

(*c*) however,

(i) for the tariff quota to transfer the full gain to the consumer in the importing country (that is, for the product to be sold at free-trade prices) a quota has to be sufficiently large to make it ineffective at least over a rather long period – this point is particularly relevant in view of some of the national European Community quotas which are being granted for the specific purpose;

(ii) if no export control can be exercised and the quota is effective, most of the advantages of the tariff quota will be reaped by the importers;

(iii) these advantages to importers may be precisely the additional incentives needed by developing countries in order to export their products to developed countries since they cause importers to prefer their products;

(iv) sometimes the preferential tariff quota may also help the less efficient exporters to develop new exports which could not be exported at all without a tariff quota;

(v) if an exporting country can influence the export price within the quota its largest gain would be from a quantitative, rather than a qualitative, quota of equivalent effect at free market prices.

If the preferred imports constitute a significant share of total imports there will be a shift of supply from developed to developing countries as long as the tariff quota is unutilised, provided the export prices of developing countries are not prohibitively high.

Furthermore, if exports of the developing countries do not exceed the tariff quota, world prices may fall in comparison to the prices that would rule under non-discriminatory and non-adjustable tariff conditions, thus increasing domestic demand in all three areas and eliminating the more expensive production in the importing country.

Thus under such circumstances tariff quotas for developing countries contribute to more liberal conditions in the importing country by shifting part of their trade to developing countries, who in turn benefit from expanded exports.

NOTES AND REFERENCES

1. Some early references to tariff quotas are Heuser, *op. cit.*, pp. 77–9 and 161–7; and S. Enke and V. Salera *International Economics*, 2nd ed. (New York: Prentice-Hall, 1951) pp. 276–7 and 286–8. A further reference to tariff quotas is included in Richard N. Cooper, 'The European Community's System of Generalised Tariff Preferences: a Critique', *Journal of Development Studies*, July 1972.
2. The demand and supply schedules can either be based on the assumption that no local production exists in the importing country and no demand in the exporting country, or alternatively on the assumption that the above schedules are derived from the basic demand and supply schedules in both countries. The derived schedules are obtained by plotting the excess of supply over demand in the exporting country on the same graph with the excess demand over supply in the importing country at each price, see for detailed description Mordechai Kreinin, *International Economics* (New York: Harcourt Brace Jovanovich Inc., 1971) pp. 240–5, deducting transport cost from the import demand by lowering the base of the graph of the importing country by the margin of transportation cost.
3. Kreinen, 'More on the Equivalence of Tariffs and Quotas', *Kyklos*, Basle, XXIII (1970) p. 76.
4. The qualitative quota is fixed in terms of value of money, thus changes in price will affect quantity in the opposite direction so that the total value will remain constant, that is, it is a unit elasticity curve.
5. If the import demand cuts the export supply in a range where the specific tariff is higher than the *ad valorem* rate the situation is reversed, and the tariff quota under a specific tariff will offer larger rewards to importers.
6. This follows, however, from the advantage of the specific tariff over the *ad valorem* tariff in the particular example and does not relate to the type of tariff quota, since these make no difference to the exporter.
7. This was the case with the woollen and worsted quota in the United States, which caused imports in excess of demand at the beginning of the period, depressing prices below the free market price, and then a much higher price than the free market price once the quota was filled.
8. The price in the importing area could be assumed to include the tariff implicitly or else, in the case of countries within a region or associated with it in one form or another, to be the equilibrium price within the area (also presumably including the tariff *vis-à-vis* third countries).
9. Many of the European Community's agreements with its associate countries or some third countries contain such tariff quotas.

10. This latter point with respect to the qualitative quota is relevant in view of the many preference schemes which are defined in terms of fixed-value tariff quotas while the value of money changes constantly.
11. It is not possible within this chapter to examine other propositions, but it should be obvious that the steadily increasing cost is not necessarily the true case in many developing countries, since plants in developing countries frequently work at under-utilised capacity. This is because of the limited internal market and the high initial unit cost which prevents them from exporting and expanding their output sufficiently to reap advantages of scale. If a preferential quota could provide a sufficient push to overcome the initial hurdle further exports could be anticipated even at the lower export price and facing a tariff once the tariff quota is expended.

PART III

Generalised Tariff Preferences

CHAPTER 7

Tariff Quotas under the Generalised System of Preferences

The purpose of this chapter, and also the one that follows, is to discuss the role of tariff quotas in the various generalised systems of preferences (GSP), both those which have been suggested and those which have been put into effect. But it seems desirable first to provide a background in the form of a few general comments on GSP. There is really no possibility of doing more than this within the framework of this book, as limitations on space prevent the extensive discussion that the subject really deserves, for this is one of the main topics with which UNCTAD has been concerned from its inception. It is sufficient to glance at the bibliography on the subject of preferences, prepared by the UNCTAD Secretariat from the documents of UNCTAD itself, to get an idea of the voluminous material available on the subject.[1] Even this bibliography in no way gives a complete picture, partly because it was made a few years ago, but also because it refers only to the documents of UNCTAD itself and not to the many other documents, books and articles which have been written on the subject.

INTRODUCTION

Demands for preferences to be given to developing countries arose before the establishment of UNCTAD and there are references to such demands in forums like the GATT and the United Nations Economic Commission for Europe (ECE) at the end of the 1950s and beginning of the 1960s.[2] But it was only within UNCTAD that this became one of the main objectives for which the organisation decided to struggle. The emphasis on this demand for the granting of general preferences to the developing countries' exports into developed countries, especially of manufactured and semi-manufactured products, was the result of the general analysis of the economic state of affairs of the developing countries. It appeared evident that the targets of the so-called development decade, of a minimum growth of 5 per cent per year in GNP, would not be possible without increasing imports from developed countries at a more or less parallel rate of growth. But it was also clear that traditional exports and existing aid would be insufficient to finance these imports.

The development of exports of manufactures was seen by the developing countries as a partial solution to bridging the gap. The rate of growth of exports of manufactures was much faster than that of primary products and their long-run prospects seemed much better. Moreover:

(a) Most developing countries principally exported a limited number of primary products, subject to large price fluctuations and a low income elasticity of demand. Diversifying their exports would reduce this burdensome dependence.

(b) The possibility of exporting manufactures would provide a spur for the development of industry generally. Often, limited internal markets alone could not justify the establishment of industrial enterprises of economic size. Moreover, employment possibilities in agriculture and other primary production were limited: a situation aggravated by technological developments, which, greatly increasing agricultural output per man, created an excess supply of agricultural labour which had to be employed elsewhere.

Yet manufactured exports from developing countries had to surmount many difficulties. In many of the countries there was no industry to speak of, and even the infrastructure necessary for industrialisation was lacking. Even where industry existed, it was mainly directed towards a small domestic market, and was of the import-substituting type, existing behind high tariff walls and receiving administrative and other indirect protection (that is, through a shortage of foreign currency). As a result, production was expensive and inefficient, and the protected enterprises lacked know-how and experience in marketing and exporting.

Hence the developing countries demanded special treatment to enable them to enter the export field. They argued that the infant industry principle, accepted in the GATT for developing countries when applied to protection against imports, should be expanded and recognised also in the field of exports. In other words, the demand of the developing world was to do away with the equal treatment of those who are unequal, a treatment presently underlined by the MFN clause of the GATT. According to the developing countries this rule is unjust. It harms the weak because it forces unfair competition between the strong and the weak.

The outcry was all the greater because the GATT agreement not only did not show preference to the developing world but in several cases actually discriminated against it. There were various reasons for this discrimination: negotiations on tariff reductions were usually conducted between principal suppliers and consequently mainly covered products of interest to developed countries; there were certain import restrictions, legal and illegal, on products of special interest to developing countries; customs unions and free trade areas *de facto* discriminated against developing countries which continued to pay the higher duty, while a significant number of the developed countries did not.

But the practical problem, after agreement in principle, was to determine the character and form of the preferences to be demanded. On this topic there was a host of shades of opinions, approaches and suggestions. Countries of the developed world had various opinions (including some objecting categorically to the principle of preference for developing countries generally); and to these were added the different approaches and opinions among the developing countries. United on the principle of preferential treatment from the developed countries, their views on practical details varied. Wide differences of interest existed between them. Some already were parties to preferential arrangements and were anxious that the benefits should not be eliminated by a new arrangement. Moreover, some were better equipped to take advantage of preferences than others, which raised the problem of equality of benefits. An outline of the principal issues discussed demonstrates the difficulties.[3]

Product Coverage. Should there be a positive selective list? Should this be uniform or not for all developed countries, or should all products in the field of manufactures and semi-manufactures be covered? How should these be defined? Are processed agricultural products also included? Can certain products be excluded *ab initio* into a negative list?

Complete free entry into all the developed countries for the exports of all the developing countries was demanded by many developing countries, at least for manufactured and semi-manufactured products. On the other hand M. Brasseur, the Belgian Foreign Trade Minister, suggested that each developed country should grant, in bilateral negotiations with specific developing countries, particular preferences which could be within the limits of tariff quotas for a limited period in specific products.[4] Another proposal was suggested[5] in the Third Committee of GATT.[6] Under this scheme a limited list would have been prepared consisting of major export products and of primary commodities which developing countries, by taking in higher stages of processing, could develop into important manufactured or semi-manufactured export items. Preferences would have been extended to all developing countries with respect to all items on the list.

Depth of Cut. What should be the preferential tariff? Should it be a given percentage cut? If so, should the cut be uniform for all products in all developed countries? Should duties on the products of the developing countries be completely eliminated? Should there be different preferential duties for different stages of development?

Safeguards. How can serious injury, or the threat thereof, be avoided? Can products be excluded partially or completely from preferential treatment? If so, how, when, under what circumstances, and by whose authority?

Beneficiaries. Who should benefit from the scheme? How, and by what methods, should a country be designated as 'developing'? Do all developed countries have to accept the same definition?

The Less Developed. How should they be determined? How should their interests be assured within the preference scheme?

The Existing Preferences for Some Developing Countries. Should they be eliminated? Should they then receive compensation and, if so, how?

Burden-sharing. Was sharing the costs of GSP among the donor countries necessary? If so, how should this be accomplished?

These were some[6] of the key questions dealt with over a period of some six years. The agreed conclusions of UNCTAD's Special Committee on Preferences were reached in 1970.

USE OF TARIFF QUOTAS AS A TOOL FOR PREFERENTIAL TREATMENT

This section reviews in more detail the use of tariff quotas as solutions to the problems above. Their use could have solved many of the main questions. An overall limitation of the volume of trade permitted under preferred terms makes more attractive the idea of wide product coverage, while unlimited one-way free trade makes it less attractive to the preference-givers. By the same token, if the quantity to be imported at preferred terms were limited, it would also facilitate acceptance of deeper tariff cuts, possibly even to zero. In addition, the number of beneficiaries to be included in a preferential scheme can be more easily extended when a tariff quota limits the overall preferred imports in total, or for a product, from all the developing world.

Tariff quotas also provide possible answers to the safeguard problem. Quotas could be stipulated when serious injury from preferential imports, threatens a domestic industry; then being invoked on an escape clause procedure basis. Alternatively, a pre-fixed tariff quota serves as a safeguard.[7]

By applying sub-quotas to sub-groups of countries, the problem of countries at various stages of development could be solved. Finally, they provide an answer to the problem of existing preferences. New preferences could be limited by a tariff quota, but old preferences unrestricted.

EARLY SUGGESTIONS OF PREFERENCE SCHEMES BASED ON TARIFF QUOTAS

Chronologically, the first proposal for a preference scheme to cover the exports of manufactures from the developing countries into developed countries based on tariff quotas was the proposal made in the *Economic Survey of Europe, 1960*.[8]

THE ECE SCHEME OF 1960

This report recognised that the developing countries needed to expand their growing exports of manufactures and acknowledged that they would only be able to do so with temporary preferential treatment from the industrial countries to help them over the initial infant industry stage. Despite this it suggested that complete abolition of tariffs and import restrictions might not be feasible.[9] However: 'Each of the industrial countries of Western Europe might agree, as a realistic gesture of immediate aid to the developing countries, to abolish all tariffs and import restrictions on such exports of manufactures by individual under-developed countries as do not, in any year, exceed a certain proportion – say, three or five per cent – of its total imports in the previous year in that commodity group.

'So long as the exports of a given commodity from any given under-developed country do not exceed the specified proportion of the European country's imports of that commodity, they would be admitted free of tariff or other restrictions. Once they exceeded the specified proportion, they would be subject to whatever tariffs, or other trade restrictions [also, it was hoped, to be gradually liberalised] that would apply in the absence of the special preferential treatment proposed.

'A move of this kind could not reasonably be regarded as spelling any threat to the domestic industries of the industrial countries: the proposed small limitation of imports would adequately guarantee this.[10] At the same time, it would be precisely the kind of help that would be needed to overcome the special infant industry disadvantages under which industrial export production in under-developed countries laboured. Once this special disadvantage was overcome, by export production reaching a significant level, the special preferential treatment would automatically lapse.'

This scheme allowed for a broad product coverage and tariff cuts to zero, but instead of free access to developed markets it provided for an overall limit to the volume of imports of *particular* products (although this was indicated only as a possibility in a footnote).[11] As individual exporting countries could only obtain a partial share of the overall preferential treatment for each product, equitable treatment of the various developing countries could be provided, and the difficulty posed by existing preferences apparently was dealt with by the quantitative limit on the new preferences. But difficulties remained.

First and foremost, the scheme required the specific determination for *each product, each year*. Thus, if commodities were narrowly defined, many tariff quotas would have to be calculated each year and the exports of each developing country kept under continual check to ensure that they did not exceed the particular ceiling; an enormous administrative task. On the other hand should product classes be more broadly defined, individual commodities within the group could constitute a much higher percentage[12] of that particular product than the 3 to 5 per cent of imports in the group, thus nullifying its safeguard properties.

Secondly, it is possible that the number of exporting developing countries, exporting within their quota limits in each product, could exceed the overall ceiling established for preferential imports from all developing countries. In such a case the individual quotas would have to be cut back proportionately, which could not only cause considerable additional administrative difficulties, but also enormous risks to the exporters of the particular products in the developing countries.

Third, by permitting only a limited preference in each particular product, developing countries could be encouraged to over-diversify. This could operate against concentration of efforts in the development of particular exports in which long-run comparative advantage might exist.

PROPOSAL OF THE AUTHOR

The second scheme of preferences, based on the principle of tariff quotas was evolved by the author of this book in 1963 as a by-product of his work as Consultant to the United Nations Secretariat,[13] in the preparation of the first UN Conference on Trade and Development.

This scheme has been presented publicly in various forms and degrees of detail both inside[14] and outside[15] UNCTAD. It is presented here again, not in all the details originally worked out in 1963, but in outline form, sufficient to show all the important elements relevant to the understanding of the scheme. The summary is given in the next section, which is followed, in turn, by a more detailed discussion of the main points.

Outline of the Scheme
(1) Duty-free global tariff quotas for imports of manufactures and

semi-manufactures from developing countries would be established in each of the developed countries.

(2) The tariff quota would be determined on the basis of a percentage (probably 10 per cent) applied uniformly in each of the developed countries to the total imports of manufactures and semi-manufactures each year. The guiding principles for the determination of the percentage would be, on the one hand, the projected long-term requirements for exports of manufactures and semi-manufactures that would be needed to fill the gap forecast for the balance of payments, if the targets of the Development Decade were to be achieved. Additionally, account would be taken of the estimated increase in imports of manufactures and semi-manufactures in the developed countries over the same period.

In order to avoid the possible disruption of markets for specific commodities resulting from preferential treatment, developed countries would have the right to intervene and limit the preferential imports when such danger arose. The procedure to be followed in such cases would be along the lines provided in Article XIX of the GATT. They would, however, apply to all developing countries on a non-discriminatory basis.

(3) The global quota of each developed country should be subdivided into two sub-quotas, each one reserved for a specific group of countries being more or less in the same stage of development, so as to permit competition by equals within the quota limits. The sub-quota percentage would also be determined on the basis of the projected export requirements which would be needed by each group in order to achieve the development decade's targets, and would be applied uniformly in each of the developed countries, in the same manner as the total quota.

(4) Safeguards limiting the threat of an over-expansion by any particular country could be included; in such a case there would be a stipulation that an overall quota should be calculated for each individual developing country. This would be based roughly on the total value of exports from the particular country to all developed countries, taken together, that would be required to achieve the desired targets of the Development Decade. Once the quota was fulfilled, additional imports from this particular exporting country would pay the regular duties. An international body — such as the United Nations Secretariat, the GATT or the Organisation for Economic Co-operation and Development (OECD) — would follow the actual import returns and make the necessary calculations.

(5) Preferential treatment would be fixed for a given period, subject to review and renewal.

Explanatory Considerations
The paragraphs in quotes in the remainder of this section refer to the

paragraphs in the outline above. In the explanations that follow mention is made of calculations, made at the time of the proposal, for the year 1970. It needs to be remembered that these were forecasts made a dozen years ago and should not be interpreted as actuals.

'Duty-free global tariff quotas for imports of manufactures and semi-manufactures from developing countries will be established in each of the developed countries.'

The global tariff quotas discussed in this scheme differ substantially from the more conventional tariff quotas since they do not refer to specific commodities but rather to a given value of total imports consisting of a multitude of commodities.

The scheme only deals with the expansion of exports of manufactures and semi-manufactures from developing countries. The problem of primary commodities is excluded from the discussion since it is treated separately elsewhere. A clear-cut definition of what constitutes manufactures and semi-manufactures is required. Specific agreement is therefore needed about which commodities ought to be included in this group. It was suggested that the SITC groups determined by the United Nations should be accepted. Thus, manufacturing and semi-manufacturing would include groups 5 to 8 and processed food products.

Furthermore, these commodities would be considered as originating from a developing country, if at least 20 per cent of the value added was[16] produced in the country, or the commodities had undergone a specific process, usually undertaken by a developing country and agreed upon before the scheme had entered into force. The low level of 20 per cent was chosen for the margin of value because in developing countries industrialisation and diversification are largely, of necessity, of the 'top-down' type: industrialisation starts with the finishing stages and assembly plants, and later develops backwards into the earlier stages of processing.

Such a low margin of added value could in principle induce developed countries to direct exports to other developed countries' markets via developing countries. Under these circumstances, however, the cost of transport would be higher and the existence of a limited quota would make such a procedure risky for exporters, and undesirable to the governments of developing countries, who might have to forgo genuine export gains.

'The tariff quota would be determined on the basis of a percentage [probably 10 per cent] applied uniformly in each of the developed countries to the total imports of manufactures and semi-manufactures each year.'

As a general principle preferential schemes should be based on simple objectives and predetermined criteria which leave as little room as possible for discretion, discrimination and arbitrary decisions. A uniform percentage for all developed countries is desirable on this principle.

It has been suggested that quotas should be established on the basis of a given percentage of national income or consumption, which would overcome the problem of actual imports reflecting the protection of the home industry. But this faces the difficulty that the relative share of imports in consumption, or national income, is not uniform for all countries, as the degree of dependence on imports is determined by such factors as the size of the country, natural endowments, customs and habits of consumption, standards of living, and so on. Despite distortions brought about by protective measures, the needs of the developed countries are reflected more accurately by total actual imports, rather than by a percentage of national income or consumption. Furthermore, the increasing liberalisation of trade between the developed countries themselves (for instance, the Regional Integration schemes) substantially reduces the degree of distortion.

A number of alternative methods for calculating yearly global quotas can be used. The percentage can be applied to the last year's actual import returns; to the average rate of increase — calculated on the basis of actual development over the most recent two or three years; or to the latest year's actual imports (multiplied annually on the basis of the past average general rate of increase and on development targets, to be established by agreement).

The third possibility seems to be the most stable solution, permitting longer-run planning on the part of developing countries. It could, however, create disparities with the actual development of imports of manufactures into the developed countries, by constituting a larger or smaller percentage than was originally intended. But whichever method is selected ought to be agreed upon in advance.

'The guiding principles for the determination of the percentage are, on the one hand, the projected long-term requirements for exports of manufactures and semi-manufactures that would be needed to fill the gap existing in the balance of payments, if the targets of the Development Decade are to be achieved. Additionally account is also taken of the estimated increase in imports of manufactures and semi-manufactures in the developed countries over the same period.'

The object was to expand the exports of manufactures and semi-manufactures of developing countries in order to fill the gap between required import payments and their normal export receipts. If the targets of the Development Decade of a 5 per cent increase in GNP each year were to be attained, then according to a very rough estimate about $10,000m worth of additional exports of manufactures and semi-manufactures to developed free market economies would be required, in order to finance the deficit in the trade balance. At the time of this calculation it was believed that $10,000m would, by 1970, equal about

10 per cent of the total imports manufactured and semi-manufactured products from all sources, according to a rough estimate based on average rates of increase of imports of manufactured products to developed countries over the preceding years. Thus, if a tariff quota was established in each of the developed countries, to the value of 10 per cent of total imports of manufactures and semi-manufactures from all sources, which would be utilised to the full, in addition to the normal imports from developing countries[17] the target of the 'Development Decade' could be achieved.

To put this into perspective exports of manufactures in 1962 from all the developing countries amounted, according to the data of the United Nations Secretariat, to about $2000m, while the imports of the developed countries amounted to $44,000m. In other words, a quota of 10 per cent of imports of manufactures would mean an immediate increase of import possibilities from developing countries of $4400m. There was no danger whatsoever that exports of manufactures from developing countries of such a size could really materialise. From the point of view of developing countries, a quota of such a size would mean *de facto* unilateral free trade. On the other hand, from the point of view of the developed countries, the scheme restricted the preferential treatment to well-defined, manageable, and not too burdensome proportions, and with a maximum limit, so that developing countries did not receive a blank cheque. This could have a very important psychological effect.

'In order to avoid the possible disruption of markets for specific commodities resulting from the preferential treatment, countries would have the right to intervene and limit the preferential imports when such danger arises. The procedure to be followed in such cases would be along the lines provided in Article XIX of GATT.' In addition, a specific, limited list of sensitive products which may seriously affect developing countries' existing preferential arrangements may also be included.

Even if there had been no 'exceptions list', the loss of existing preferences by developing countries would not be significant for the following reasons:

> (a) the important preferences were mainly in the field of primary commodities;
> (b) the imports from developing countries were limited within the global quota, while the preferred countries benefit from unlimited access to the individual country; and
> (c) in exchange for limited concessions on their preference in one specific market, they would enjoy preferences in other markets.

The primary danger of maintaining a global quota in terms of total import value is the overflow of imports in a selected number of items, such as textiles. It is, therefore, absolutely essential to such a preference scheme that some kind of an escape clause should be introduced that would protect the importing country from serious injury. But the criteria for the invocation of the escape clause should be strict and clearly defined, so that it is used only when really justified; and it should be subject to the review and the control of the GATT, or some other appropriate body. If such a review should find that the action taken was unwarranted or excessive, a recommendation could be made for its modification or withdrawal, or for the provision of appropriate compensation to the exporting country (or countries) affected by the maintenance of the restriction.

The relatively meagre share of developing countries in exports of manufactures to developed countries suggests that the danger of serious disruption is limited in the short run. But even in the long run the dangers under this scheme would be less than under others. The range of goods permitted duty-free entry into a developed country would be unlimited, so that concentration on the production of specific items by the developing countries is unnecessary. The possibility that use could be made of the exception might in itself be sufficient to meet the problem.

'The global quota in each country should be subdivided into two sub-quotas each one reserved for a specific group of countries being more or less in the same stage of development, so as to permit competition by equals within the quota limits.'

Actually, the global import quota, together with the safeguards provided to prevent cases of serious disruption of the market, might be a sufficient preference scheme and a better one because of its simplicity. The subdivision of developing countries could create difficulties and breaches in the united front of developing countries. But lack of subdivision has the disadvantage of treating unequals equally. On this ground, the total global quota in each developed country should be divided into two sub-quotas, each for a specific group of countries in more or less the same stage of development.

An alternative solution, proposed elsewhere,[18] is the allocation of a global quota[19] for each developing country in each developed country, in accordance with objective and predetermined criteria.[20] This kind of solution suffers from the disadvantage that large numbers of individual quotas would have to be determined each year through international agreement, a procedure possibly requiring a substantial amount of negotiation. Even if this were not the case, and the predetermined criteria permitted a clear-cut allocation of individual quotas for a number of years in advance, there would still be the question whether this type of allocation would really be in the best interests of the developing countries: it is difficult to predict what the export of each developing country to each individual developed country ought to be, and from this standpoint the quota distribution could well be arbitrary.

The advantage of the solution proposed here is that, within the framework of a large global quota, competition between more or less equals would permit each of the developing countries to concentrate on those particular markets and products in which they had a comparative advantage.

'The sub-quota percentage would also be determined on the basis of the projected export requirements needed by this group in order to achieve the Development Decade's targets.'

The projection of the total gap between future import requirements and normal export receipts, though highly tentative and intended for illustrative purposes only, nonetheless involved a number of detailed estimates suitable only for an overall model. In other words, the calculation of the overall gap, based on these calculations, did not lend itself to a precise breakdown into groups of individual countries. Nevertheless, such a method could well be essential for more restrictive schemes of preferences, and it is necessary to find a principle for allocating global quotas within the two sub-groups (as well as to individual developing countries in case a need for such allocation may arise, which is improbable).

Such a principle of allocation could be based on a method which, though less accurate, would at least try to approximate in a most general way to the purpose of the preference scheme, but would have the advantage of being more expedient, predetermined, uniform and simple. Essentially it is based on the fundamental assumption that the relationship between gross domestic product (GDP) and imports remains more or less stable[21] over an extended period of years and that, therefore, an annual increase of 5 per cent in gross domestic product would be accompanied by an annual increase of 5 per cent in imports.

It would, therefore, be possible to calculate the import requirement of the developing countries (as a whole as well as of each individual country) for, say, 1970 on the basis of existing import data, assuming the minimum rate of increase of 5 per cent postulated in the Development Decade target. Thus, for each individual country, the total import requirements for 1970 would be computed on the basis of the latest import returns shown in the *United Nations Yearbook, International Trade Statistics*, in dollar terms, assuming an annual rate of growth of 5 per cent.[22] Net import requirement would be the difference between these total import requirements and actual export receipts. This gap, expressed as a percentage of the total net import requirements of all the developing countries (calculated in the same way) would represent the percentage of the total quota allocations to the individual country.[23] Since the total global quota for all the developing countries is expressed in value terms for each year, the relative share of each developing country in value terms could also be determined, and therefore that of the sub-groups.

The main advantage of allocating individual quotas along these lines is that they would approximate the long-run requirements[24] of individual countries, and take into account the different relationships between imports and GDP for individual developing countries. It is clear-cut and predetermined, and the information required is readily available, accurate and unalterable. Furthermore, even if the targets themselves have to undergo changes in the light of criticism,[25] the estimate can very easily be adjusted to take account of these changes.

'The percentage of the sub-quota would be applied uniformly in each of the developed countries in the same manner as the total quota.'

If a particular group of countries had a total quota of a given percentage of total manufactured imports in all the developed countries, this group of countries would have the same quota in each of the developed countries. This would not mean that each individual developing country in the group would have the same individual quota in each developed country; as the groups are large and geographically dispersed, each individual country would be able to concentrate on those markets in the developed countries of most interest to it.

'Safeguards could be included which would limit the threat of an over-expansion by any particular country; in such a case there should be a provision which would stipulate that an overall quota should be calculated for each individual developing country. This would be based roughly on the total value of exports from the particular country to all developed countries taken together, that would be required to achieve the desired targets of the Development Decade. Once the quota was fulfilled, additional imports from this particular exporting country would have to pay the regular duties.'

Individual global quotas would only be introduced as a desirable refinement to prevent over-expansion of particular countries. Initially there would be little need for them, with a global quota five times as large as the actual imports of manufactures from the developing countries in 1962. But they provide a means of checking the over-expansion of individual countries, should it be necessary in the future.

It is important to emphasise that the quotas suggested here would not be individual quotas determined for each developed country but rather overall quotas of each developing country for *all* the developed countries taken together. While it is difficult to predict the direction of trade, it is easier to estimate, albeit roughly, the overall export requirements of each developing country that would be needed to fill an anticipated gap. Finally, having group quotas seems preferable even when individual global quotas have been introduced since it provides the less developed countries as a group more opportunity in *all* developed countries' markets.

'An international body (such as the United Nations Secretariat, GATT or OECD) would follow actual import returns and make the necessary computations for the purposes referred to in the preceding paragraph.'

As long as a preference scheme consists of global total import quotas, administration is relatively simple. No more is needed than up-to-date statistical tabulations in the developed countries, showing imports at the preferred rate. The necessary administrative machinery needs to be more elaborate once more detailed provisions and refinements are introduced.

A central computing agency would be required to ensure that individual developing countries did not exceed their overall global quotas. This could be one of the agencies of the United Nations, the GATT or even OECD. Its essential service would be to monitor continuously overall actual import returns for each of the developing countries on the basis of overall data transmitted to it by individual developed countries' importing authorities, and it would notify all developed countries when a particular developing country's global quotas had been filled.[26]

Global tariff quotas, under a first-come-first-served rule applied to imports actually crossing the border, are claimed by critics[27] to give unfair advantage to neighbouring countries, and also to distribute imports unevenly, with the bulk coming at the beginning of the period. As the global quota is open in each of the developed countries, one developing country having an advantage here and another there, it could be argued that the first of these criticisms is not valid. The quotas too, are sufficiently large in most developed countries to permit imports even from distant lands to come in duty-free without utilising the quota to its fullest extent. This also provides a partial answer to the second criticism. If total imports are insufficient to utilise a quota fully, there is really no need for any particular rush to get in ahead of anybody else. If a quota is effective, then the yearly total import quota could be divided into half-yearly, quarterly, or monthly quotas as required, so permitting a more even distribution of imports.

'Preferential treatment should be fixed for a given period, subject to review and renewal. It would seem desirable that the termination of preference should be phased out over a period of years.'

If it should be decided to terminate preferences for a particular developing country, it might be desirable to avoid abrupt termination by eliminating the preferential individual global quota by stages over a period of years, each year reducing the overall quota by a given percentage. This would, in the first place, immediately stop preferred exports expanding further and would also allow the developing country's export industries to adjust themselves slowly to the new conditions. The percentage and duration of the phasing out are matters to be determined by common agreement.

In summary all developed free market economies would extend to all developing economies preferential treatment in all manufactures and semi-manufactures, with occasional exception on an *ad hoc* basis to prevent market disruption, and the loss of existing preferences in particularly sensitive commodities. The quota should be based on 10 per cent of imports of developed countries, subdivided into two groups, the tariff to be zero within the quota, and the period to be fixed for, say, ten years, but subject to renegotiation.

To summarise the advantages of the scheme:

(*a*) It facilitates the development of industrial exports by the developing countries.

(*b*) The limited quota avoids substantial interference with other preferences. This is because access to members of customs unions is unlimited, whereas access to these markets from developing countries is restricted.

(*c*) It could, to some extent, prevent the diversion of existing trade or the worsening of the terms of trade in third countries in the developing stage, when customs unions are formed among developed countries.

(*d*) Within the limits of the quota the escalation of the tariff is eliminated, so there are no additional discouraging obstacles to prevent the development of higher stages of production.

(*e*) The unlimited range of potential exports from developing countries would enable the developing countries to specialise in those industries in which they have a comparative advantage.

(*f*) It is administratively simple. It is uniform, predetermined and based on objective criteria, and leaves little room for arbitrary interference and discriminatory power in the hands of importing authorities.

Finally, inaccuracies in estimating the required percentage for quotas would minimise any possible harm and serious mistakes in forecasting would not categorically determine actual developments; imports of commodities in excess of the limited quantity are possible, provided a higher duty is paid.

While the advantages of the scheme have been discussed fairly extensively it seems proper to point to some of the problems which the proposed scheme raises even in its simplest and primary form.

One characteristic of this form of global quota (as well as of the ECE scheme) has been criticised both in the Secretariat paper[28] as well as in the report of the Secretary General of UNCTAD,[29] which presents a preferential scheme for manufactures along otherwise similar lines. This relates to the use of the percentage of imports of the manufactures in developed countries as the basis for calculating and determining the overall quota. The disadvantage of this method is that the developed countries with a very low import coefficient would have a relatively small quota of preferential imports. Thus the real benefit would be to the highly protectionist countries, where high tariffs prevent substantial imports. The argument of the Secretariat papers was in a similar vein. Therefore other possible criteria for the determination and distribution of the overall quota have been suggested, such as production, or consumption, or a combination of these with imports.[30]

The need to make use of escape clauses as additional safeguards forms the basis of a second criticism. The tariff quota relates to overall imports, not to individual commodities, and therefore, serious injury (or threat of injury), would require application of an escape clause. This eliminated the possibility of doing away with pressure group demands for cancellation of preferential treatment,[31] which was one of the main advantages of tariff quotas in the eyes of some of its proponents. Finally, the overall tariff quota could be said to limit preferential imports unnecessarily, being applied in the absence of injury, and thus restricting total preferential imports below the level they might otherwise have attained.

DRAFT PROPOSAL OF THE LATIN AMERICAN COUNTRIES

Before discussing these criticisms, it is useful to introduce a third scheme[32] of preferences, submitted by nineteen Latin American countries in the second committee of UNCTAD I as a Draft Proposal.[33] This scheme originally constituted part of the Charter of Alta Gracia, a programme agreed upon for UNCTAD by the Latin American States members of the Organisation of American States (OAS), in a Conference held in Alta Gracia at the end of 1963.[34]

The relevant features of the scheme were:

(*a*) Developed countries should accord preferential treatment on a non-reciprocal basis to imports of manufactured (and semi-manufactured)[35] products, from the developing countries. The preference should be granted *by all the developed countries in favour of all developing countries.*

(*b*) Industrialised countries should forthwith grant entry, free of duties and other charges of equivalent effect, to imports of all finished manufactured products from the developing countries, whenever such imports represented for each product not more than 5 per cent of the *domestic consumption* of the importing country concerned. Moreover, any industrialised country could grant similar preferences to imports that exceeded the above mentioned limit, without extending them to other industrialised countries.

(*c*) The duty-free import quotas referred to in (*b*) above would not include imports from developing countries which already enjoyed previously established preferences.

The Latin American scheme answers some of the criticisms directed against the global overall tariff quota. Most important, the basis of calculating the tariff quota *ceilings relates to consumption*. When quotas are calculated on the basis of production, countries not producing a particular item might escape granting preferences on such items,[36] and when imports are used as a basis, protectionist countries could take advantage of their general restrictive policy for continuing to exclude imports from developing countries. Moreover, 3 to 5 per cent of consumption would generally imply a substantially higher import percentage.[37]

The Alta Gracia proposal provides for the tariff quota specifically as a safeguard, in place of an *escape clause*, which solves the problem of pressure groups seeking the elimination of the preferential imports. And, thirdly, the Alta Gracia proposal does not require the application of tariff quotas in a *mandatory* manner. Like the ECE proposal it is open-ended in two different senses:[38] the volume of imports is not limited, and in some specific products no tariff quota need actually be applied.

But there are also drawbacks to the Alta Gracia scheme. First, it is very difficult to determine the percentage of consumption for *each product*, for detailed statistics of such a character are rarely available even in highly developed countries. Even to attempt to obtain consumption data indirectly, by adding production and imports together and deducting exports, would cause considerable difficulties.[39]

But the use of consumption as a base causes misgivings from a more fundamental point of view. The relative share of imports in relation to consumption or production is not uniform for all developed countries, for the degree of dependence on imports is determined by the size of the country, the availability of natural resources, the customs and habits of consumption, standards of living, and similar factors. Total actual imports of the product (or, in the case of overall tariff quotas, of manufactures generally) would seem to reflect the needs of developed countries more accurately despite the distortion brought about by protective measures) than a percentage of consumption, or for that matter of production. Furthermore, increasing liberalisation of trade between the developed countries themselves, and particularly within the regional groups, reduces the degree of distortion substantially.[40] These considerations, coming with those of practical administration, explain why the import base prevailed.[41]

Moreover, the use of such tariff quotas as safeguards might not be acceptable to developed countries. The difference between this and the previous scheme is that the overall tariff quota was not suggested as a safeguard measure, but rather as a means of facilitating the acceptance of preferences in the developed countries, who might fear an unlimited flow of imports from developing countries. To the extent that such psychological assurance was not needed, the overall quota was really superfluous. On the other hand the safeguard measure in the form of a tariff quota might, in reality, be much more restrictive, as there would be no freedom left to the individual exporting country to concentrate in a particular market in a specific commodity for which it might have an advantage. Through the introduction of the *non-mandatory* requirement clause an element of arbitrariness is introduced into the automatic formula of the safeguard.

These criticisms of the scheme are additional to those which have already been referred to in the ECE scheme, with respect of the determination of the product groups.

TARIFF QUOTAS IN UNCTAD DISCUSSIONS

The various Preference Committees (or groups), as well as the Second Committee of UNCTAD (Committee on Manufactures) spent much time and effort in clarifying the general issues involved in the granting of preferences to exports from developing countries, and in elaborating the technical aspects of the problem in particular. These discussions continued after the first Conference until agreed conclusions were accepted in 1970. Much of this discussion was summarised, and the problems analysed further, in the Secretariat's documents prepared for these meetings. While these documents dealt with *all* the problems of preferences, they also gave quite an important place to the various issues involved in the use of tariff quotas within the GSP.

Most of the discussions repeated earlier points, although elaborating, refining and clarifying them, and there is no need to repeat them here. But one major issue must be mentioned, in view of its importance and the substantial disagreement among the major donor countries in the committee. This is the alternative method of safeguards.

It is obvious that no GSP would be introduced if the developed countries were unable to protect their domestic industry from serious disruption or threat of injury, or from safeguarding the legitimate interests of third exporting countries. A method had therefore to be devised which would take care of these apprehensions. Theoretically, there were various possibilities: limiting the number of products to which preferences are granted to a selective list; excluding *ab initio* the most competitive products; only reducing the duty to a limited extent; or introducing a safeguard to be applied fully, or partially, against all beneficiaries or against individual major suppliers among the beneficiaries, whenever serious disruption or threat of injury occurred. Another possibility could be the use of a tariff quota method to fix in advance the volume that could be imported preferentially.

Tariff Quotas under Generalised Preferences

Since the starting-point for the discussions, particularly during 1966–67, was the examination of a duty-free preferential treatment applied generally to all manufactures and semi-manufactures, the two alternatives receiving the most attention came to be known as the 'escape clause' system, and the 'tariff quota' system.[42]

The debate at the Group on Preference[43] really centred upon a comparison of the advantages of an escape clause system, applied *a posteriori* in case of serious injury or threat thereof, as opposed to an automatic predetermined system of tariff quotas, to be applied generally whenever imports of a particular commodity reach a given volume or value. The representatives of some donor countries[44] favoured a uniform tariff quota system. For the developing countries such a system would ensure a fixed volume, or value, of imports which would be treated preferentially, and the application of the safeguard would be known. It would thus offer some guarantee of security for the investment made in the industrial plants in the developing country while at the same time taking into account the interest of suppliers from third countries (and of the domestic industry). The automatic safeguard of the uniform tariff quota had the merit of avoiding the uncertainties arising from an escape clause unilaterally applied,[45] and possibly more important, it prevented the intrusion of vested interests in the developed countries.[46]

Opponents of this tariff quota safeguard system[47] argued that such a system would introduce an unnecessary and arbitrary element right from the start, by applying the quota to products, and at levels, which were not really necessary. If, however, the system was not to be applied to all products, then arbitrariness would be introduced by the selection of the products to which it would be applied. There was also the question as to how to treat those cases of serious injury which might arise when a tariff quota proved insufficient to protect a specific industry. Was there not a need in such cases to be able to take a unilateral decision to apply an escape clause, or should quotas remain unaffected by an escape clause even in emergency situations?

Furthermore, the tariff quota system involved difficulties of administration and of fixing a uniform percentage in all developed countries, and they also pointed out that experience with the escape clause system had shown that such clauses were rarely invoked and no serious uncertainties had arisen from their invocation in international trade. Accordingly, they questioned the desirability[48] of the tariff quota system.

The issue was also a bone of contention among the group of experts in the OECD. This became evident from the report by the Special Group on Trade with Developing countries of the OECD transmitted to the New Delhi Conference[49] of UNCTAD, which stated:

Although the group devoted a considerable part of their time to examine the merits and shortcomings of the different methods of providing against the possible dangers referred to in paragraph 27 [the need to mitigate the possible effects of increased competition in the donor market] they were *not able* to reach agreement that any one method was so demonstrably superior to the others or was so sufficiently free from risks or difficulties of its own that they could recommend it for general acceptance.

There were also *differences as to whether it would be necessary for the same or a substantially similar arrangement to be adopted by all donor countries* and whether it would be possible, assuming that it could be made consistent with the other principles generally accepted for different countries to adopt arrangements which they found individually suitable to their own circumstances.

On these matters the groups are agreed that there should be further discussions among prospective donor countries.

The issue was finally resolved with the agreed conclusions of the Special Committee on Preferences, for the donor countries submitted schemes with different characteristics, which nevertheless have been found to be mutually acceptable to all. In other words, the demand to have a uniform system of preferences in all donor countries was dropped and it had been recognised that different schemes may have different kinds of safeguards.[50] Once there were the agreed conclusions from the fourth special session of the Special Committee of UNCTAD the way was finally paved for the introduction of the GSP in the donor countries.

NOTES AND REFERENCES

1. *Generalised System of Preferences: Cumulative List of Documents* (Geneva: UN, April 1971), and addenda. This source should be consulted for the full titles of UNCTAD document numbers.
2. An account of the early discussions of the preference issue can be found in Gardner Patterson, *Discrimination in International Trade – The Policy Issues 1945–65* (Princeton: Princeton University Press, 1966) Chapter VII. A further discussion appeared in Hebrew – Rom, *UNCTAD and the Problem of Preferences for Exports of Manufactures from Developing Countries* (Tel Aviv: Export Institute, November 1965).
3. This took place over a number of years in the Committee of Manufactures, the Committees on Preferences and the Special Groups on Preferences of UNCTAD.
4. See the mimeographed statement by Mr P. A. Fortthom on Preferences for Industrial Development in Developing Countries, in the *Second Committee at UNCTAD I* (Geneva: UN, 22 April 1964) pp. 9–11; also outline of the Brasseur plan submitted by the Delegation of Belgium, United Nations TD/B/C2 Add. 1: and TD/B/AC1/4, Add. 1, p. 68.
5. *GATT* L/1969, Committee III, and supplement to the list of 25 March 1963, COM3/105.
6. There were many other questions involving the duration of the scheme, the institutional arrangements, the problem of reverse preferences, the determination of

Tariff Quotas under Generalised Preferences 175

rules of origin and so on, but these are not relevant to the subject being discussed here.
7. See later discussion, page 167.
8. *Economic Survey of Europe 1960* (Geneva: UN, 1961) Ch. V, pp. 49–50.
9. The Report sees minimal damage to the developed countries, with few exceptions, if they followed such a policy, see p. 49.
10. As an additional safeguard, it might be agreed that if the total exports of a particular commodity group from all under developed countries taken together should exceed a certain ceiling (say 20 or 30 per cent of the total imports of a particular industrial country for that commodity group), the countries concerned should negotiate such a reduction in the maximum percentage of imports for each exporting country below 3 or 5 per cent sufficient to keep the total exports of the group of under-developed countries within the limit of 20 or 30 per cent.
11. While the analysis in that part of the report refers to commercial policy in Western Europe, the policy conclusions apply *mutatis mutandis* with no less force to developed countries outside Europe, in particular, to the United States.
12. An illustration of this point is the example of chemical exports to the developed countries as a whole. While in 1962 the imports of chemicals to the developed countries from developing countries as a whole amounted to $250m, or 4.9 per cent of the total imports of the developed countries in this branch, the imports of one subbranch, namely dyeing and tanning extracts, amounted to $14.9m, or 38.6 per cent of the total imports of developed countries in this sub-branch.
13. The author is indebted to the United Nations for the opportunity it afforded him in 1963 of preparing the original (more extended and detailed) draft of this paper. The views expressed in it are, however, his own. They do not necessarily reflect the views of the institutions with which the author was in the past, or is at present, connected.
14. First time in 29 April 1964 the Second Committee of UNCTAD I. Speech and S. R. of UNCTAD E/Conf., 46/C2/SR26, 29 April 1964; then the Special Committee on Preferences of UNCTAD, June 1965, New York.
15. See *Aussenwirtschaft*, St Gallen, Switzerland, No. 1/1966, pp. 43–53, and in Rom, *UNCTAD and the Problem of Preferences, op. cit.*, pp. 48–64.
16. Value added in the sense of total export value of the product less the import content of that product. This definition follows along the lines used in the Basic Agreement of EFTA, Article 4, para. 1(c). Source: *European Yearbook*, Vol. VII, *op. cit.*, p. 665.
17. The duty-free tariff quotas for the additional export from developing countries assume that their normal exports of manufactures would continue, despite the duty being paid. A problem is created, however, if the normal exports traditionally enter at zero duty. If they are included in the calculations they may (at least in theory) fill the total of the preferred quota and there could be little or no additional import of semi-manufactured or manufactured goods entering in at the preferred rate (in some cases there could be even less than previously). This obviously is not the intention of the scheme. But the complete exclusion of duty-free imports would punish to some extent those developing countries which have maintained a more liberal trade policy. The practical solution seems to be the exclusion from the scheme of duty-free imports up to the value of the past year.
18. See *Trade and Development* (Geneva: United Nations, 1964) Vol. IV, pp. 26–35.
19. Global in the sense that many commodities could be imported within the quota. This kind of tariff quota is sometimes termed General Tariff Quota.
20. The criteria being based on such factors as population and national income.
21. This was established as being roughly true over a period of nine years for a number of individual countries as well as for the less developed countries as a whole, as can be seen from the *World Economic Survey, 1962, op. cit.*, pp. 1 and 5, where development of imports (at constant prices) and GDP (at constant prices) increased by 4.6 and 4.65 per cent respectively.
22. The assumption of a minimum 5 per cent increase per annum does not mean that this would be the actual rate of increase of the GDP, or of imports of the individual

countries. They may have rates far exceeding this rate, or far below it. In the first instance, it would only mean that preferential treatment would be applied to a minimum, the rest having to develop under normal conditions. In the second instance, the quota might be ineffective.
23. The overall total global quota was calculated to be only a part of the total difference since the overall projection takes account of normal increases in exports, and other receipts, but the relative share of the developing country remains the same.
24. The method is only a rough approximation for the following reasons: (*a*) The propensity to import which is here assumed to be fixed, may change. (*b*) Net import of services, contrary to what has been assumed here, may also have to be financed by exports of commodities, or vice versa; net exports of services may foot the bill of import requirements. (*c*) The data for the base year may not be representative of the general situation of the country, but rather reflect some special accidental developments in that particular year. There may be actual cases where more detailed consideration would be justified; for example, should the rough method of calculation demonstrate that no quota should be allocated to the developing country. A quota would not be allocated, as income from exports would seem to be sufficient to cover long-term requirements of imports. This would need to be more thoroughly verified.
25. See, for example, 'The Criticism of the Brazilian Delegation' in the *United Nations General Assembly's Eighteenth Session of the Second Committee* (Provision A/C/2/SR.894), 17 October 1963, p. 4.
26. If supervision over the global quotas proceeded along the lines suggested above, it would also be possible to deal with the problem of *existing* duty-free imports into developed countries. This could be by excluding existing duty-free imports into developing countries from the calculation of the global quota of the developed countries, as well as from the individual global quotas of each developing country up to the value of the past base-year performance. This could be simply done if the developed countries did not report to the central authority in charge of supervising the scheme the particular imports of duty-free items from each of the developing countries, up to the value of past trade with them. Similarly, these amounts would not be included in the calculation of the global import quota of the developed country. This could mean that the global quota in developed countries would only refer to the additional trade.
27. L. W. Towle, *International Trade and Commercial Policy* (New York and London: Harper Brothers, 1947) p. 446.
28. *Trade and Development*, Vol. IV, *op. cit.*, pp. 26–35, especially p. 33.
29. Report of the Secretary General; *Towards a New Trade Policy for Development* (E/Conf. 46/3) (Geneva: UNCTAD, 1964) pp. 70–2.
30. See further discussion on pp. 170–71.
31. See discussion, pp. 171–72.
32. Chronologically this scheme was developed, to the best of the author's knowledge, in Alta Gracia at the end of 1963.
33. See UNCTAD E/CONF 46/62/L23.
34. See UNCTAD E/CONF 46/100 of 10 April 1964 – also reprinted in UNCTAD, *Trade and Development*, Part I., *op. cit.*, pp. 57–66.
35. See UNCTAD E/CONF 46/62/L23.
36. See UNCTAD, Second Session, New Delhi, *Problems and Policies of Trade in Manufactures and Semi-manufactures*, Vol. III, p. 20 (New York: UN, 1968).
37. The relative importance of actual imports from developing countries as a percentage of production, total imports and consumption is presented for Germany, the United States and Japan, in 1965, in Tables 12, 13 and 15 of United Nations TD/12/Supp. 2, reproduced in *ibid.*, pp. 63–6.
38. This by the way, it true also in the ECE Scheme if the footnote to that proposal is accepted as an integral part of that scheme. But the ECE scheme puts the major emphasis on the limitations of preferential imports from a *particular* developing

country, thus assuring other developing countries their preferential access. Primary emphasis in the 'Alta Gracia' scheme is on the safeguard aspect of the overall tariff quota for the specific product, from the point of view of the importing developed country.
39. See the discussion in Chapter 5 which shows the problems involved in determining the 5 per cent production of woollen and worsted in the United States. This only refers to one product group; the problems would be multiplied many times with the vast increase in the number of quotas that this method implies.
40. Various alternatives have also been suggested in the Secretariat paper UNCTAD E/CONF 46/6, p. 33, and in the Secretary General Report UNCTAD E/CONF 46/3, p. 71. Among these were for instance, the formula in which total consumption of manufacture and imports from the developing countries would be weighted together. (This proposal referred to the overall quota base – but the same considerations could also apply to individual product quotas.)
The same objection can be made to such a method as to the consumption base alone.
41. Strangely enough, in the Group of Experts' Report, United Nations TD/56, the tariff quotas referred to in paras 28–9 are based on percentages of consumption or production.
42. As was, in fact, suggested in the Draft Proposal of the first Conference.
43. See United Nations TD/B/C2/AC/10, pp. 5; also TD/C/C2/AC1/SR15, pp. 3–11.
44. These representatives were spokesmen of the European Community member countries, and in particular the French delegate, Mr Kojeve.
45. United Nations TD/B/C2/AC1/10, p. 7.
46. See United Nations TD/B/C2/AC1 SR 15 p. 4.
47. The main spokesman was the American delegate Mr Props. See *ibid.*, p. 4, and TD/B/C2/AC1 SR 19, pp. 9–10.
48. It should be mentioned that most representatives from the developing countries favoured the escape clause system, but with appropriately objective criteria by which to judge whether those escape clauses should be invoked, which would only be after consultation among the parties concerned, and in international forums.
49. United Nations TD/56, included in 'Problems and Policies of Trade in Manufactures and Semi-manufactures', *op. cit.*, pp. 78–84, especially pp. 82–3.
50. See United Nations TD/B/332 Decisions, Suppl. 1, Annex, p. 3, III, 'Safeguard Mechanisms'.

CHAPTER 8

Systems of Generalised Tariff Preferences for Developing Countries

The various proposals in the international organisations about the form that any scheme of preference for the less developed countries might take have been discussed at some length in the previous chapter. These proposals, and the argument of their supporters and detractors, provided a good appreciation of the problems that would follow the introduction of any such scheme, and also demonstrated the attendant advantages. This discussion helped to establish the climate necessary for the actual introduction of such schemes. Three of these – that of Australia, the European Community and Japan, all based on tariff quotas – are outlined in this chapter and are considered in the chronological order in which they were introduced.

AUSTRALIAN SCHEME

This was originally presented in May 1965 in outline form to a meeting of the United Nations Special Committee on Preference in New York, a few days after it had been announced in the House of Representatives in Australia. This unilateral decision of the Australian Government was intended, on the one hand, to express support for the need of preferential treatment to new exports from developing countries who could not compete on an equal footing with the more advanced countries. At the same time it formally introduced a reservation to Article XXXVII of the new Part IV of the GATT which was too far-reaching for a country like Australia, which claimed that her stage of development was more in the middle-zone position. Although Australia is a developed country in terms of per capita income, it is still industrialising and trying to avoid an excessive dependence on a limited range of primary products for its export earnings, and felt it was not able to accept the same obligations as the highly developed industrial countries.[1]

It therefore introduced a limited preference scheme, based on a

Systems of Generalised Preferences 179

selective list of products in which less developed countries had a particular export interest and in which they faced a competitive disadvantage. Furthermore, the scheme was not to conflict 'with the long-standing Australian policy of protection for economic and efficient industry',[2] nor should it jeopardise the essential interests of the existing exporters to the Australian market.

In the light of these considerations an initial list of products was drawn up after consultation with representatives of Australian industry and taking account of the products which the less developed countries indicated as being of special interest to them. (The scheme envisaged that additional products could be added to the list from time to time, and the Australian Government was prepared to consider suggestions from developing countries in this respect.) From this list the Government selected certain products on which duties on imports from less developed countries could be reduced without serious detriment to Australian industry. These reductions were made possible because 'with few exceptions protective duties in the Australian tariff have been fixed on the basis of the competition offered by producers in the industrialised countries. They are therefore frequently higher than are needed to afford reasonable protection against the generally less competitive industries'[3] of the less developed countries.

If an individual less-developed country were to export certain items which were already competitive without the preference, then it would have those items excluded from the preferential treatment. Furthermore, preferential rates would usually be subject to tariff quotas, not only to provide an additional safeguard for Australian industry, but also to ensure that the preferences did not disrupt or cause serious damage to the trade of third countries.

Initially, the proposed scheme envisaged a list of products of about sixty items, or groups of items.[4] Australia's total imports of these items in the financial year 1964/65 were approximately Aust. £55m (or about A$125m) of which under Aust. £5m came from developing countries. Since preferential treatment for developing countries was contrary to the MFN clause of the GATT, the Australian Government had to obtain a waiver from that organisation in order to put the scheme into operation. A request for the granting of a waiver to Australia, under the provisions of Article XXV(5), was submitted on 26 May 1965 and discussed by the GATT Council, which set up a working party to consider the request. This met on three occasions[5] between June and December of that year. During this period some slight modifications were introduced into the initial list of products by the Australian Government and the list of beneficiaries was extended.

The list consisted of 28 tariff quotas for items, or groups of items, which were admitted duty-free within the quota limits (the total value of these quotas amounting to Aust. £4,470,000 – or A$10m) and 31 tariff quotas for items, or groups of items, which were admitted at a preferential rate of duty within the quota (the total value of which was Aust. £2,140,000 or A$4,793,600). Thus the total value of imports available within tariff quotas was Aust. £6,610,000 or A$14.8m. In addition, two groups of items of handicraft were to be imported duty-free without quota limitations.[6] The scheme was to be applied to all developing countries. Even at the initial stage of submission the scheme was criticised,[7] not only as to the principles on which it was based but also with respect to the concrete proposals.

According to the critics of the principles, the preferential tariff quotas for specific products to all developing countries would provide an undesired incentive for the *same* products to be developed in *all* the developing countries, although in the long run such countries might have no comparative advantage in these products. In the view of these critics the smaller the list of products, and the greater the number of beneficiaries, the greater would be the danger of overproduction of these products in the developing countries. Since only a limited quantity of each product would be imported at preferential rates, there could be substantial uncertainty as to the tariff that would be applied to the product.

It was also maintained that such an arrangement would discriminate against the less developed among the developing countries, as it treated unequals equally and the chances for the more developed to capture the quota were greater both in the short and long run. It would require simultaneous introduction in all developed countries to avoid a situation in which countries would be discriminated against through greater distance from a particular market, for this might cause difficulties in competing within the quota in view of the cost of transportation.[8]

In their view the scheme would constitute an undesired precedent as it put very strong power into the hands of the importing country alone. The unilateral right to determine the products and the quantities in each product, regardless of any objective or predetermined criteria, would enable the importing country to influence the development of industries in the developing countries arbitrarily, and through product selection, also discriminate among the developing countries.

With respect to the actual proposals themselves it was argued that the scheme gave very little practical encouragement (Aust. £6m) to developing countries, that the products included on the list favoured a particular, limited, number of countries, and the list of beneficiary countries was criticised. Further, the fact that a developed industry in a developing country was excluded (Hong Kong is an example), was contrary to the basic purpose of the scheme. These were intended to encourage export earnings of developing countries, or infant economies, and not infant industries. It was not clear what criteria had been used to determine that, for instance, Hong Kong textiles had reached a stage of development that required no preference.

They argued that it was illogical to encourage the development of a product by a developing country at the expense of another developing country which could produce the same product efficiently, although not in sufficient quantity. It was likely that once the preferential treatment had ceased, and competition was on an equal footing, it would no longer be able to compete with the efficient developing country.

Despite the criticism and reservations, the scheme was nevertheless approved and the waiver granted on 28 March, 1966,[9] and the developing countries welcomed it as the first breakthrough in the battle in favour of preferences for them. They therefore supported the Australian request, despite their feeling that the scheme should be improved in certain respects.

This particular scheme of preferences was in operation from July 1966 up to the end of 1973 when it underwent fundamental changes in order to improve and liberalise the offer of preferential access to the exports of developing countries. While this scheme was in operation the list of products was continually enlarged, quotas increased and duties reduced. By January 1973[10] the number of preferential products, which originally consisted of some 60 items, included 120 specified manufactured and semi-manufactured products admitted duty-free without quota limitations, and 326 groups of specified manufactured and semi-manufactured products admitted at preferential rates of duty up to the level of annual quotas; the total value of these annual quotas amounted to $55.5m. In addition, 65 categories of specified handicraft products were admitted duty-free without quota limitation.[11]

ADMINISTRATION OF THE SCHEME

Before summarising the actual experience with the scheme a brief account of its administration[12] will be helpful.

The quotas for the manufactures and semi-manufactures on the selective list are fixed on an annual basis for administrative purposes but the quota year is divided into two six-monthly quota periods, the first from 1 July, the second from 1 January. For each quota group of products, half of each annual quota is made available for the first quota period, and the remaining half of the annual quota (plus any part of the quota not allocated in the first period) then becomes available in the second period. Any unallocated part of the quota lapses at the end of the second period in each quota year. About two months before the beginning of each quota period invitations to apply for quota allocations are circulated in the Customs and Excise Notices issued by the Australian Department of Customs and Excise, which mainly reach Australian importers.

Quotas are allocated only to *importers resident in Australia*. In consequence exporters wishing to benefit from the preferences have to contact importers in Australia, or else establish an import agency there. The quota allocation to importers is made at the beginning of each period. To minimise any wastage of quotas, and also to act as a safeguard against speculation, quota-holders are required to submit evidence of intention to import. If this is not provided by a certain date (usually within a few months of the beginning of the quota period) the allocation is cancelled and reallocated among the eligible applicants.

All applications from importers are granted in full if the total value of applications received for a particular product group is less than the available quota. In all other cases the available quota is allocated equitably[13] among the applicants, the allocations not being restricted to traditional importers. Quota-holders are required to import the goods concerned within *twelve months* from the beginning of the six-monthly quota period for which the quota allocation was granted.

In order to benefit from preferences, documentary evidence has to be submitted certifying that the product originates in the developing country. A product is considered to originate from a developing country when the final process is performed in the developing country which exports the goods, and not less than half of the factory or works cost of the goods is represented by the value of labour and materials of developing countries and/or Australia. For handicraft products certification is required confirming that they are hand-made, and that they are traditional products of a cottage industry in the exporting country. The certificate for handicraft products must be made by an authority in the exporting country approved for this purpose by the Australian authorities.

ACTUAL EXPERIENCE WITH THE SCHEME

Table 8.1[14] summarises some actual trade results of the scheme for the period 1966/67 to 1971/72.[15]

While the value of available quotas had been constantly increased by the Australian Government,[16] in no year were they fully utilised; even the allocation of quotas never reached more than half. But the figures reveal an even more serious shortcoming, namely that actual total imports under the quotas were usually less than half of the total value of allocation. An examination of the detailed data for 1970/71 and 1971/72 shows that this state of affairs holds true not only for the totals, but also for most of the individual items. For example, out of 240 tariff quotas available in 1971/72, in only one case was a quota both fully allocated and actually utilised. In 82 cases the quota was fully allocated, but preferential imports from developing countries were not fully utilised within the allocation. Actual imports fell substantially short of the allocation.[17] In about some 67 cases no allocations were granted, whereas in 90 cases the allocation in each quota was less than the full quota available.[18]

TABLE 8.1
Australian Trade under GSP, 1966–71

	A$m (A$1 = US$1.12)					
	1966/67	1967/68	1968/69	1969/70	1970/71	1971/72
Quotas available	13.3	20.4	30.1	36.2	47.0	44.0
Quotas allocated	3.7	9.1	14.6	17.7	22.7	21.7
Percentage unallocated	72.0	55.0	51.0	51.0	52.0	51.0
Imports under quota[a]	1.7	5.0	7.6	9.8	11.9	9.7
Imports as a percentage of available tariff quotas	2.8	24.5	25.2	27.1	25.3	22.0
Handicraft imports	0.6	1.3	2.1	2.5	4.2	7.0
Total preferential imports	2.3	6.3	9.7	12.3	16.1	16.7

Source: United Nations TD/B/C5/9, Annex II, p. 2.
[a] The fall in the value of quotas available in 1971/2 was due to the implementation of MFN duty-free Kennedy Round Concessions.

It was argued[19] that the shortfall in the utilisation of quotas could be attributed, *inter alia*, to a lack of knowledge of the arrangements among exporters in developing countries; a lack of selling experience and know-how among exporters in some developing countries; reluctance among some importers to take the necessary action to obtain quotas; and the inability of developing countries to compete with other suppliers on certain products, despite their enjoying a preference.

These explanations, while perhaps true in some individual cases, do not seem to constitute the whole explanation, not only because the products for which preferential import quotas were granted were nominated by developing countries, or by importers in Australia, as being of present or *potential interest*, but also because, for many products, allocations were granted which were not fully utilised, while at the *same time* there were exports of these products from developing countries at non-preferred rates. It seems reasonable, therefore, to examine the administrative arrangements to see whether they provided the barriers which prevented the utilisation of the preferences.

Theoretically the prior allocation system could permit importers to block preferential imports for a considerable period. There is reason for thinking that this could be one cause for the unutilised allocations which had been granted, if, in practice, there was no follow-up and cancellation of unutilised tariff quotas and their transfer to other applicants. Furthermore, the need to find a resident importer interested in applying for the prior allocation before an exporter can start to penetrate the market at preferential terms could well provide a relevant explanation for those cases where no prior allocation took place. This need to find a resident importer could have a deterrent effect, especially among the newcomers of the less developed countries who have to start from scratch in establishing themselves in the market.

Another possible drawback of this particular practice of prior allocation is that the *past* trade efforts of an importer within the scheme were ignored. If an importer had made an effort and had received a substantial quota allocation in the first year he could none the less find himself with a negligible quota in the following year if more countries — and more importers in each country — applied. This reduced the incentive to develop preferential imports within the quota.

All these criticisms refer specifically to the administration of the quotas in accordance with the given prior allocation procedure. But it should also be pointed out that the prior allocation system, in contrast to the greyhound system of allocation, has the advantage that the importer will have more definite knowledge beforehand about the treatment the goods will receive on arrival. While these explanations mainly refer to the method of prior allocation as the obstacle to the utilisation of the scheme, there seem two other possible explanations which have not been mentioned so far.

An important part of the list of products for which tariff quotas were granted, though perhaps of potential interest to developing countries in the future, was not of any *immediate* benefit to them, and they were unable to make use of the preferences offered. These were mainly the more sophisticated products for which rather big quotas were granted, but yet were not allocated at all or only to a very limited extent. Examples are: 84.62.200 precision-ground steel ballbearings (A$1m) or 84.52.000 calculating and statistical machines (A$2.9m).

The 'origin' requirement, discussed a little earlier on page 182, also imposed constraints. Most manufacturers in developing countries are of the 'top-down' character, which means that they frequently import the product in a semi-finished state, and then complete or assemble it. Only as industrial development advances are more and more stages of production carried out in the developing country itself. It seems possible, for many of the products for which preferential tariff quotas were granted, that the value added in the developing country did not reach the required 50 per cent.

The factual data of GATT Document L/3798, Annex D, also provides an interesting breakdown of the actual total developing countries' preferential imports by country of origin.[20] The data show that, in 1971/72, India (25 per cent), Taiwan (17.9 per cent) and Hong Kong (11.2 per cent) together enjoyed more than half of the total benefits from the scheme. If imports from Thailand (6.1 per cent), Pakistan (5.2 per cent), Philippines (5.0 per cent), Singapore (2.3 per cent) and South Korea (2.3 per cent) are added, then it becomes evident that the South

East Asian region enjoyed more than three-quarters of the preferential import benefits. The only two major exceptions were the more developed among developing countries, Spain (11.3 per cent) and Mexico (4 per cent). This seems to corroborate some of the earlier apprehensions about the geographical advantage of proximity, and the need for simultaneous application of preferential schemes in all developed countries. While in this particular instance earlier apprehensions were substantiated, little evidence can be found in support of some of the other criticisms which were voiced initially. Some of the expected long-run effects of the scheme were mitigated by the fact that quotas were not utilised, that other major donor countries had in the meantime introduced different GSP schemes, and that, in some important instances, some specific industries of a developing country originally excluded had eventually been included.[21]

The Australian authorities themselves reviewed the experience of the scheme and, in an effort to improve their offer of preferential access to developing countries in the Australian market, they introduced a new scheme[22] in January 1974. Among the most important features of this scheme are the reduction of import duties on a wide range of products included in the revised scheme, by one-third to three-quarters of the pre-July 1973 rates. Furthermore, about 860 items, or approximately one-third of the total items in the Australian tariff, are free of duty when imported from beneficiaries. This is in addition to 325 items, including some items under Chapters 1-24 of the BTN, which are duty-free when imported from any source.

Certain products are excluded either because they are subject to revenue duties (such as tobacco products, beer and spirits), or because, in the view of the Australian Government, developing countries are already competitive or are likely to become quickly competitive on the Australian market at the general tariff rate of duty.[23] All products of the original Australian GSP have been incorporated in the revised scheme, mostly without a *quota limitation*. Tariff quota limitation only exists in the new scheme for a list of 43 cases, consisting of both old and new products; in the case of the old product items, the ceilings have usually been increased.

The GSP duty is usually 10 per cent *ad valorem* lower than the MFN duty, and in those cases where the MFN is $12\frac{1}{2}$ per cent or less the preferential duty was reduced to zero. Handicrafts continue to be imported duty-free without quantitative limitations.

Australia introduced a safeguard by reserving the right to modify, withdraw, suspend or limit preferential treatment at any time for any item, with respect to any beneficiary country. Such action, which would arise from serious injury (or threat thereof) to domestic industry, would only be taken after full consideration of all circumstances.

From the outline of the revised scheme it is clear that the role of tariff quotas has been substantially reduced and that today they are more in the nature of an exception for particularly sensitive products. It is, therefore, safe to conclude that, in Australia, the tariff quota system of preferences actually served more as a transitory safeguard measure. This enabled the Australian Government to take a limited risk and to plunge into a new unconventional venture of commercial policy. The effects of this policy were at that time unknown, and the tariff quotas are being phased out increasingly as experience proves that their use as safeguards is superfluous.

THE EUROPEAN COMMUNITY'S SCHEME

Although the European Community's scheme[24] was the first among the major developed countries, being introduced in 1971, it was nevertheless only decided upon after long deliberation. In the OECD, discussion among the developed members had taken place since 1965, mainly on two basic types of GSP the so-called escape clause and the tariff quota.

The Community chose the second type since it had the advantage of offering greater certainty and was easier to administer overall. Any other choice would have encountered a lot of complications. One donor country can very quickly decide on an exception from a preferential system, but in a customs union, which is one step on the way towards an economic union, such decisions would require very long, tedious and problematical negotiations[25] among the member states, and the time required for such negotiations would not be available. Furthermore, basic doubts were expressed as to the suitability of applying escape clauses, as these could provide a precedent which would create an insoluble conflict in aims between the internal Community interests and external political requirements.

On the other hand tariff quotas and quantitative ceilings, as chosen by the Community as a basis for the GSP, have the advantage of an automatically applied escape clause which avoids the need to decide in each individual case,[26] by weighing internal and external interests. Following its choice of a tariff quota system, the basic scheme was submitted in outline form to the OECD Secretariat in March 1969, as a preliminary proposal.

As a general rule,[27] preferential treatment would be given to all industrial manufactures and semi-manufactures in Chapters 25–99 of the Brussels Tariff Nomenclature originating in the developing countries, and would take the form of exemption from customs duties. Ceilings would be set for preferential imports, in value terms, and these would be calculated on a common basis for each product: but preferential imports of a given product from a single developing country should not, as a general rule, exceed 50 per cent of the ceiling fixed for that product, so that the preferences granted to the more competitive developing country or countries could be limited and a substantial quota be reserved for the less competitive.

Annual ceilings would normally be calculated in accordance with the formula of c.i.f. value of imports from beneficiaries under the system (basic quota), plus 5 per cent of the c.i.f. value of imports from other sources (supplementary quota). Subject to improvements being made to the basis of calculation after several years of operation, the basic quota would be a fixed amount which corresponded to imports in a reference year. The supplementary quota would be variable, being recalculated annually on the basis of the latest available figures, but without, however, reducing the ceiling.

For cotton textiles covered by the Long-term Agreement, customs exemption would only be granted to beneficiary countries taking part in the Long-term Agreement, and then only by virtue of the special provisions in that Agreement, or by bilateral arrangement. For coir and jute products, customs exemption is also envisaged under specific measures to be arranged with the exporting developing countries.

The Community would grant tariff preference for a certain list of agricultural and processed products, with the rate for each product given in the list. While for industrial manufactures and semi-manufactures the safeguard mechanism was the direct result of the system chosen by the Community (predetermined import ceilings), an escape clause would apply for processed agricultural products.

This set of preliminary proposals was submitted subject to any modifications that might have to be made following the consultations which the Community was obliged to hold with some of its associated countries, in accordance with the provisions of the Association Agreements.

The basic principles were reiterated a year later in document TD/B/AC2/34, Addenda 1, with one modification. This referred to cotton textiles and stated that 'preference may also be granted for the same period in accordance with terms and procedures to be agreed bilaterally by countries which are beneficiaries under the system of generalised preferences but not signatories to the Long-term Agreement which give similar undertakings *vis-à-vis* the Community to those given in the Long-Term Cotton Textile Agreement.'

These principles still underlie the fundamental approach to the GSP by the Community, but many additional important features were introduced when the scheme was put into practice. The first was for the establishment of separate lists of products and groups of products for preferential treatment.

Originally there were eight such lists of industrial[28] products, composed of four main groups, each of which was subdivided. The main subdivisions were cotton textiles and substitutes; other textiles and footwear; iron and steel products; and other industrial manufactures. There were a variety of reasons for this classification; in some cases, the beneficiaries under the scheme differed, and in others the administrative authority was the reason — for example, the ECSC. The *official* subdivision was into two categories, sensitive products and non-sensitive products, but in fact a three-way subdivision of the preferential products developed for administrative purposes. This was into sensitive, semi-sensitive and non-sensitive product lists, and each category was treated differently.

For the *sensitive* products, predetermined Community tariff quotas (and fixed export country amounts) were fixed, which, according to the preamble to the relevant regulations, appear to be generally calculated according to the ceiling formula described above, and are administered very strictly. Information about the utilisation of the quota and the export country amount is transmitted immediately. Once the quota, or export country amount, is filled, the MFN rate of duty is automatically applied to additional imports of that product from all beneficiaries or that particular country.[29]

On the other hand semi-sensitive and non-sensitive products are imported duty-free, theoretically up to the limits of the ceilings (and the fixed export country amount to 50 per cent for the individual exporting country), calculated on the basis of the formula mentioned. Control over the ceilings is normally exercised, however, on the basis of trade statistics which frequently lag behind actual imports. In such cases the normal MFN rates are not reintroduced as long as a Community Regulation is issued, and preferential imports can continue, despite the fact that actual imports are in excess of the ceilings.

The difference between the semi-sensitive[30] and non-sensitive products lies mainly in the special surveillance procedures introduced for the semi-sensitive products. This enables the Commission to monitor closely the import figures for these products, through a more rapid statistical reporting system. Nevertheless, in practice, the semi-sensitive products are administered in a flexible way by the Commission, and imports may be allowed to continue above the ceiling, as long as there is no request from a member state to re-establish MFN rates of duty, nor has any decision to that effect been taken by the Commission.

Ceilings for non-sensitive products are usually neither calculated nor applied, and import possibilities are unlimited in practice.[31] Although a ceiling should be calculated in individual, justified, specific cases by the statistical office of the Commission in Strasbourg, the chances of this happening are extremely unlikely, and, if it should happen, the product would be reclassified as a semi-sensitive product.[32]

Another feature of the scheme in practice has been that the maximum amount limitation for export countries, for many tariff quotas, has been reduced to 30 or 20 per cent of the total quota, instead of a limit of 50 per cent.

A newer, and most restrictive, feature of the GSP in the Community was the fixed allocation of shares for member countries of the tariff quota and ceiling, which was established on the basis of some kind of weighting of GNP, population and foreign trade. By using this method, and before the accession of the new member states, the fixed share allocation for most products was based on the following percentages: West Germany, 37.5 per cent; Benelux, 15.1 per cent; France, 27.1 per cent, and Italy, 20.3 per cent. Each member country could import only their fixed percentage of the overall quota for each product, regardless of the actual trade flows in any particular product, and there was no Community reserve to enable any adjustment in this automatic allocation to be made. The justification advanced for this procedure was that there was no time to calculate a detailed allocation for each product, as is required for a normal community tariff quota, as the necessary statistical and other information was lacking.

Another important feature of the scheme were the rules of origin. With certain exceptions these are based on the principle that a product is defined as originating in a beneficiary country if it is totally produced there or, if the final product is classified by a different Brussels Tariff Nomenclature (BTN) item, then the BTN classification of the imported inputs of that product.

ADMINISTRATION OF THE TARIFF QUOTA

As has been stated the overall Community tariff quota is subdivided according to fixed proportions, into national tariff quotas, and the administration of these are left to the individual member governments. This differs from country to country. In Germany, originally, all tariff quotas, except for ECSC products, were allocated on the basis of the 'combined procedure'. This granted prior import licences for specific quantities, or value, within the national tariff quotas, but did not specify a specific beneficiary source. The national tariff quota was allocated on the basis of an adjudication during a limited period of some twenty days, during which applications by importers were submitted. Eighty per cent of the total quota was distributed to traditional importers in the proportion of their respective shares over the last three year period, and the remaining 20 per cent to newcomers. To the extent that the total applications from traditional importers exceeded the sum available for them, their allocations were cut back *pro rata*.

Although national tariff quotas were allocated on a prior licensing basis and therefore importers were assured of their preferential imports, partial use was also made of the greyhound procedure, in view of the fact that the 'maximum amount limitation' of a particular beneficiary was determined for the Community as a whole, based on the actual order of imports from that particular beneficiary. But, while the importer may not be able to import from that particular beneficiary at a preferential rate, his prior licence certificate entitles him to import the product under preferential terms from the other beneficiaries.

During 1972 some of the sensitive German tariff quotas were changed to the greyhound procedure,[33] and since the beginning of 1973 the 'combined procedure' has only applied to a quarter of the sensitive products of manufactures. In these cases the principle of allocation has been modified by only allocating to traditional importers 50 per cent of the national tariff quotas, while allocating the other 50 per cent equally between all the applicants who submitted requests for imports within the quota, during a given specified period.

In Belgium, Luxemburg and Italy the rule is first come, first served, without prior licences, and computation is based on products presented to Customs.[34] In the Benelux the quota was subdivided equally between the Netherlands and the Belgium and Luxemburg Economic Union, but a reserve of 20 per cent of the total was established for eventual reallocation between the two.[35] In the Netherlands the procedure of allocation to importers is based on prior licensing, whilst in France, on the other hand, quotas are allocated in close consultation with domestic industry and importers,[36] and no clear criteria of allocation can be ascertained.

Before attempting to appraise the operation of the scheme some background data on the overall magnitude will be helpful. This information is only available for 1967, from various sources,[37] and so has been used instead of 1968, which was the actual base year for the scheme.

Table 8.2 indicates on the one hand that the preferences shown as Item 25 represent a very small[38] percentage of the import from the developing countries. The same is true if the overall imports of manufactures, either from third countries or developing countries, are compared with their preferential import (Item 26). Much use has been made of these figures by critics of the scheme, both inside UNCTAD and outside it.[39] But this picture can mislead for a number of reasons.

A comparison of dutiable and overall imports from beneficiary countries shows that more than two-thirds of the imports are duty-free on the MFN basis and that if the preferred imports are also added, then more than three-quarters of the 1967 imports would have been duty-free. The scheme was originally intended to give preferential treatment to manufactures and semi-manufactures, and the dutiable manufactures included in the scheme constitute two-thirds of the total dutiable manufactures imported by the beneficiaries ($444m out of $688m). The additional ceiling, based on the 5 per cent applied to the third countries (other than the beneficiary) for the same products, allows the exports of

Systems of Generalised Preferences

TABLE 8.2
European Community Imports, 1967 ($m)

1.	Total Imports	54,938
2.	manufactures (BTN 25–99)	42,991
3.	agriculture (BTN 0–24)	11,947
4.	From Member Countries	24,163
5.	manufactures	21,003
6.	agriculture	3,160
7. (1–4)	From Third Countries	30,775
8. (2–5)	manufactures	21,998
9. (3–6)	agriculture	8,787
of which		
10.	From Developing Countries – Total	11,527
11.	manufactures	7,791
12.	agriculture	3,736
of which		
13.	From Associated Countries	2,279
14.	manufactures	1,329
15.	agriculture	950
therefore		
16. (10–13)	From Beneficiaries	9,248
17. (11–14)	manufactures	6,462
18. (12–15)	agriculture	2,786
19. (7–16)	Total Third Countries + Associated imports	21,528
20. (8–17)	manufactures	15,536
21. (9–18)	agriculture	6,001
from beneficiaries		
22.	Total Dutiable Imports	2,703
23.	manufactures	668
24. (22–23)	agriculture	2,035
25.	of agriculture and manufactures enjoying preferences	475
26.	of manufactures enjoying preferences	444

Source: Statistisches Amt der EWG, Aussenhandel. Analytische ubersichten Import 1967, I–XII, pp. 3–5. Taken from *Aktuelle Beiträge zum Wirtschafts und Finanzpolitik*, No. 128, 2 October 1972, p. 4, or derived from them.

these manufactures to be more than doubled.[40]
 This last point would have been true if the overall quota of over $1000m had really been freely available for the utilisation of exports of manufactures from developing countries, without any additional constraints. But this was not the case, because of the additional limitations

of individual commodity tariff quotas, export maximum amounts and the allocation of shares among member countries. These points are discussed more extensively a little later on. Even assuming for the moment the absence of this additional constraint, the above overall quota and supplementary amount would constitute a preferential margin for double the exports of the beneficiaries only in the base year. The chances of its becoming a more severe constraint on preferential imports long before the intended termination of the GSP would be a very real danger.

The first to demonstrate this point was R. M. Cooper[41] who calculated the number of years it would take for imports from beneficiaries to surpass the quota. Assuming that total imports would grow at 10 per cent a year (as they did on the average in the 1960s), he calculated the number of years it would take for imports to reach the duty-free quota, making various assumptions about the initial share of imports from the beneficiaries, and the annual rate of growth of imports from them. With an initial share of imports from beneficiaries of about 5 per cent,[42] and taking 15 per cent as the annual rate of growth of these imports (which is about the rate European imports of manufactures from these countries grew during the 1960s) it would require only six and a half years to exhaust the overall quota.

An additional constraint in the basic formula, even in its broadest and more general interpretation (taking the total import of manufactures and semi-manufactures from the beneficiaries as a whole) is the fixed value of the basic quota, which usually relates to imports in a reference period of a number of years. If there should be substantial price rises[43] then the real value of the preferential imports within the basic quota is reduced. This is not as serious a disadvantage in the supplementary amount of the ceilings since they are adjusted according to the most current statistics available. Even here the time-lag until the data becomes available could produce a similar effect as in the basic quota, although in a less severe form. In any event there is no compensation for the reduced value of the basic quota.

As a solution to this problem it was suggested in the Special Committee on Preferences[44] that, if the present basic quota system were maintained, at least the reference year should be advanced to a more recent period and that in future this basic quota should be *linked* to an index which would guarantee the basic quota in real value terms.

With all the criticism voiced against the formula there is one point in its favour which deserves mentioning. This formula (as in the case of the national tariff quota for bananas in Germany[45]), permits some degree of certainty,[46] for it fixes for a number of years ahead a minimum assured level of preferred imports in value terms, while additional imports may still be possible. This characteristic would allow importers to plan their imports in a more orderly way within the quota, if only they

Systems of Generalised Preferences

were not confronted with the other uncertainties of the scheme, such as the maximum amount limitation, as well as administrative uncertainties.[47]

Until now the overall quota has been discussed as if it were the only constraint.[48] There are, however, additional limitations and constraints which do not allow the full utilisation even of this restrictive overall quota. The first of these relates to the fact that the formula, at least in theory, does not apply to the overall total imports of manufactures and semi-manufactures from beneficiaries but to individual products or product groups. As has been pointed out elsewhere[49] the more minutely the items are differentiated, the smaller are the tariff quotas and the maximum export amounts. It makes a certain difference whether a ceiling or maximum amount is based on textile products as a group, or only on cotton products, cotton yarns or cotton yarns of a specific size. If the exporter is a substantial exporter of the specific cotton yarns then the preferred quota share increases the more broadly the product group is defined and is used as a basis for the computation of the quota. Unfortunately the Community GSP has no clear cut policy. In some cases it defines product groups at the 6-digit BTN level, in some, for example textiles, even more minutely, while others, mostly the non-sensitive products, are defined at chapter level of two digits although they may be subdivided at a later year into more minute classification groups.[50] There is, therefore, the theoretical possibility that all 6-digit level items (close to 2000 for BTN – Chapters 25–99) might constitute separate tariff quotas based on the formula.

Needless to say the subdivision of the overall quota into product quotas creates a severe restriction on the developing countries' preferred exports, since they do not produce the whole range of products in Chapters 25–99. So, instead of using the overall preference to develop exports of those products in which they have a comparative advantage, they have to over-diversify if they want to utilise the preferences, or else substantial quotas will be unutilised while their export products have to be exported at MFN rates of duty. Yet this is not the whole story. Since the ceilings are computed on the basis of the fundamental formula there is a bias against products in which developing countries have a comparative advantage and would like to develop their exports still further. This can be illustrated by the following example.

A developing country is the major supplier ($900,000) of a particular product, whereas other countries are minor suppliers (only $100,000). If total imports of that product in the next year increase by 20 per cent then the quota would look as follows compared with the original quota:

$900,000 + $5000 = $905,000 (in the base year 5 per cent of $100,000 = $5000).
$900,000 + $6000 = $906,000 (in the next year 5 per cent of $120,000 = $6000).

Whereas total demand increased to $1,200,000 assuming a percentage increase of 20 per cent, exports of beneficiaries increased to $1,080,000 while the quota increased by only a small fraction of one per cent to $906,000. This example shows that quota increases are somewhat limited,[51] precisely in those products in which the beneficiaries have a comparative advantage and in which they would like to increase their exports. On the other hand tariff quotas are quite substantial for those products which are hardly exported and come primarily from other third countries.

This is not the end of the story, for there is an additional constraint, namely the 'maximum amount limitation' which any exporting country is permitted within each quota or ceiling. Here again, the 50 per cent of the quota (or, in some cases, the 30, 20 or 10 per cent limitation) does not refer to the overall exports within the overall global tariff quota[52] but rather to the tariff quota of each individual produce or product group. This again restrains more severely those products of particular interest to developing countries for which the overall quotas may be smaller, as explained above.

When the maximum limitation is applied to specific product groups it may not only reduce overall preferential imports for the main exporter, but also leave many of the ceilings unutilised, for lack of other exporters among the beneficiaries able to utilise this preference.[53] This fact is indicated by the number of those limitations applied without the ceiling of the product group being applied against all beneficiaries.[54]

The Community's justification for the mechanism of the 'maximum amount limitation' is that it provides an 'equitable sharing of the benefits among beneficiaries having different levels of development and different degrees of competitiveness', and as such it also promoted development effort.[55] It is however questionable whether such a sharing of the benefits should be carried out at the level of the individual product or product group. If the quotas and ceilings refer to more detailed and smaller commodity groups, then the chances of their being utilised very quickly may also increase, at least for those products for which several developing countries are suppliers. This fact increases the risks of importers and exporters in view of the uncertainty of treatment the product will receive on arrival. It will contribute either to the price being offered by importers assuming they have to pay the full duty – thus shifting the forgone customs revenue from the government to the importers – rather than to the exporting country. The importers might even try to cancel the order once the duty increases.[56]

While these constraints and limitations apply to all the manufactured and semi-manufactured imports from beneficiaries, there is an additional constraint which applies only to the sensitive products.[57] For these products the tariff quotas which have been established by the Community are subdivided into national tariff quotas, but unlike the European Community tariff quota discussed in Chapter 4,[58] there exists no Community reserve. In addition almost all products have been allocated among member countries in a standard manner regardless of the actual trade flows in these commodities. The implications of this allocation can best be illustrated by comparing the allocation of quotas with the actual percentage of trade flows of some specific products.[59]

TABLE 8.3
European Community Imports subject to Tariff Quotas, 1969 (%)

	Allocation of tariff quotas	(87.10) Bicycles	(70.13) Glassware	(40.11) Rubber tyres and tubes
France	37.5	23.0	83.2	70.5
Italy	27.1	13.7	7.7	20.8
Benelux	20.3	–	2.5	6.1
Total	100.0	100.0	100.0	100.0

Source: UNCTAD TD/C5/3, p. 21., para. 73.

In the first place it becomes evident that national quotas can limit actual export possibilities even more severely than the overall quota limitation or maximum amount limitation. In fact, despite the ability of a particular exporting country to export its products, even within the maximum amount limitation, and despite the fact that the importing country may wish to import it, the national tariff quota prevents this, even though the overall tariff quota is not fully utilised, since other member countries do not require the product.[60] Secondly, and this has worried the Commission, this allocation of the overall tariff quota into national tariff quotas is contrary to the rules of the Community, for reasons discussed fully in Chapter 4.[61]

The reasons for allocating the overall tariff quota into national tariff quotas can be questioned, as there is free movement of goods between member countries and once the product has entered the Community border anywhere, it should be possible to ship it to another member state duty free. In practice, cases have been reported[62] where an exporter in a developing country, finding the national tariff quota of one member country exhausted, has channelled his product through another member country where the quota had not yet been utilised. Nevertheless, this is a cumbersome procedure, and requires correspondents in the various member countries; it also adds to the cost and can eliminate the advantage inherent in the preference. Furthermore, according to Article 115 of the Treaty of Rome, it is possible for member states to thwart such circumvention.

Finally, mention must be made of the fact that the administration of the national tariff quota is left to the individual member countries, as has been described previously[63] and the different administrative procedures may provide an additional restraint against the utilisation of preference by exporters. The administrative obstacles can include the need to comply with different administrative requirements and regulations in each member country, including difficulties in obtaining a prior licence in some countries, and the possibility of quotas being blocked by vested interests.[64] Furthermore the compliance with origin rules can also constitute a substantial obstacle to the utilisation of the preferences.

Also doubts about the treatment of the product when it arrives in the importing member country, in those cases where the greyhound procedure prevails, can also serve as a deterrent to exports, particularly in view of the absence of public information on the state of utilisation of quotas and ceilings.

THE SCHEME FROM 1971 (2ND HALF) TO 1973

When examining the operation of the GSP of the original six member countries of the Community two different aspects need to be distinguished: the trend of development in the various main features of the scheme, and the effects of the scheme in practice.

Trend of Development

A comparison of the European Community's annual regulations which govern the scheme reveals that some changes over time have been introduced, which are summarised below. Table 8.4[65] presents the number of tariff quotas for sensitive items, as well as the number of items subject to ceilings as semi-sensitive products. The data are given for the four categories of product groups, for 1971/73.

The figures show that, while there was an increase in the *overall total*, the sensitive product tariff quotas declined in 1973 as compared to 1972, mainly due to the reduction of some Long-term Agreement sensitive tariff quotas, although the number of semi-sensitive products subject to ceilings in this group doubled. More interesting, however, than the number of tariff quotas and ceilings is the comparison of the total value, or volume, of these over the period. Unfortunately as part of the data refers to value and part to quantity, two separate presentations must be made. (See Table 8.5.)

This increase in the total preferential exports possible within these tariff quotas and ceilings is not at all impressive if the increase in the rate of inflation is taken into account, as well as the actual export performance. For the industrial groups by value, past performance of exports from beneficiaries for the same products increased between 1967 and 1970 at an annual average rate of 40 per cent.[66] Figures presented by the Community itself for 1971 (first half), 1972 and 1973, giving information for all industrial products (except the textile sector)[67] in value terms, show that total tariff quota and ceilings had amounted to 340m units of account (ua) in 1971, 780m ua in 1972, and 900m ua in 1973. In textiles the tariff quotas and open ceilings increased from 19,429 tons in the second half of 1971, to 39,944 tons in 1972 and 42,631 tons in 1973.[68]

TABLE 8.4
European Community Tariff Quotas 1971–73

		1971 (2nd half)	1972	1973
Sensitive products				
I	Industrial products other than textiles, shoes and ECSC products	44	52	53
II	Long-term Agreement cotton and substitutes	15	17	14
IIIa	Other textiles	17	18	18
IIIb	Shoes	4	4	4
IV	ECSC iron and steel products	5	5	4
	Total: sensitive products	85	96	93
Semi-sensitive products				
I	Industrial products other than shoes and ECSC products	40	61	54
II	Long-term Agreement cotton and substitutes	12	10	20
IIIa	Other textiles	5	6	8
IV	ECSC iron and steel products	2	3	2
	Total: semi-sensitive products	59	80	84
	TOTAL	144	176	177

Source: UNCTAD TD/C5/23, p. 22. Table 1; and pp. 29–30, Table 3.

While these figures are substantially higher, their rates of growth from 1972 to 1973 are not markedly different from those shown in Table 8.5. In the group of products other than textiles the rate of growth by value was 15 per cent, or slightly higher than in the data presented previously. The data for the textile products in quantitative terms increased only by some 8 per cent between 1972 and 1973, or slightly below the data presented previously. Both cases support the argument that the increase

TABLE 8.5
European Community Tariff Quotas 1971–73
By value[a] ($'000)

		1971 (2nd half)	1972	1973
Sensitive products				
I	Industrial products other than textiles, shoes and ECSC products	82,966	183,343	198,335
IIIb	Shoes	4,730	10,091	10,402
IV	ECSC iron and steel products	14,191	28,381	31,160
	Total: sensitive products	101,887	221,815	239,897
Semi-sensitive products				
I	Industrial products other than textiles, shoes and ECSC	36,358	89,920	99,162
IV	ECSC iron and steel products	1,658	3,311	16,389
	Total: semi-sensitive products	38,016	93,231	115,551
	TOTAL	139,903	315,046	355,448

[a] Rate of growth between 1972 and 1973 was 12.8 per cent.

By weight [b] (tons)

		1971 (2nd half)	1972	1973
Sensitive products				
I	Industrial products other than textiles, shoes and ECSC products	5,453	11,030	10,797
IIIa	Other textiles	11,150	22,500	23,265
	Total: sensitive products	16,603	33,530	34,062
Semi-sensitive products				
II	Long-term Agreement cotton and substitutes	715	705	2,832
IIIa	Other textiles	670	618	1,099
	Total: semi-sensitive products	1,385	1,323	3,931
	Total	17,988	34,853	37,993

[b] Rate of growth between 1972 and 1973 was 10.9 per cent.
Source: UNCTAD TD/B/C5/23.

in preferential quotas did not keep pace either with actual development or with the increase in the rate of inflation.

Some changes were also introduced in the 'maximum amount

limitation' between mid-1971 and 1973. Table 8.6 shows a definite trend towards a more severe limitation of the maximum amount of tariff quotas and ceilings between 1972 and 1973.

TABLE 8.6
Limitations on European Community Tariff Quotas, 1971–73

Maximum amount (%)	Tariff quotas		
	1971 (2nd half)	1972	1973
Sensitive products			
10	1	1	
20	28	39	44
30	37	40	38
50	19	16	11
Total: sensitive products	85	96	93
Semi-sensitive products			
20	–	6	7
30	2	10	17
50	57	64	60
Total: semi-sensitive products	59	80	84
All products			
10	1	1	–
20	28	45	51
30	39	50	55
50	76	80	71
TOTAL: all products	144	176	177

Source: UNCTAD TD/B/C5/23.

The explanation for this trend may be found in the statement of the Parliamentary Under Secretary at the Federal Ministry for Economics, Philip Rosenthal, in the German Bundestag. This was in reply to questions numbers 42 and 43 of Representative Seiter. He had asked whether the German Government was aware that among the beneficiaries of the GSP there would also be countries which might disrupt the German market with dumping-type practices, or through especially competitive advantages. He also questioned whether the Government was aware that, by forgoing any exceptions and the possibility of exclusion from the scheme it might bring about the liquidation of individual branches of industry. Mr Rosenthal answered that this would not occur as the Government would aim to reduce the level of 'maximum amount limitation' from 50 per cent to some lower percentage, and it was reasonably sure that it would achieve this.[69] In other words the reduction of the 'maximum amount limitation' was mainly introduced as an additional protective device for domestic industry, and not in the interest of permitting the expansion of exports from other developing countries, as has often been argued.[70]

Effects of the Scheme

Although the GSP scheme has been in operation since July 1971, there is still no adequate information available as to the actual results of the scheme. In the first place nothing is available that measures the Community preferential imports within the scheme, either generally or broken down by country and commodities. There is also nothing that specifically demonstrates the utilisation of the tariff quotas or their use by member countries. All that is being published regularly, in the Regulations and in statements given in the official journal of the European Community, relates to the application of the ceilings and maximum amount limitations.

Various attempts have therefore been made[71] to evaluate the performance of the scheme by comparing actual trade flows, although these do not accurately reflect the trade covered by the scheme. One such attempt has been made with respect to the 1972 scheme. This compares 1970 imports from beneficiaries of products subject to ceilings or tariff quotas in 1972, and the results are shown in Table 8.7.

TABLE 8.7
European Community Imports in 1970 subject to 1972
Ceilings or Tariff Quotas ($m)

Product group	Imports covered by the scheme		
	Sensitive (tariff quota)	Non-sensitive	Semi-sensitive (ceilings)
Cotton textiles subject to the Long-term Agreement and substitutes	39.2(14.0)	5.3	0.7(3.5)
Other textiles and footwear	149.2(128.6)	14.4	3.1(3.5)
Iron and steel products governed by ECSC	32.3(28.4)	0	3.3(3.3)
All other manufactures and semi-manufactures	249.1(183.2)	236.2	61.2(89.9)
Total	469.9(354.2)	255.9	68.3(100.2)

Source: UNCTAD TD/B/C5/8, p. 35.

This table gives some idea of the restrictiveness of the tariff quotas for the sensitive products and shows that they are fully utilised even when the trade flows in these products of two years earlier (1970) are compared with the ceilings. On the other hand actual trade flows of semi-sensitive products for the same period were far below the ceilings for this group. Another interesting feature of the table is the relative distribution of preferred imports by degree of sensitivity. This shows that prior to the introduction of the scheme less than a third (32.2 per cent) of those imports were of the non-sensitive products, the sensitive products accounted for some 60 per cent, and the semi-sensitive for 8.6 per cent.

From this evidence it could be argued that the quotas do not provide any increase in preference since they are close-ended, even on 1970 figures, which are most certainly lower than the 1972 actual import data for the same products. Thus these imports would have to come in at MFN rates. Such a conclusion, however, would be premature in view of the level of aggregation of the tariff quotas and ceilings, and the disregard of the other constraints that might affect the preferential imports.

Table 8.8 presents the aggregated trade flows of sensitive and semi-sensitive imports from beneficiaries, by product groups for 1970 according to the 1972 scheme, and their breakdown into preferential and MFN treatment.

The table is very revealing for it makes it abundantly clear that the overall comparisons between columns 3 and 4 (which provide the basis for Table 8.7) do not give a correct picture of the actual effects of the tariff quotas and ceilings. For example, although total 1970 imports from beneficiaries, as well as total imports of each product group of the sensitive products, are larger than the tariff quotas, it becomes clear from column 5 that in *none* of the product groups did preferential imports utilise to the full the overall tariff quota allocated to the group. For the semi-sensitive products, the excess of ceilings over actual imports (columns 3 and 4), whether in total or in most product groups, must not be taken to mean that none of these products came in at MFN rates. In fact, the table shows that although there were unutilised ceilings in each group there were also imports at MFN rates, and that total MFN imports were about 70 per cent of the preferred imports.

There are a variety of reasons for this. Aggregation, for instance, conceals different quotas, some of which are restrictive, and cases where imports enter in substantial amounts despite the MFN rate, whereas other tariff quotas are not being fully utilised at all.[72]

Furthermore, as the table makes clear, while the ceilings play a role in restricting preferential imports in some products, there are cases where the major supplier may be restricted without other suppliers being able to make full use of this tariff quota. Thus the maximum amount

TABLE 8.8
European Community Imports in 1970 of Sensitive and Semi-sensitive Products as defined by the 1972 Scheme ($'000)

Product group	Beneficiaries share of total (%)	Total 1970 Import from beneficiaries	1972 Quota or ceilings	Under preference scheme	1970 Import from beneficiaries Total	Due to ceilings	Due to max. amount under/MFN	Due to allocation
1	2	3	4	5	6	7	8	9
Sensitive products								
Long-term Agreement cotton textiles and substitutes	6.3	39,249	14,025	8,861	30,388	26,415	1,186	2,787
Long-term Agreement non-textiles and footwear	4.8	149,218	128,631	54,940	94,278	25,258	53,241	15,779
Iron and steel products	1.0	32,274	28,381	10,961	21,313	8,476	5,405	7,432
All other manufactures and semi-manufactures	4.5	249.126	183,229	77,542	171,584	91,322	53,364	26,898
Total	3.8	469,867	354,266	152,304	317,563	151,471	115,196	52,896
Semi-sensitive products								
Long-term agreement cotton textiles and substitutes	0.2	674	3,490	629	45	0	45	—
Long-term Agreement non-textiles and footwear	1.0	3,109	3,409	1,105	2,004	1,075	929	—
Iron and steel products	0.9	3,332	3,311	1,832	1,500	162	1,338	—
All other manufactures and semi-manufactures	1.5	61,153	89,920	36,452	24701	13,530	11,171	—
Total	1.3	68,268	100,230	40,018	28,250	14,767	13,483	—

Source: UNCTAD TD/B/C5/3, p. 57, Tables 10 and 11.

constitutes a restraint although the tariff quota remains open-ended, yet the major supplier of the beneficiaries continues to export at MFN rates, even in substantial quantities.[73]

The allocation of the tariff quota and ceilings among the member countries of the Community is another factor which explains the gap between their overall utilisation and the actual preferential trade within the scheme. While no details are available for the actual comparison of preferred imports according to product and the share of the member states in the quota, some conclusions can be drawn from the UNCTAD calculations of 1969 trade flows in relation to the 44 analysed tariff quotas for 1971.[74] That comparison indicated that some 40 per cent of the import would have been subject to MFN rates of duty, through the share allocation of member states failing to correspond with the actual flows of imports into member countries.

On this basis, the Federal Republic of Germany appears to be the major importer affected by this limitation, as 50 per cent of its imports from the beneficiaries would be subject to MFN treatment; Benelux is similarly affected with some 44 per cent of its imports having to pay MFN rates. At the other extreme, France would have a substantial overall net excess share of unutilised imports at preferred rates of duty. In other words, the possibility of unutilised overall tariff quotas due to the fixed country allocation and the absence of a Community reserve is another important restraint.

Other interesting information can be obtained from Table 8.9 and the data[75] on which it is based. This relates to the role played, according to these calculations, by the 1970 preferred imports from the beneficiaries as compared with the tariff quotas and ceilings, and shows the total imports of beneficiaries in these products, and those of the rest of the world.

These comparisons reveal what is now the obvious fact that the quotas and ceilings, which in themselves constitute a small share of the world imports (2.5 per cent) or 8.8 per cent of third countries' imports, do not adequately reflect the actual preferences granted. The various restrictions within quotas restrain imports to 42.3 per cent of the quota and ceilings, or to 3.8 per cent of third countries' imports or an even smaller share of the total import of these products.

They also show that a substantial part of the imports in these products (68 per cent) comes from the Community itself, and that therefore it makes a difference whether the 5 per cent supplementary amounts of the quotas are determined on the basis of total trade, or only in relation to third countries' trade. This fact becomes all the more important when the enlargement of the Community reduces the number of third countries, by including among the member states important trading nations like the United Kingdom.[76]

TABLE 8.9
European Community Imports, 1970, by Source ($'000)

Product Group	Total Imports	From the European Community	From third countries other than beneficiaries	From beneficiaries	Under tariff quota	Preferred
Sensitive	12,480,649	8,690,080	3,320,703	469,867	354,266	152,304
Semi-sensitive	5,245,589	3,382,445	1,794,876	68,268	100,230	40,018
Total	17,726,238	12,072,525	5,115,579	538,135	454,496	192,322

Source: UNCTAD TD/B/C5/2 p. 57, Tabs. 10 and 11.

MAIN CHANGES IN 1974

In 1974 some modifications to the scheme were introduced[77] and at the same time it was extended to include the three new members of the European Community (Denmark, Ireland and the United Kingdom). These countries adopted the scheme of preferences from 1 January 1974. The list of sensitive products was reduced compared to 1973 with 82 instead of 93 tariff quotas in the sensitive products, while the semi-sensitive products only increased from 84 to 89 products.

While the system of ceilings, tariff quotas and maximum amount limitation which was used in 1973 was maintained in 1974, certain improvements in the calculations of the ceilings were introduced, by changing the reference year for the basic amount from 1968 to 1971, and, in the case of the supplementary amount, from 1970 to 1971. For textiles, the reference year for the calculations of the basic amount continued to be 1968, while for the supplementary amount the reference year remained at 1970, as it had in 1973. However, a lump sum increase of 50 per cent of the 1973 ceilings was made for these products.

The overall increase in the tariff quotas and ceilings in 1974, as compared to 1973, is shown in the following table. The overall ceilings, including the non-sensitive products, are substantially higher.[78]

TABLE 8.10
European Community Tariff Quotas and Ceilings, 1973–74

Category	1973	1974
Sensitive ($'000)	239,897	293,205
Semi-sensitive ($'000)	115,517	352,935
Total ($'000)	355,414	646,140
Textiles		
Sensitive (tons)	34,062	21,329
Semi-sensitive (tons)	3,931	25,728
Total (tons)	37,993	47,057

Source: UNCTAD TD/B/C5/23, p. 57, tables 10 and 11.

A new scale for the distribution of preferred imports within the sensitive tariff quotas among the member countries was established and different shares for textiles, plywood and some other products fixed. The general allocation was changed to: Benelux 10.5 per cent, Denmark 5.0 per cent, France 19.0 per cent, West Germany 27.5 per cent, Ireland 1.0

per cent, Italy 15.0 per cent, and the United Kingdom 22.0 per cent. For textiles the shares were: Benelux 10.0 per cent, Denmark 7.0 per cent, West Germany 27.0 per cent, and Italy 14.0 per cent, with the remaining countries as before.

Other changes relate to the addition of new agricultural products, the reduction of some tariffs on these products, the extension of the list of beneficiaries, and, in particular, the enlargement of beneficiaries in the textile and footwear products. Since none of these improvements constitutes a major departure from the scheme as originally instituted, there is no need to discuss them here in detail.[79]

PROPOSED CHANGES FOR 1975

At the time of writing this book no details were available about any proposed changes in the scheme for 1975. However, from a news item in the *Financial Times* of 14 November 1974 it is evident that the Council of Ministers agreed on 12 November 1974 to extend the scope of its trade preferences for developing countries for 1975 and to take early steps to review the system in general to see how it might be improved. The decisions, which were in line with the British 'renegotiations' demands and at the Dutch insistence, permit industrial imports to enter under preferential duties to the value of some 2800m units of account and agricultural imports to increase to between 450m and 600m units of account – the overall increase is estimated by the Community to reach 15 per cent.[80]

More relevant to the discussion here is the fact that the Ministers also agreed to reduce the community list of sensitive products. At the same time there will be an increase in the tobacco quota[81] to 30,000 tons, most of which will go to India. Another concession to the British demand was the inclusion of plastic and rubber footwear from Hong Kong in the community scheme. With respect to the above decision it should be mentioned that due to the lack of details it is impossible to compare the data with the proposals of the Commission,[82] which contained, however, some interesting changes. What is of great interest is that Community reserves have been proposed for some tariff quotas.

The proposals also introduced a new feature into the semi-sensitive lists with respect to the maximum amount limitation. This would limit, for certain products, the exporting countries' share to 15 per cent, if they have either reached the maximum amount for a given product successively in 1972 and 1973, or appear on the basis of the most recently available statistics to supply the Community with at least 40 per cent of its total imports of the said product. But, in order to avoid damaging the interest of the less favoured among these beneficiary countries and territories, this limit of 15 per cent of the maximum amount does not apply either to those which have a very low *per capita* gross national product, or to those whose charges against the preferences for a given product represent at least 10 per cent of their supplies to the Community of manufactured industrial products eligible under the Community's preferential scheme.

Furthermore this maximum amount limitation of 15 per cent is applicable, or becomes applicable, only when it is higher in absolute value than the amount laid down under the 1974 preferential scheme, in order not to reduce the maximum amount laid down hitherto. The whole purpose of this limitation, according to the proposal, is to ensure a more balanced distribution of the advantages granted to all beneficiaries.[83] To what extent this is really the case may be questioned in view of the earlier discussions.[84]

JAPANESE SCHEME

The basic principles of the Japanese scheme of preferences resemble those of the GSP of the European Community, as is evident from the revised submission of the Japanese proposal in the OECD.[85]

Products falling within Chapters 25–99 of the Brussels Tariff Nomenclature
1. Duty-free entry will be granted in principle to all goods falling within Chapter 25–99 of the Brussels Tariff Nomenclature.
2. In spite of paragraph 1 above, a 50 per cent tariff reduction will be made for selected products, a list of which is attached as Annex I, and apart from hydrocarbons, which are subject to customs duties of a fiscal character, a very limited number of products listed in Annex II will be excluded from preferential treatment.
3. In granting preferences, a ceiling will be set for each product, which will be calculated as follows: the value of the quantity of imports from beneficiaries in a reference year (basic quota) plus 10 per cent of the value or quantity of imports from sources other than beneficiaries in the latest year for which statistics are available (supplementary quota).
Preferences will be suspended if preferential imports of a particular product from a given beneficiary exceed 50 per cent of the ceiling in the course of a year.
The supplementary quota will be revised every year, and it will not be less than that of the preceding year.

Products falling within Chapters 1–24 of the BTN
1. Preferences will be granted to the agricultural products lists in Annex III.
2. As to the products included in the list referred to in paragraph 1

above, a safeguard mechanism will be of an escape clause type which can be invoked *vis-à-vis* specific product of a specific beneficiary.

Even at this stage there are some differences between this proposal and the European Community scheme: that is, the supplementary quota is not 5 per cent, but 10 per cent, of the value (or volume) of imports from sources other than beneficiaries; a list of *ab anitio* exclusions has been determined; and, some of the products falling within Chapters 25–99 of the BTN only enjoy a 50 per cent reduction within the quota. More important than these, however, are the differences in the scheme which evolved in the course of the elaboration of the details[86] for implementation.

The scheme, which came into force in August 1971 (a month after the Community scheme) for a duration of ten years, established for the entire range of industrial products (those in Chapters 25–99 of the BTN) which were enjoying preferential tariff treatment, 214 groups of products for which annual ceilings are pre-calculated and published.[87] Among the product groups there were 57 groups to which a duty reduction of only 50 per cent applied, while for the rest the tariff quotas are duty-free.

Excluded from preferential treatment are the following products: petroleum oils – crude (27.09), petroleum spirits (27.10) and petroleum gases (27.11) subject to customs duties of a fiscal character; gelatine and glues derived from bones *et cetera* (35.03); articles of apparel and clothing accessories of leather (42.03); plywood (44.15); raw silk (50.03–3); woven fabric of silk (50.07); footwear of any material except metal (64.05).[88]

Despite the existence of ceilings as the *a priori* method of a safeguard mechanism for industrial products, the Japanese scheme provides for an emergency tariff measure applicable to products in BTN Chapters 25–99. This measure is essentially an escape-clause safeguard which could be invoked, although so far it has not been made use of, and no administrative guidelines exist for its application.

ADMINISTRATION OF CEILINGS

The scheme provides that the control of ceilings and 'maximum amount limitations' will be administered according to one of the following three methods (depending on the product group):[89] daily control; monthly control; or a prior allotment. Preferential imports will be determined on the basis of the date of the import declaration (the date of application for approval of entry into bonded warehouse or bonded manufacturing warehouse in the case of imports kept in such warehouses). The value (or quantity) of preferential imports of each product group will be announced monthly in the *Official Gazette*.

Preferential treatment under the *daily control* method is granted on a first-come-first-served basis. The value (or quantity) is computed daily and preferences are suspended two days after the aggregate of value (or quantity) exceeds the ceiling. The same applies for the determination of the 50 per cent maximum allocation of an individual beneficiary in this group. Initially this method covered 95 product groups. Under the *monthly control* method preferential treatment is granted on a first-come-first-served basis, but the value (or quantity) is calculated monthly. Preferences will be suspended on the first day of the month following the month in which the aggregate value (or quantity) has exceeded the ceiling. The same applies to the maximum amount limitation. Initially this method applied to 108 products.

Under the *prior allotment* method preferential treatment is granted to imports for which importers received from the Japanese Government an advance allotment of value (or quantity), not exceeding the ceiling. Initially only some 11 product groups were administered under this scheme. For 8 of these the ceiling was divided into a general quota (85 per cent) and a reserve quota (15 per cent). For the general quota, allotment is made on the basis of a formula which takes account of past trade, whilst the reserve quota is allotted contract by contract. For the remaining three product groups a similar procedure applies, but there is no allotment prior to receipt of application. The maximum amount limitation still exists under the prior allotment method but there is no competition among exporters on a first-come-first-served basis, since the importer, who has the monopsony buying power of his allotment, determines from whom (and at what price) to buy.

Despite the fact that, with a few exceptions, the industrial products cover all tariff items 25–99, the overall ceilings when computed on the basis of actual Japanese imports in 1970[90] from the beneficiaries account for only some 22 per cent of the dutiable products in BTN Chapters 25–99. Thus the role of preferential imports can be seen to have been limited if the existing structure of exports remain unchanged. This is explained first by the important role played by those dutiable products excluded from the scheme *ab initio*.

Secondly, 1970 imports do not reflect the permissible, preferential imports within ceilings but rather the *actual* trade pattern included in the ceilings. There are important commodity groups where the available preferential ceilings would be much larger than the actual imports from beneficiaries, due to the substantial imports from other countries, which determine the supplementary quota. Thirdly, it is worth remembering that about 42 per cent of the total imports of industrial products (BTN 25–99) from beneficiaries in 1970 came in duty-free.

Although only 22 per cent of total dutiable imports from beneficiaries enjoyed preferences in 1970 – and this seems to reveal a somewhat disappointing magnitude for the scheme – such a static calculation may be misleading since the 1970 data do not reflect the effects of the preference. It could be that *because* of the duty structure many industrial products would not have been exported from the beneficiaries in the past, and it is precisely so that the commodity composition of exports can be altered that preferences are needed. It is therefore important to examine in the future the effects of preference on the trade structure and the overall development in exports.

Particularly meaningful, however, are the characteristic features of the scheme which put constraints on the potential utilisation of the preferences. Since many of these have been discussed in detail with respect to the Community scheme they will be mentioned here only in summary form. As mentioned already in connection with the Community scheme, the preferential ceiling available is related not only to the initial share of imports of the product from the beneficiary but also to the rates of growth of the imports from the beneficiaries and from the rest of the world. With a given rate of growth in the rest of the world, the more rapid the rate of growth of beneficiaries and the higher their initial share in the total import of the product, the more rapidly actual imports could surpass the ceiling.[91]

This is all the more so because the basic quota was fixed in 1968: not only was no account taken of changes in normal real growth, but neither were changing prices and increased imports which resulted from changes due to the revaluation of the yen (for instance in 1972). One conclusion that can be drawn from this is that the more that imports came traditionally from developing countries, the more these potential preferential imports were restrained within the ceilings.

The second point to mention is the division into product groups for the purpose of ceilings. The 214 product groups are not all equally defined. In some cases large sections of two digits of the BTN are considered as one group, while in others there are minute items singled out as a product group for the purpose of ceilings. As a result some quota groups are substantial while in others the quota is very small.

A comparison of the 1970 trade data, carried out by the UNCTAD Secretariat with the available ceilings for the 214 products, is summarised in Table 8.11, which lists imports of all products into Japan, from all beneficiaries, which exceeded $5m in 1970.

The table shows that, while the overall imports (column 2) from beneficiaries (including copper) in 1970 exceeded the annualised ceilings for 1971 (column 3) by 52 per cent, actual imports of 1970 that would have benefited from the scheme only amount to $208m out of the $490m ceiling, or less than 43 per cent, whilst at the same time substantial imports would have taken place at MFN rates. This is also apparent in the Community scheme and is the result of sub-classification of the overall preferred imports into commodity groups to which the ceilings apply. In some quotas imports exceed the ceiling or the maximum amount limitation, in others the ceiling remains unutilised. For a very

Japanese Imports of Products in 1970 under the 1971 System of Ceilings, annualised ($m)

Product groups	Imports from World (1)	Imports from Beneficiaries (2)	1971 Ceilings annualised (3)	Under the scheme (4)	Imports from beneficiaries Under MFN Total (5)	Due to ceiling (6)	Due to max. amt. (7)
Copper (154, 155)	474.0	410.0	0	0	410.0	410.0	0
Iron and steel products (153)	237.0	49.0	63.0	47.0	2.0	0	2.0
Precious and semi-precious stones (140)	109.0	44.0	30.0	30.0	14.0	14.0	0
Knitted outer garments (111)	46.4	20.4	3.8	3.8	16.6	16.6	0
Wooden sheets of Lauan, etc. (58)	13.2	12.8	6.0	6.0	6.8	6.8	0
Cotton yarn (85)	11.1	10.7	10.4	10.0	0.7	0.3	0.4
Copper, scrap (156)	67.7	10.7	nil	nil	10.7	10.7	0
Aluminium (166, 167)	133.5	9.3	26.5	9.3	0	0	0
Cotton woven fabrics (86)	28.4	8.3	4.7	4.7	3.6	3.6	0
Electrical machinery and equipment (188, 189 and 195)	187.4	8.2	13.8	8.2	0	0	0
Ferro-alloys (147)	37.1	6.7	3.0	3.0	3.7	3.7	0
Silver, unalloyed (141)	22.2	6.6	10.8	5.6	1.0	0	1.0
Wigs (134)	9.0	6.5	0.5	0.5	6.0	6.0	0
Machinery and mechanical appliances (184)	993.5	6.3	80.8	6.3	0	0	0
Organic chemicals (17)	289.6	6.2	25.8	6.2	0	0	0
Sheep and lamb leather (43)	6.2	6.2	6.9	5.8	0.4	0	0.4
Ferro-manganese (145)	7.0	6.2	0.3	0.3	5.9	5.9	0
All other products	2557.7	114.9	203.7	61.3	53.6	46.4	7.2
Total	5230	743	490	208	535	524	11
Total excluding copper	4756	333	490	208	125	114	11

Source: UNCTAD TD/B/C5/6, Annex III, p. 25.

Systems of Generalised Preferences 211

few product groups (153, 166, 167, 184, 17), which comprise $196.1m, or 40 per cent of the ceilings, the total excess of preferential ceilings reached $126.1m or some 45 per cent of the unutilised ceilings.[92]

During 1968 and 1969, copper, which is subject to a sliding tariff, was imported duty-free on an MFN basis. Since these were the years for the establishment of the quota and a supplementary quota, there is a zero ceiling for 1971, despite substantial imports from beneficiaries in 1970 paying a duty.

The effect of the maximum amount constraint is shown in Table 8.11 to be very limited. This is because the method here has been to take account only of those cases of maximum-amount limitation that are not eliminated by the ceiling limitation. In other words, in those cases where more than one beneficiary used the ceiling to the full, then, despite the fact that one exporting country was restricted by the maximum-amount limitation, this has not been considered as sterilising trade since its effect is simply to split up the preferential trade among at least two beneficiaries.

Even in the case where there is only one supplier, it could be possible that exports from it might have exceeded not only the maximum amount limitation but also the ceilings. It would, therefore be necessary to attribute to the maximum amount only that part of the total exports beyond the maximum-amount limitation within the ceiling, attributing the exports in excess of the ceiling to the ceiling limitation. It therefore follows that, if the maximum-amount limitation had been the sole constraint, it would have been responsible for a much higher share of the exports of MFN than is reflected in the table.

CHANGES IN THE SCHEME

The Japanese Government introduced, during the operation of the scheme, certain changes which were intended to improve it. Product groups were consolidated for the purpose of setting ceilings, and were steadily reduced, first from 214 to 211 in the second fiscal year, then to 189, and finally to 182 product groups in 1974.[93] This consolidation provides increased export opportunities for it allows the unutilised portion of product group A to be used for product group B. An additional improvement has been the transfer of some products from the daily to the monthly control system.

In 1973 items which were subject to ceilings were placed under a system of flexible administration. Under this system preferential rates of duty are continued to be applied to the product from beneficiaries, even when ceilings, and maximum-amount limitations, are exceeded. The number of product groups to which this system applied had reached 116 out of 182 in 1974, or nearly two-thirds. The purpose of this scheme was to provide a pragmatic way of increasing export opportunities without having to change the reference year of the quota, which would have required the revision of the law concerning the entire provision of the scheme.[94]

The number of products to which only a 50 per cent reduction applied was reduced, and, by 1974, the list contained only 48 products, compared with the original 57. Other changes in the scheme include the splitting up of a few textile overall quotas into half-yearly tariff quotas so that imports could be distributed more evenly. Finally, in a few cases from amongst the overall tariff quotas which were under the flexible administration system, particular sub-items were singled out and put within a separate tariff quota.[95]

OPERATION OF THE SCHEME

There is scanty information available at present in English on the actual operation of the scheme. One set of data which appears from time to time in UNCTAD documentation[96] is the translated information drawn from published sources[97] relating to the application of ceilings, and of maximum-amount limitations, under the scheme. Some of this information is summarised in Table 8.12 for the fiscal year 1972 and 1973.[98]

TABLE 8.12
Number of Product Groups for Ceilings in Japan, (BTN: 25–99), 1972–73.

	1972	1973
Total number of groups	211	189
Ceilings applied	76	66
Maximum-amount limitations applied	13	34
Ceilings surpassed	–	15

Source: UNCTAD TD/B/C5/17.

The result of the flexible administration was that total imports into Japan increased in 1973 under the GSP to nearly $1000m, representing an increase of 2.7 times over the fiscal year 1972. For those products affected by the flexible administration of ceilings, imports under the GSP amounted to $630m in the fiscal year 1973, representing an increase of 3.2 times over 1972.[99]

It has been agreed by the Japanese representative on the committee that, although factors other than preferences might also have been at work, there had been trade diversion in favour of the beneficiaries since the implementation of the scheme. The percentage share of beneficiaries in total imports had steadily risen from 36.5 per cent before the initiation of the scheme, to 40.8 per cent in 1972 and to 45.6 per cent in 1973, reflecting also a rate of growth which is much higher than the rate of growth of imports from non-beneficiaries.

He also pointed out that his country's scheme was truly generalised because the products imported under the scheme covered an extensive range and the benefits in 1973, had not been limited to a small number of countries or to any one region. Twenty-one countries exceeded $10.0m in their preferential exports to Japan, and a large number of countries had experienced a sharp increase in their preferential imports.

But the maximum-amount limitation was increasingly applied against one particular country of the region, namely the Republic of Korea. In 1972, six out of the thirteen maximum-amount limitations were applied against this country while two were applied against India, and one each against the following five beneficiaries: Bulgaria, Chile, Hong Kong, Portugal and Spain. By 1973, 21 out of 34 maximum-amount limitations were applied against the Republic of Korea, while three were applied against Spain, two each against India and Brazil, and one each against Colombia, Paraguay, Peru, the Philippines, Portugal and Singapore.

It is interesting to note that, during 1973, in some ten product groups out of the 83 products which were subject to flexible maximum amount limitations, MFN rates were introduced. In some of these products individual beneficiaries exceeded not only the 50 per cent limitation, but the ceilings too.[100] For concluding remarks the reader is referred to Chapter 10.

NOTES AND REFERENCES

1. See Peter J. Lloyd, 'The Australian Preference Scheme for Developing Countries', *Journal of World Trade Law*, Twickenham, United Kingdom, May–June 1970, pp. 461–2.
2. See United Nations TD/B/C2, Addenda 1; and TDB/AC1/4, Addenda 1, Annex B. p. 3.
3. *Ibid.*
4. Source, see United Nations TD/B/AC1/SR12, p. 7.
5. For details, see *Basic Instruments and Selected Documents, op. cit.*, pp. 162–77.
6. For details of the list, see *ibid.*, Annex, pp. 27–31.
7. For example, Rom, *UNCTAD and the Problems of Preference, op. cit.*; also *ibid.*, pp. 163–4; and *GATT* L/2 527, Annex C and D.
8. Since the scheme proposed a system of prior allocation of preferential imports within the quota, the time-element of distance was not an issue.
9. *Basic Instruments and Selected Documents*, 14th Supplement, *op. cit.*, p. 23.
10. Notifications of additional products, further increases in quotas, and reductions in duties took place on 23 July 1973. See *GATT* L/3584.
11. From the Australian Department of Trade and Industry, *Australian System of Tariff Preferences for Developing Countries* (Canberra: Australian Government Printing Services, 1969), pp. 3–5.
12. From a statement by the Australian Delegation. See United Nations TD/B/C5/9, Annex II, p. 1.

Systems of Generalised Preferences

13. Usually the allocation procedure is to allocate 20 per cent of the quota on a country basis and the rest between the importers. Therefore, if allocation was requested for five countries by one, four, ten, twenty and 45 importers respectively, a quota of $1m would be allocated as follows:
    Country A: to one importer 40,000 + 10,000 = 50,000 to one importer.
    Country B: to each of the four importers 10,000 + 10,000 = 20,000.
    Country C: to each of the ten importers 4000 + 10,000 = 14,000.
    Country D: to each of the twenty importers 2000 + 10,000 = 12,000.
    Country E: to each of the 45 importers 888 + 10,000 = 10,888.
14. From United Nations TD/B/C5/9, Annex II, p. 2.
15. Unfortunately no report was submitted by the Australian Government to the contracting parties about the experience in 1973. On 4 January 1974 a new scheme was introduced.
16. See p. 179.
17. It is interesting that, in all but one of these cases, imports from beneficiaries also entered at non-preferential rates.
18. From *GATT* L/3798, Annex A and C.
19. See United Nations TD/B/C5/9, Annex II, pp. 2–3.
20. See *GATT* L/3798, Annex D, which also provides a breakdown of developing countries' total preferential trade into quota products and handicraft products. But the picture is not sufficiently different to warrant specific discussion here.
21. See, for example, *GATT* L/2832, where Australia notified the contracting parties that, after consultations with Britain on behalf of Hong Kong (under paragraph 4 of the waiver, relating to the threat of substantial injury to Hong Kong's trade in certain products), Australia had agreed to extend to Hong Kong the tariff preferences under items 55.09.390 and 97.04.900 (the latter for a trial period of a year, to be reviewed).
22. For details see United Nations TD/B/480.
23. This list contains not only traditional items such as textiles, but also amplifiers, radios, televisions and components, cathode ray tubes, steam locomotives, mechanical trains and so on.
24. Only a brief description of the GSP elements relevant to the discussion can be given here. For a more detailed account, see United Nations TD/B/C5/3; TD/B/C5/23; TD/B/AC5/34 and Addenda 1; TD/B/373; TD/B/396; TD/B/444; and TD/B/481. The last four documents show the European Community schemes for the years 1971–4.
25. Translated from J. K. Jurgen Kuhn, 'Hauptelemente der EWG Zollpreferenzen: Neue Phase der Aussenwirtschaftspolitik', *Ausenhandelsdienst*, Vol. 29, 1972, pp. 675–6.
26. It is interesting to note the shift of emphasis from the case-by-case negotiations originally suggested by the Belgian Foreign Minister to the automaticity advantage – a point stressed by the French representative to the various committees of UNCTAD.
27. The phrase 'as a general rule' implied that a very limited number of exceptions might be introduced in the light of consultations to be held with the other OECD members.
28. There was also the additional positive list of agricultural products mentioned earlier. These complete lists are reproduced in English for 1971 in UNCTAD TD/B.373, Addenda 1.
    The document contains the following regulations:
    I Instruments for which publication is a condition of their application:
    (EEC) Council Regulation No. 1308/71 of 21 June 1971 concerning the establishment, sharing and management of Community tariff quotas for certain products originating in developing countries.

    (EEC) Council Regulation 1309/71 of 21 June 1971 concerning the establishment of tariff preferences for certain products originating in developing countries.

    (EEC) Council Regulation 1310/71 of 21 June 1971 concerning the establishment, sharing and management of Community tariff quotas for certain textile products originating in developing countries.

(EEC) Council Regulation 1311/71 of 21 June 1971 concerning the establishment of tariff preferences for certain textile products originating in developing countries.

(EEC) Council Regulation 1312/71 of 21 June 1971 concerning the establishment, sharing and management of Community tariff quotas for certain textile and footwear products originating in developing countries.

(EEC).Council Regulation 1313/71 of 21 June 1971 concerning the establishment of tariff preferences for certain textile and footwear products originating in developing countries.

(EEC) Council Regulation 1314/71 of 21 June 1971 establishing a system of generalised preferences in favour of the developing countries for certain products falling within Chapters 1–24 of the common customs tariff.

II Instruments for which publication is not a condition of their application:
Council 71/232/CECA: Decision of 21 June 1971 of the representative of the Governments of the States members of the European Coal and Steel Community meeting in Council concerning the establishment, sharing and management of tariff quotas for certain iron and steel products originating in developing countries.

71/232/CECA: Decision of 21 June 1971 of the representatives of Governments of the States members of the European Coal and Steel Community meeting in Council concerning the establishment of tariff preferences for certain iron and steel products originating in developing countries.

Similar regulations appear in UNCTAD TD/B/396; TD/B/444; and TD/B/481, for later years.

29. Whenever imports of a product subject to a tariff quota from a *beneficiary* reaches the 'maximum-amount limitation', the Commission must immediately inform the member states of the date on which the normal rate of duty must be reimposed in respect of that beneficiary. This information is published in the official journal of the Community.
30. The semi-sensitive list for 1973 was provided in the BFA Zollinformation, *ibid.*, Annhang VI fuer 1973, and is marked with an asterisk (there were 72 such items). For 1974 the list is reproduced in the Community Handbook on the scheme, *infra.*
31. *Handbook on Scheme of the EEC* UNCTAD/TAP 164, April 74.
32. United Nations TD/B/C/5.23 p. 20.
33. In answer to an inquiry in the German Bundestag, a spokesman for the Minister of Economy and Finance stated that the 'greyhound' procedure had been applied to 25 out of 96 tariff quotas, as this method is only suitable for products for which demand can be expected to be relatively restrained. This was the case with these 25 products in the second half of 1971. In such cases the system has advantages for the developing countries without the drawbacks of hasty overflow of imports which could cause disturbances (see Deutschebundestag 6 Shalperioide Drucksache VI/3/33 Sachgebiet 6 13, Bonn, 8 February 72).
34. The information is based on *The EEC on the Move*, Special Report (Geneva: Business International, June 1972) p. 69.
35. According to UNCTAD TD/B/C5/3, pp. 22–3. It is also stated there that in the Netherlands the national tariff quota system is based on the greyhound procedure.

36. UNCTAD TD/B/C5/3, p. 24.
37. *Statistiches Amt der Europäischer Gemeinschaften*, Analytische Ueberschichten Import 1967, I–XII, pp. 3–5. Taken from *Aktuelle Beiträge zum Wirtschafts und Finanzpolitik* No. 128, 2 October 1972, p. 4, or derived from them.
38. The fraction is even more significant if preferences are compared with total overall imports of the Community, or the imports of third countries.
39. See, for example, Tracy Murry, 'How Helpful is the Generalised System of Preferences to Developing Countries?', *Economic Journal*, Cambridge, June 1973, pp. 450–1; and United Nations TD/B/C5/3, p. 30; TD/B/C5/16, Addenda 2, p. 10; and TD/B/C5/22, pp. 18–19.
40. See *Zwischenbilanz der Preferenzverhandlungen*, Ministerialrat Jürgen Kühn (Bonn: BWM, 1971). The figure of dutiable imports from third countries in manufactures is not available. Total manufactured imports (dutiable and duty-free, including raw materials) indicates a $776.7m additional ceiling. While this is probably over-estimated, available data for dutiable manufactures from third countries in 1968 show that the additional ceiling amounted to $565m, compared to the original basic quota of the preferred exports from beneficiaries of $446m. Thus the total preferences in 1968, for semi-manufactures and manufactures, amounted to $1011m, or more than twice the actual exports of these products.
41. See Cooper, *op. cit.*, p. 380. It is true that he refers not to an overall tariff quota, but to one for each commodity group. Since the different shares and rates of growth of the individual categories must be assumed, the average rates applied by Cooper seem to approximate more closely to the calculation of an overall tariff quota than individual commodities.
42. This obviously refers to the basic quota in relation to total dutiable products covered by the scheme coming from other third countries in the basic reference year.
43. In 1973 for instance, the reference period for the basic quota was the level of imports from beneficiaries in 1968. Between these years the price rose 20 per cent (see TD/B/C5/3, p. 8, para. 62). Thus, in real terms, the value of the basic quota amounted only to 83.3 per cent.
44. See United Nations TD/B/C5/SR51, p. 87.
45. See Chapter 1.
46. As compared with the uncertainties of the United States tariff quota for woollen and worsted fabrics.
47. See p. 196.
48. In fact, it is debatable whether there is an overall constraint, as non-sensitive products are not closely monitored. There could be two interpretations of this: (i) that the products are on the non sensitive list as very few of these items are produced by developing countries; and (ii) that these products, regardless of the amount imported, for various reasons do not affect the domestic producers or other important importers, and will therefore not even be restricted within ceilings. The second interpretation has rather important implications for the scheme.
49. See previous chapter.
50. United Nations TD/B/C5/3, para. 63.
51. This is another example of the relationship between the initial share and the rate of growth discussed earlier. In this particular example, the decisive factor seems to be the high initial share.
52. As was suggested in the scheme on p. 167.
53. This raises the interesting question as to the economic relationship between the closed-ended tariff quotas from the minor suppliers and the open-ended ones for the beneficiaries. It was argued in United Nations TD/B/C5/3, p. 17, para. 58, that it would be possible to have a situation where the degree of trade discrimination against the major supplier among the beneficiaries, in favour of the minor suppliers, would substantially reduce the advantage which the major supplier can derive from the scheme.

54. See United Nations TD/B/C5/23, Annex III.
55. See United Nations TD/B/C5/L16, Addenda 2 (A), p. 2, para. 7.
56. See the Draft Report of the Special Committee on Preferences on its sixth session, *ibid.*, where a representative of one developing country complained that the tariff quotas for some of its exports were so limited that they had been exhausted in the first few months of the scheme and, in certain cases, orders originally placed had been cancelled by importers in the European Community, resulting in financial loss to the exporters. He added that only 8 to 10 per cent of the cotton textiles his country exported to the Community received the benefit of GSP treatment, because of the restrictive quotas.
57. While the list of sensitive products is quite small, imports of such products were more than 60 per cent of total imports from the beneficiaries, a considerable share of the preferred imports.
58. See p. 85.
59. Taken from United Nations TD/C5/3, p. 21, para. 73.
60. This point of criticism was first voiced at the third UNCTAD conference. See United Nations TD/111/C2, Sr. 5, p. 48.
61. See p. 85 passim.
62. See *The EEC on the Move*. Special Report 72-1 (Geneva: Business International, June 1972), p. 68.
63. See pp. 80-2.
64. See, for example, United Nations TD/B/C5/3, p. 24, para. 85.
65. Source: United Nations RD/B/C5/23, Tables 1 and 3.
66. *Ibid.*, p. 21.
67. Presumably including, in value terms, the non-sensitive products also.
68. United Nations TD/B/489; and TD/B/C5/29. The Report of the Special Committee on Preferences on its sixth session, issued provisionally as United Nations TD/B/C5(VI), Misc. 2, GE74-46181, p. 26.
69. See Deutscher Bundestag 6, Whalperiode 79 Sitzung Bonn, 12 November 1970, pp. 44-63.
70. See, for example, Murry, 'How Helpful is the Generalised System of Preferences to Developing Countries?,' *op. cit.*, p. 450.
71. United Nations TD/B/C5/3; and TD/B/C5/22. Also, see Cooper, *op. cit.*, and Murry, *op. cit.*
72. A more detailed disaggregation, carried out by the UNCTAD Secretariat for the 44 sensitive products, compared the 1969 trade flows with the 44 tariff quotas, annualised for 1969. It revealed that, if the scheme had been in operation in 1969, only 22 products would have filled the tariff quota, and exports beyond that would have taken place at MFN.
73. United Nations TD/B/C5/23, para. 105, states that an 'analysis of the actual application of the maximum amount shows that the number of products affected increased from 37 in 1971, to 48 in 1972 and 56 in 1973. The maximum amount of 20 per cent was applied to nearly two-thirds of all products affected. Despite the low 'maximum-amount limitation' *only exceptionally was more than one beneficiary affected by such a maximum amount* under each tariff quota. Under the 1971 scheme two beneficiaries were affected by maximum-amount limitations in the case of only four tariff quotas, and three beneficiaries in the case of one tariff quota under the 1972 scheme and two beneficiaries in the case of eight tariff quotas. In 1973 two beneficiaries were affected in the case of six tariff quotas and three in the case of one tariff quota. This seems to suggest that the products subject to certain tariff quotas have been narrowly defined with the purpose of limiting preferential imports from specific countries. In fact in a number of cases *there were practically no other beneficiaries capable of utilising the remaining 70 or 80 per cent* of the quota to any meaningful degree which therefore was largely sterilised. (In two-thirds of the products no ceilings were applied).

74. See United Nations TD/B/C5/3, paras 137–9; and *ibid.*, p. 24, para. 99.
75. United Nations TD/B/C5/2, Tables 10 and 11.
76. It would seem that a use of the formula in relation to the third countries including Community imports would be more in line with the arguments.
77. Source: United Nations TD/B/C5/23.
78. According to the representative of the European Community on the Special Committee on Preferences, sixth session, total tariff quotas and ceilings, with the exception of textiles, had been increased to 2000m units of account in 1974, against 900m in 1973. As for textiles, they reached 68,205 tons, compared with 42,631 tons in 1973. See United Nations TD/B/C5(VI), Misc. 2, GE74–46181, p. 26.
79. There are major changes in respect of the GSP of the new member countries of the Community. Their previous schemes of preference seem to have been more liberal. See United Nations TD/B/C5/23, p. 17. Comparison of these schemes with the Community GSP is outside the scope of the present discussion.
80. According to that source, the Netherlands criticised the increases as barely keeping pace with world inflation, and therefore pressed for an early review of the scheme.
81. First established in 1974 for 30m units of account, not exceeding 22,000 tons, and allocated mainly to the United Kingdom. This was one of the four tariff quotas established in Chapters 1–24 of the BTN for cocoa butter, soluble coffee, preserved pineapple and raw tobacco. For details, see United Nations TD/B/C/5 23, pp. 5–6.
82. See *Official Journal of the European Communities*, Vol. 17, No. C110. Also *ibid.*, p. 13.
83. It is true that experience has shown that there is a concentration of preferential imports in a limited number of beneficiaries who account for a major share of the preferential trade. This is evident (for lack of any other details) from the application of the maximum-amount limitation. See United Nations TD/B/C5/23, Annex III.
84. The argument that the tariff quota system avoids unilaterally discriminating and arbitrary action loses much of its value in view of the constant changes in conditions and size of the maximum-amount limitation. In the final analysis an exporting country is interested in the tariff quotas as it is applied to its exports. The worsening conditions under which it may be permitted to continue its exports makes the system as uncertain for the planning of future development of exports as is the case with the escape clause system.

    It could no longer be claimed, as was argued by proponents of the tariff quota system, 'that whereas in the so-called safeguard clause system the application of the safeguard clause was left to the importing countries' discretion so that the volume of goods was variable and unpredictable . . . in the latter case the volume was fixed and announced in advance and the application was purely automatic and independent of the wishes of the countries applying it.' United Nations TD/B/C2/38; and TD/C2/AC1/10, p. 9, para. 23.
85. See United Nations TD/b/AC5/34, Addenda 7.
86. For details, see United Nations TD/B/373, Addenda 7.
87. *Weekly Tariff Bulletin* (in Japanese) of the Ministry of Finance.
88. See United Nations TD/B/C5/6, p. 7.
89. For details, see the list of product groups for setting ceilings in United Nations TD/B/373, Addenda 7, Annex 3, pp. 57–77.
90. See United Nations TD/B/C5/6, Table 1. Out of the total imports from beneficiaries in 1970 of $6906m, $5847m were products included in BTN Ch 25–99. Out of total dutiable products of $3984m, $3344m were products included in these chapters. $743m of the products in Chapters 25–99 were covered by the ceiling.
91. For the calculation of the year in which this might happen under hypothetical assumptions of the Japanese growth rate of imports from beneficiaries, when the growth rate of imports from the rest of the world are assumed to be given and assuming a different percentage of Japanese imports originating in the beneficiaries, see United Nations TD/B/C5/6, pp. 14–17.

92. In actual fact detailed data show that actual trade in 1970 would have exceeded the ceiling of 1971 in 89 product groups where preferential imports were $90m and the total imports from beneficiary countries in these 89 products accounted for $200m (excluding copper). In the other 125 commodity groups preferential trade totalled $133m, and the ceilings were open-ended.
93. See *UNCTAD Report on Special Committee on Preferences*, Sixth Session, *op. cit.*
94. *Ibid.*, p. 43.
95. See, for example, rubber tyres in group 31, on which the MFN rate was re-established despite the fact that the total group of rubber articles is placed under flexible administration. See United Nations TD/C/C5/117, Addenda 8, pp. 1–2.
96. *Ibid.*
97. *Japanese Ministry of Finance, Weekly Tariff Bulletin*, 1973, No. 1072.
98. Based on data from United Nations TD/B/C5/17, Addenda 4, 6, 8, 9 and 12.
99. See *Customs Tariff Schedule*, Tokyo, *op. cit.*
100. See, for example, United Nations TD/B/C5/17, Addenda 12, p. 2, para. 6.

PART IV

Some Final Thoughts

CHAPTER 9

Responses of Exporting Countries to Tariff Quotas

As a tariff quota is an instrument of an importing country, discussion is liable to centre on the details of its operation there and the effect it could have on that particular country. Problems posed by the administration of such a quota, when examined from the viewpoint of an exporting country, are frequently overlooked and are not given the attention they deserve. As many of these are not self-evident they need to be explored more fully.

There is no single best administrative policy that can be adopted by a government's export licensing authority in the field of tariff quotas which will apply in every case, for there are many different influences that need to be considered. Among other things, the specific conditions and circumstances of the exporting country itself, and the objectives that the authorities wish to attain, have to be taken into account, as does the type of tariff quota and the purpose for which it has been granted abroad.

If, for example, a tariff quota was granted globally on a first-come-first-served basis, and exporters in many countries were competing to utilise this same quota, the best policy for the licensing authority would be to abstain from any intervention that might hamper or delay the export from the country. On the contrary, it ought to ensure, by all means that are available, that its goods are exported as quickly as possible, so that it may gain as large a share as possible of the quota, ahead of its competitors from other countries. In these circumstances it does not matter whether these are the most desirable exports for the country, or not.

The policy would, however, be different when a tariff quota is granted solely, or mainly,[1] to one exporting country and the structure of the industry in that country happens to be such that there are a number of producers capable of exporting the product; and the total exporting capacity of the industry is greater than the tariff quota. The export licensing authority may then have a problem to decide the best administrative method to adopt for allocating the tariff quota. Theoretically there are a number of possible procedures, and the decision as to which to choose depends first on the objective which the licensing authorities wish to attain. If, for instance, the main objective is to achieve orderly exports abroad within the quota, with the minimum of interference at home and keeping the administration as simple as possible while still maintaining a competitive spirit, then the allocative principle that would seem appropriate should be based on the first-come-first-served principle.

Under this system there are two sub-groups that can be distinguished in practice and each of these has a number of possible variations:

(a) The quota benefits to be allocated to the first-come-first-served exporters as and when the exports leave the country's boundaries; and

(b) issuing licences to exporters, on a first-come-first-served basis, prior to the exports being made.[2]

The advantages of the above systems, as already pointed out, are their ease and simplicity of administration, speed and competitive nature, but they do have substantial drawbacks. The first sub-group causes the exporter substantial risks and uncertainty until the export leaves the country's boundaries, while the second may raise the problem of quota blocking, where the company which wishes to export first may ask for the whole quota.

Certain things can be done which will mitigate some of these difficulties, such as issuing monthly or quarterly sub-quotas, limiting the validity of licences to very restricted periods, or limiting the amount each exporter is entitled to obtain in each application. But the main disadvantage here is that the quota benefits would be allocated to those who are the quickest to export or to apply for licences. As experience has shown,[3] competition based on speed has not always been the most desirable form of competition, either for the exporting or for the importing country. It may lead, for instance, to exports of inferior quality or cheap goods, where higher-value and better-quality products may be required.

There are other possible systems of allocation, which get away from the first-come-first-served principle, and which may perhaps seem to export licensing authorities to be appropriate. One of these is the system of the prior allocation of the tariff quota by issuing licences based on the principle of past trade. Such an approach is based not only on the desire to interfere as little as possible in the existing export structure of the industry, but also by the wish to maintain the *status quo* and the relative relationships of the individual exporting firms in the economy. The maintenance of the *status quo*, in addition to relatively simple administration, is a possible advantage[4] compared with the first-come-first-served alternatives, but under this system of allocation no attempt is made to maximise receipts of foreign exchange.

If the tariff quota is a quantitative one a third approach would be to give preference within the tariff quota to those exporters whose export price is the highest. This presupposes that the exporting country enjoys in the tariff quota a real preferential advantage which it should exploit. Such an approach — which is, in fact, customary in some countries — is probably based on the assumption that the higher price received per unit of weight ensures a higher total income of foreign receipts from the tariff quota. This, however, is only correct, under highly restrictive conditions of *ceteris paribus*, in the sense that the only differential feature is the price. Usually there are variations between different products and in different factories in the value added: that is to say in the net foreign exchange resulting from the difference between the foreign exchange export price of the final product, and the direct and indirect costs in foreign exchange of the raw materials, semi-processed products and services, which enter the final produce as input. Consequently, despite the higher price of an export product, the net foreign currency contribution from it may be smaller[5] than one where the price is lower yet the value added is higher.

Similarly, the quantitative tariff quota may contain a range of different products on which the tariff rates themselves can differ.[6] Under these circumstances it may be thought sensible to maximise the tariff proceeds saved, other things being equal, and to allocate the quota to those items which save the highest tariff payment per kilogram. In the light of these two reservations it will be seen that an approach based solely on the export price criterion may not prove to be the best method of allocation, except under extremely restrictive assumptions.

In order to maximise foreign exchange earnings *within the quantitative tariff quota*, it is necessary to be clear as to what exactly is meant by the export price. This could be the price ex-works (or f.o.b.)[7] which the producer has to charge in order to cover all costs and to make a normal profit. It could also mean the price which he can obtain abroad for his product, after deduction of transport and insurance costs as well as the payment of the duty, or it could mean the price he could obtain abroad after deduction of transport and insurance, but assuming that no duty has to be paid. These three different meanings are important since all of them (as will become evident later) play a role in the determination of the allocation of the quota.

The ex-works, or f.o.b., price is needed in the first instance to indicate the minimum profitability under which the firm is willing to produce for export. If the price abroad is lower than this domestic f.o.b. price, there will be no production for exports. Secondly, the value-added data are usually based on cost calculations computed for the ex-works price, and not for the particular price it can fetch temporarily in a specific market. As a later example will show, the rate of duty with reference to this price[8] is also significant in some specific instances.

On the other hand the price quoted abroad (quoted after deduction of transportation and insurance costs) represents to the exporter the total receipts per unit which he can get for his exported product, provided that there is no duty to be paid. This price has first to be compared with the ex-works price in order to eliminate those products where the price abroad is not sufficient to cover costs plus normal profits. But a ranking of the remaining products, by prices quoted abroad in descending order of value, would still not provide the best criteria for allocating exports within the tariff quota. To maximise the receipts of net foreign exchange from this source requires the deduction of the value of the foreign exchange component of input from the foreign exchange price of the final product.[9]

Only by ranking the net value added, in descending order by value of unit, can the maximisation of the net foreign exchange within the tariff quota be achieved; that is, by allocating export permits to the products in descending order of value per unit, until the quota is filled.[10]

If the export licensing authorities are really interested in maximising total foreign exchange earnings, then to attempt to maximise the earnings *within the quota itself* may be undesirable. Maximisation within the tariff quota ignores the fact that, while some products may be exported only within the quota, others may also be exported quite profitably while paying the full duty, despite their also being the top earners within the quota. In this case the total net revenue of foreign exchange may be higher even though the export receipts within the tariff quota may not be at the maximum. In other words, account has to be taken of the elasticity of the demand abroad for the products, the rates and sizes of the tariff, the margin of profit between the ex-works price, and that obtainable abroad, inside or outside the tariff quota.

To calculate such a maximisation becomes a rather complicated problem when the number of product items involved is relatively large, even when highly simplified assumptions are used about the elasticity of demand abroad and the linearity of cost relations. A hypothetical example of a limited number of products can, however, be presented without the use of mathematical techniques,[11] and this, though using highly restricted assumptions, can nevertheless be quite realistic in specific circumstances. The example which follows was to some extent constructed on the basis of elements of a concrete case.

The information used in the example is all summarised in Table 9.1. The top line sets out the various enterprises which can export the products. The second gives a listing and an account of the commodities which can be exported. Line (iii) shows the export capacity in tons; (iv) provides the minimum export price; and (v) the foreign price, less transport and insurance costs. Line (vi) states the value added based on the minimum cost price; and line (vii) gives the tariff rate charged in the importing country beyond the tariff quota. The data presented in the

TABLE 9.1
Optimising Export Receipts

(i)	Enterprise	A	A	B	B	C	D	D	E
(ii)	Commodity and listing	A (1)	B (2)	A (3)	B (4)	C (5)	D (6)	E (7)	F (8)
(iii)	Export capacity (tons)	120	79	192	171	50	140	20	50
(iv)	Export price f.o.b. (per kg.)	$3.60	$4.20	$3.50	$3.88	$2.50	$3.20	$10.00	$5.00
(v)	Foreign price (including duty), less transport and insurance	$4.00	$5.00	$4.00	$5.00	$2.75	$4.00	$14.00	$6.50
(vi)	Value added based on f.o.b. price	70%	60%	80%	70%	100%	100%	50%	50%
(vii)	Customs duty	15%	12%	15%	12%	13%	20%	20%	17%
(viii)	Foreign exchange input in f.o.b. price (100 less value added)	30%	40%	20%	30%	—	—	50%	50%
(ix)	Foreign exchange input in f.o.b. price in absolute terms	$1.08	$1.68	$.70	$1.16	—	—	$5.00	$2.50
(x)	Total value added plus excess profit: line (v)–(ix)	$2.92	$3.32	$3.30	$3.84	$2.75	$4.00	$9.00	$4.00
(xi)	Foreign price (less transport and insurance) minus duty: line (v)–(vii)	$3.32	$4.46	$3.32	$4.66	$2.43	$3.33	$11.66	$5.55
(xii)	Total value added: Line (xi)–(ix)	$2.24	$2.78	($2.62)	$3.30	($2.43)	$3.33	$6.66	$3.05
(xiii)	Duty on export price f.o.b. (per kg.)	$0.54	$0.504	0.525	$0.466	$0.325	$0.64	$2.00	$1.00
(xiv)	Exports at f.o.b. price + duty as compared to foreign price and duty line (iv) + line (xii) as compared to line (v) Yes (+), No (–)	—	+	—	+	—	+	+	+
(xv)	Difference between value added inside and outside the quota	$2.92	$0.54	$3.30	$0.54	$2.75	$0.67	$2.34	$0.95

table assume constant cost and that the demand conditions abroad are completely elastic.[12]

In order to obtain a tabulation which compares the contribution of each product to the foreign exchange earnings, inside and outside the tariff quota, additional data had to be derived from the original information. First, the relative and absolute foreign exchange input component in the price had to be calculated, and the results are shown in lines (viii) and (ix). From the demand price (less transport and insurance costs) the value of the foreign exchange components of input was deducted (line (x)). This assumes no payment of any duties and therefore only applies to exports within the tariff quotas.

If exports are to take place despite the duty, the demand price given in line (v) must consist of the export price plus the duty. In the case of product (1) for example, the $4.00 shown would represent 115 per cent, and not 100 per cent. This latter price has been calculated and is shown in line (xi), as are similar prices for other products. Line (xii) establishes the value added for the prices derived in line (xi). Line (xiii) computes the tariff rates for the f.o.b. prices. This permits an approximate[13] comparison of the price offered abroad with the minimum price demanded at home. In the example, the first product will not be exported outside the tariff quota, since the f.o.b. price (line (iv)), plus the duty (line (xiii)), is higher than the price offered (line (v)). Line (xiv) indicates, by a negative sign, that no exports are possible without the tariff quota, and the same is found to be true for the third and fifth products shown.

The final line tries to establish the difference between value added inside and outside the quota. It is the ranking of this difference in a descending order which will determine the allocation of exports within the quota. From the table it becomes clear that maximum overall gains would have been obtained if the following products were included within the quota:

	Value Added	
Product (3)	192 tons × $3.30 per kg. =	$633,600
Product (1)	108 tons × $2.92 per kg. =	$315,360
Total	300 tons	$948,960

Outside the quota the following products would be exported:

	Value Added	
Product (7)	20 tons × $6.66 per kg. =	$133,200
Product (8)	50 tons × $3.05 per kg. =	$152,500
Product (6)	140 tons × $3.33 per kg. =	$466,200
Product (4)	171 tons × $3.30 per kg. =	$564,300
Product (2)	79 tons × $2.78 per kg. =	$219,620
		$1,535,820
		+ 948,960
Overall total value added		$2,484,780[14]

Value Added

For comparison, the maximisation of the tariff quota itself would be:

Product (7)	20 tons × $9.00 per kg. =	$180,000
Product (8)	50 tons × $4.00 per kg. =	$200,000
Product (6)	140 tons × $4.00 per kg. =	$560,000
and part of		
Product (4)	90 tons × $3.84 per kg. =	$345,600
	300 tons	
Total in the tariff quota		$1,285,600

Outside the quota the following exports would still take place:

Product (4)	81 tons × $3.30		
	per kg.	= $267,300	
Product (2)	79 tons × $2.78		
	per kg.	= $219,620	
		$486,920	$486,920
Overall total			$1,772,520

This comparison makes the point quite clearly that maximising net income within the tariff quota is not necessarily the best solution.

This discussion by no means exhausts the subject, for government licensing authorities could well have aims other than the short-run maximisation of foreign exchange income.[15] The same is true with respect to the system of administration, where many solutions, other than those mentioned, are possible.[16]

It is hoped that even this brief review will help to arouse interest and focus attention on one aspect of tariff quotas that frequently gets overlooked. It is important enough to be explored and examined more closely by those who are in charge of administering them than is usually the case.

For the reader who is mathematically inclined attention is drawn to Appendix I, where the problem of maximising total foreign exchange income is further elaborated.

NOTES

1. There are cases where a tariff quota, which was not granted to one country exclusively, nevertheless chiefly benefits a single country due to its having a particular comparative advantage in the production of the specific product. This was the case with the stainless steel table flatware from Japan exported to the United States in the late 1950s and early 1960s.
2. If either condition (a) or (b) are absent, the problem does not exist: in the first case the monopolist will enjoy the tariff quota and, in the second case, the quota is not effective and all exporters may enjoy its benefit. The explanation for the lack of utilisation of

the tariff quota may be lack of supply or the inability to compete, either with more efficient exporters in other countries (despite the higher duty they have to pay), or with the domestic producers in the importing country, or other beneficiaries who may enjoy the same, or even greater preferences. Conversely, a tariff quota granted solely to one country does not ensure it a real preference. It may be that other beneficiaries enjoy the same preferences, not within tariff quotas but on an unlimited basis.

3. See the case of the cheap woollen and worsted fabrics imported into the United States from Italy discussed in Chapter 4.
4. It is possible that receipts from exports within the quota under this scheme might be higher than that under the first-come-first-served scheme since not speed but past exports will be the criterion for inclusion.
5. See, in the table of the example which follows, product 8 in comparison to product 6.
6. For instance the quantitative tariff quotas of the European Community, for certain Mediterranean countries in cotton fabrics of BTN item 55.09, contain three different tariff rates beyond the quota limits or 13 per cent, 14 per cent and 15 per cent.
7. To emphasise the domestic price in the discussion, no differentiation is made between 'ex-works' and 'f.o.b.'.
8. See line (xiii) in Table 3.1.
9. See line (x) in Table 3.1.
10. In the example which follows this would mean the inclusion of the products 7, 8, 6 and partially, 4.
11. For a more elaborate mathematical note, see Appendix.
12. This assumption is quite plausible for exports from a small country to a large developed country. Also, the variation as to the value added, prices and tariffs seems plausible, for the higher quality type of products may require a more expensive special type of raw materials and semi-processed imported materials. The degree of backward integration may also explain the variations between different factories in costs, value added, and so on, of identical products.
13. It is an approximation because the prices are f.o.b. or ex-works, and not c.i.f.
14. It is interesting to note that the only product which will not be exported at all is product 5, with 100 per cent value added due to its low price.
15. Suppose the purpose in granting the tariff quota to a country was to permit it to develop and expand a particular branch of industry, by giving new infant firms access to the export market of the developed country at the preferred terms. It would then seem a mistake for the export licensing authority to grant these advantages to old-established plants despite their possibility of earning higher receipts in foreign exchange.
16. Suffice it to mention one theoretical possibility of the auctioning of the right of export within the tariff quota.

CHAPTER 10

Summing Up

Before attempting to draw together the many threads of discussion that make up this book it will be useful to look at the development of those preferential schemes based on tariff quotas in operation and to see what particular advantages and disadvantages are emerging. At the outset it has to be stressed that it is still relatively early days for these schemes and there is insufficient data and evidence to permit any hard-and-fast conclusions to be drawn. At the very best little more can be done than to indicate the way things have been developing, and also to suggest where additional work and study could usefully be employed.

It will be recalled that the examination of the GSP of the European Community and its actual operation, which has been discussed in considerable detail in Chapter 8, showed that much vital information is still missing. Nothing is available about the preferred imports within the scheme or about how the sensitive tariff quota have been used. Additionally, the actual shares of the preferred imports by major export suppliers are also lacking. Furthermore, there is no data which measures the economic effects of the preferences offered upon export or import prices – or on any possible disruptive influence that preferences may have on the internal market.[1] Most important of all, no information is available about the evolution of the *non-sensitive* preferred imports. Even a clear allocation of the commodity groups, which is necessary before imports can be compared with ceilings,[2] does not exist.

Nevertheless, some tentative conclusions begin to emerge by examining such evidence as there is, going back to the early period of the GSP scheme of the Community as originally constituted, and utilising the analysis that the UNCTAD secretariat has carried out on the basis of actual trade data for the years before the GSP was introduced. From this examination of the European Community scheme it would seem (i) that the total values of the preferred imports are inadequate; and (ii) that even these theoretical levels are so hedged about with further restrictions (which are inherent in the scheme) that actual imports of these preferred items are even more restricted.

This restriction is really brought about by using the instrument of the tariff quota three or four times on the same set of data. First there exists a general formula which forms a theoretical overall quota. This is then broken down into individual commodity quotas to which the formula applies and, within each of these, the maximum allocation is made, which is virtually a tariff quota. Finally there is even an allocation into individual member country quotas in some cases.

Examining the actual trade flows can lead to some rather pessimistic conclusions. In fact some commentators have considered the Community GSP to be little more than a relatively small aid programme which, in 1971 allowed $53m[3] of the Community's customs revenue to be transferred to the beneficiaries. In fact it is doubtful whether all of it went to the beneficiaries, who often exported the same commodities at MFN rates, thus creating a closed-ended tariff quota for most of the imported product. It seems likely that a sizeable proportion of the gain from the lower duty probably went to the importers rather than providing a stimulus to investment and expansion of exports, as was intended.

This conclusion may be too pessimistic. Perhaps the actual trade flows give too much weight to the sensitive and semi-sensitive products and pay insufficient attention to the potentials of those products and exporting countries for which preferential imports could develop in the future; these would fall in the non-utilised, or non-sensitive, category. The issue then would be not whether more than two-thirds of the preferential imports are restricted as sensitive, or semi-sensitive, products as they are today, but rather what will happen to that part of the exports which might develop in the future in the non-sensitive sector.

If a product is classified as sensitive, or semi-sensitive, it immediately becomes a substantial export item of a beneficiary, and thus becomes subject to various limitations, there is obviously little incentive for expansion, and the pessimistic view is justified. But if the opposite should happen and new export items, which are today classified as non-sensitive, are permitted to enter even beyond the theoretical ceiling, then the pessimistic view is perhaps unjustified and the scheme may provide a stimulus for investments and expansion of exports. Under these circumstances it is possible that the ceilings and limitations for the sensitive and semi-sensitive products would become a sort of escape clause for a limited number of them. This would have the advantage that commodities, instead of being totally excluded *ab initio*, would be permitted to enter preferentially, although only within quantitative limits.

If this second development proves to be correct then many of the arguments in favour of the adoption of the tariff quota system as opposed to the escape clause system lose much of their value. One of the strong arguments in favour of the tariff quota system is that it provides a high degree of certainty for both importers and exporters. If tariff quotas are not used systematically and automatically (and this has been the tendency) then they no longer have the merit of avoiding the uncertainties that the unilateral application of a ceiling imposes.

A further point which has to be kept in mind is that using a predetermined tariff quota system instead of an escape clause system does not always provide the protection that is expected. Within a product group the overall ceiling may be set too high in order to prevent any damage being done to one of its component products. Furthermore, the tariff quota in value terms can conceal considerable fluctuations in the quantities that are imported, which are the result of changes in the price of the product. If the price of the product exported is charged in its domestic currency, any devaluation of that currency could substantially increase the quantity exported within the quota limit, and could, in theory, disrupt the internal market of the importing country unless some other limitation is introduced. From all the above it becomes evident that a predetermined tariff quota system seems less desirable than an escape clause system which imposes a limit only where there is real need. As has been shown, tariff quotas are not in all cases the most suitable system. Nevertheless, wherever possible tariff quotas, instead of quantitative restrictions or *ab initio* exclusions, should be used.

It should be mentioned here that the aspects of the Community scheme that are under discussion are very closely paralleled in the Japanese scheme. Here, too, in practice the scheme has moved towards a sort of 'escape clause' system, although it is based on a similar sort of system to that of the Community, where broad commodity group ceilings are determined with, in some cases, a safeguard procedure, limiting not only overall preferential imports but also the import of specific items within the broad groups. In practice, some imports are permitted beyond the ceilings and 'maximum-amount limitations', whilst in other cases restrictions are placed on imports within the permitted tariff quotas and maximum limits. It would seem that for both these areas the arguments point towards the likelihood that the GSP based on a tariff quota system as at present constituted is unduly severe, and that it should be considerably improved and liberalised.

The possibility of moving to a system, both in the Community and Japan, which only employs a limit in cases of real necessity makes particular sense in the light of the actual experience that some other donor countries, some of them quite small, have had with GSP. They have been able to grant unrestricted duty-free imports for manufactures without experiencing any serious difficulties, with the escape clause rarely being invoked. It is worth emphasising that trading conditions have been changing over recent years with virtually free trade amongst the industrialised West European countries. There seems a sad irrationality in maintaining discriminatory tariffs against the developing countries, when the more developed can compete more favourably anyway.

It cannot be emphasised too strongly that these comments on the GSP should be regarded as only a very preliminary judgement on the effect of using tariff quotas in the various preference schemes. This is partly because the schemes have only been in operation for a relatively short time, partly because they are continually being modified but mainly because the available data necessary for sensible measurement is so inadequate. Much more information is required covering a longer period of time, and a considerable amount of analytical work needs to be done on it, before firmer conclusions can start to be drawn.

GENERAL CONCLUSIONS

It will be evident from material presented in this book that tariff quotas have *indeed been used* and are likely to continue to be used increasingly as a tool of commercial policy despite the meagre attention paid to them in the literature. It is equally obvious that there are many kinds of tariff quotas and that they are merely a technical neutral tool which can be used for different purposes, even contradictory ones. Their desirability and adequacy as a tool depends on the specific conditions and aims and has to be judged from case to case in the particular setting in which they are being applied. No absolute value judgement can be made.

This last conclusion is corroborated by an examination of the case studies, where examples of both success and failure have been shown. While much further work remains to be done in order to pinpoint more specifically the elements which contribute to the success or failure of a tariff quota in a specific situation, there can be no doubt that the tool is operationally workable in many situations. And it is worth remembering that, from an analytical point of view, one of the findings has been that tariff quotas are a more liberal form of trade restriction than either quotas or even tariffs.

Such conclusions are particularly relevant in the context in which the whole issue arose originally, which was the prevention of the trade-diverting effects inflicted on third countries in the case of the establishment of a customs union. It is also in this context that the place of tariff quotas in the GATT has been examined. Although under certain circumstances they conform with its articles, the particular case of establishing a tariff quota for a third country is not in conformity with the GATT from a legal point of view, even though it has been found to be justified economically and is in line with the spirit of the agreement, and would require a change in Article XXIV.

As has already been explained in earlier paragraphs discussing the role of the tariff quota in the GSP, it seems that its excessive use in the schemes of some major donor countries could be too restrictive at present, though this perhaps may be too premature a judgement. Much depends on the treatment of the non-sensitive imports in the future and it is hoped that the unnecessary and severely restrictive element will be eliminated. In this respect it is encouraging to observe the experience of Australia, who used the tariff quota as a transitory safeguard measure and who now only uses it as an exception. This experience, which could be shared by other major donor countries in the future, gives substance to the original idea that the use of the tariff quota would help to overcome the psychological fears and objections of domestic industry and labour to the introduction of preferences.

In theory at least tariff quotas are also used at present as automatic predetermined safeguards, as opposed to escape clause procedures. It would seem desirable for them not to be applied in this automatic way in the future but only to be available as a safeguard under *escape clause procedures*. Where imports have to be limited, tariff quotas should be used *instead* of the *ab initio* exclusions.

Finally, it has been demonstrated that the correct utilisation of a tariff quota for maximising foreign exchange need not necessarily lead to the maximisation of foreign exchange earnings of the quota itself for an exporting country.

It will be obvious that the present volume has only made a start at dealing with the whole subject and that it ought to be studied and analysed further. The more that is known about it the better can the tool be used in specific situations.

NOTES

1. As was pointed out in Chapter 7, the disruptive effect on the internal market and dissatisfaction of importers and exporters alike were a major cause of the elimination of the scheme. No study has been made by the Community, or by UNCTAD, to examine if, and to what extent, there are similar disruptive effects in the GSP in the Community.
2. United Nations TD/B/C5/3, p. 34, para. 117.
3. Tracy Murray, 'How Helpful is the Generalised System of Preferences to Developing Countries?', *op. cit.*

APPENDIX I

Mathematical Note to Chapter 9

PREPARED BY R. HAIMI-COHEN

Assume that a quota of k is given to m different products. The usual tariff on the jth product is t_j per cent. The price $p_j(s)$ of the jth product in the importing country is a function of the supply S of this product.

In the exporting country there are n different producers. The maximal output capacity of the ith producer in the jth product is Aij ($Aij = 0$ means he does not produce that product at all), and his foreign exchange expenses on that product are s_{ij} per unit. The minimal price that the ith producer will sell the jth product for is M_{ij}.

The export of the ith producer in the jth product inside the quota is denoted by q_{ij}. Q_{ij} is his total export of the jth product.

The price that the ith producer gets for the jth product inside the quota is:

$$p_j \left(\sum_{k=1}^{n} Q_{kj} \right)$$

The price he gets outside the quota (that is, before paying the tariff) is:

$$\frac{100}{100 + t_j} \cdot p_j \left(\sum_{k=1}^{n} Q_{kj} \right)$$

His total expenses in foreign exchange on this product are:

$$s_{ij} Q_{ij}$$

The aim here is to maximise the total foreign exchange income of the whole export. Hence the object function y is:

$$y = \sum_{i=1}^{n} \sum_{j=1}^{m} \left[q_{ij} + (Q_{ij} - q_{ij}) \frac{100}{100 + t_j} \cdot p_j \left(\sum_{k=1}^{n} Q_{kj} \right) - Q_{ij} s_{ij} \right]$$

where y is the sum of the foreign exchange income net (the value added) of each producer on each product. The constraints imposed on the variables q_{ji}, Q_{ji} are:

Mathematical Note to Chapter Nine 237

(a) $0 \leq q_{ij} \leq Q_{ij} \leq A_{ij}$ $1 \leq i \leq n,$ $1 \leq j \leq m$

(b) $\sum_{i=1}^{n} \sum_{j=1}^{m} q_{ij} \leq K$

(c) $Q_{ij} p_j (\sum_{k=1}^{n} Q_{kj}) \geq q_{ij} M_{ij}$ $1 \leq i \leq n,$ $1 \leq j \leq m$

(d) $(Q_{ij} - q_{ij}) \dfrac{100}{100 + t_j} pj (\sum_{k=1}^{n} Q_{kj}) \geq (Q_{ij} - q_{ij}) M_{ij}$

Constraints (c) and (d) express the fact that if the price received in the importing country (after substracting the tariff, in case the export is outside the quota) is less than the minimal price M_{ij}, the producer will not export this product (not, that is, outside the quota).

In the general case this is a non-linear programming problem and the way to attack it depends on the nature of the functions $p_j(s)$. In the special example in the text (p. 224) these functions were constant — $p_j(s)$ was the world price of the jth product which was constant because of the assumption of completely elastic demand – and thus it was a linear programming problem and could also be handled in the usual way of solving such problems.

It is assumed that the output capacities A_{ij} are constant. Sometimes, however, they can be variables which the government may control by raw material distribution. One may assume that the amount of output is proportional to the amount of raw materials invested in it, hence for each type of raw material there is a linear constraint of the form:

(e) $\sum_{i=1}^{n} \sum_{j=1}^{m} a_{ij} A_{ij} \leq b$

Here a_{ij} is the quantity of material required by the ith producer to produce one unit of the jth product.

APPENDIX II

Tariff Quotas and Rates of Duty, 1973

TSUS Items	Description	Tariff quota	Within quota	Over quota
100.40	Cattle Weighing under 200 lb. each	Quantity limited to 200,000 head in the 12-month period beginning 1 April	1.5¢/lb.	2.5¢/lb. (TSUS 100.43)
100.53	Weighing 700 lb. or more each (not including cows imported specially for dairy purposes)	Quantity limited to 400,000 head entered in the 12-month period beginning 1 April, of which not over 120,000 shall be entered in any quarter beginning 1 April, July, October or January. Cattle have been subject to a tariff quota since 1 January 1936. These rates have been in effect since 1 January 1948, following concessions granted by the US under the GATT.	1.5¢/lb.	2.5¢/lb. (TSUS 100.53)
110.50	Fresh chilled or frozen fillets, steaks and sticks of cod,	Quantity to be determined annually – not more than a quantity equal	1.7/8¢/lb	$2\frac{1}{2}$ ¢/lb.

Tariff Quotas and Rates of Duty, 1973

TSUS Items	Description	Tariff quota	Within quota	Over quota
	cusk, haddock, hake, pollock and Atlantic ocean perch (except frozen into blocks weighing over 10 lb. each)	to 15% of the average aggregate apparent annual consumption of such fish during the 3 calendar years immediately preceding that in which the imported fish are entered or 15,000,000 lb., whichever quantity is greater, of which total quantity not over one fourth shall be entered during the first 3 months, not over half during the first 6 months, and not over three fourths during the first 9 months of the year.		
112.30	Fish prepared or preserved in any manner not in oil in airtight containers. Tuna: in containers weighing with their contents not over 15 lb. each	Quantity entered in any calendar year not to exceed 20% of the US pack of canned tuna during the immediately preceding calendar year as reported by the US Fish and Wild Life Service.	12.5%	25% (TSUS 112.34)
		Tariff quota became effective 14 April 1956.		
115.10	Fluid milk and cream fresh or sour (except	3,000,000 gall. entered in any calendar year. This	2¢/gal	6.5¢/gall, (TSUS 115.15)

TSUS Items	Description	Tariff quota	Within quota	Over quota
	buttermilk) containing over 1% but not over 5.5% of butterfat.	item has been subject to a tariff quota since 1 January 1936.		
137,20	Potatoes white or Irish Certified seeds.	114m lb. in each 12-month period beginning on 15 September in any year. Potatoes have been subject to tariff quotas since January 1936.	37.5 per 100 lb.	75¢ per 100 lb. (TSUS 137.21)
137.25	Other seeds than such certified seeds.	45m lb. in each 12-month period beginning 15 September in any year. If for any calendar year the production of white or Irish potatoes including seed potatoes in the US according to the estimate of the Dept. of Agriculture made as at 1 September is less than 21,000m lb., any additional quantity of potatoes equal to the amount by which such estimated production is less than the 21,000m lb. shall be added to the 45 lb. provided in TSUS 137.25 for the year	37.5¢	75¢ per 100 lb. (TSUS 137.28)

Tariff Quotas and Rates of Duty, 1973 241

TSUS Items	Description	Tariff quota	Within quota	Over quota
		beginning the following 15 September (potatoes the product of Cuba shall not be charged against the quota of 45m).		
	Brooms and brushes consisting of vegetable materials bound together but not mounted or set in a block or head with or without handles; brooms wholly or in part of broom corn	(The quantities specified below may be modified as provided under head note 3 (a) to schedule 7 pt. 8 sub-part A of the TSUS).		
750.26	Whisker valued not over 32¢ each.	Up to 115,000 dozen per calendar year. Whisker brooms (classified under items 750.26 to 750.28 inclusive)	per 20% ad val.	32¢ (TSUS 750.27)
750.29	Other brooms valued not over 96¢ each	Up to 205,000 dozen in one calendar year (classified under items 750.29 to 31 inclusive)	20% ad val.	32¢ each (TSUS 750.30)
	The following references for the Philippines only in accordance with the Philippine Trade Agreement Revision of 1955.			
170.22 170.26 170.31	Scrap tobacco and stemmed and unstemmed	If entered on or before 31 December 1973 during each	Duty-free	

TSUS Items	Description	Tariff quota	Within quota	Over quota
170.36 170.42 170.47 170.62	filler tobacco	calendar year 1971–3 1.3m lb.		
170.72	Cigars	If entered on or before 31 December 1973, during each calendar year 1971–3, 40m cigars.	Duty-free	
176.05 176.08 176.12	Coconut oil	Dutiable at preferential rate if entered on or before 1 December 1973 but the total quantity entered at such preferential rates during each calendar year 1971–3 not to exceed 40,000 tons.		
745.21	Pearl or shell buttons	If entered on or before 31 December 1973 in each calendar year 1971–3, 170,000 gross buttons	Duty-free	

Selected Bibliography

Set out below is a selected bibliography of those major volumes referred to in the text.

WILLIAM ADAMS BROWN, *The United States and the Restoration of World Trade* (Washington: Brookings Institution, 1950).

The EEC on the Move, Special Report (Geneva: Business International, June 1972).

LYNN R. EDMINSTER, *Agricultural Stake in the British Agreement and the Trade Agreement Program* (New York: International Conciliation, Carnegie Endowment for International Peace, 1939).

S. ENKE and V. SALERA, *International Economics*, 2nd edition (New York: Prentice-Hall, 1951).

PAUL ERDMAN and PETER ROGGE, *Die Europäische Wirtschaftsgemeinschaft und die Drittländer* (Basle: 1960).

FRANK ISAIAH, *The European Common Market – An Analysis of Commercial Policy* (London: Stevens, 1961).

GOTTFRIED HABERLER, *Quantitative Trade Controls, their Causes and Nature*, Economic and Financial II A5 (Geneva: League of Nations, 1943).

——, *A Survey of International Trade Theory*, revised edition (Princeton: Princeton University Press, 1961).

——, *The Theory of International Trade*, 3rd impression of English translation (New York: Macmillan, 1950).

H. C. HAWKINS, *Commercial Treaties and Agreements, Principles and Practice* (New York: Reinhart, 1951).

H. K. HEUSER, *Control of International Trade* (London: Routledge, 1939).

Non-tariff Obstacles to Trade. Report of Meeting of 28 April 1969; Brochure 258 (Paris: International Chamber of Commerce, May 1969).

JOHN H. JACKSON, *World Trade and the Law of GATT* (New York: Bobbs-Merrill, 1969).

MORDECHAI KREININ, *International Economics* (New York: Harcourt Brace Johanvanovich, 1971).

IAN M. D. LITTLE, *A Critique of Welfare Economics*, 2nd edition (Oxford: Oxford University Press, 1960).

JAMES E. MEADE, HANS LEISNER and SIDNEY WELLS, *Case Studies in the European Economic Union*, issued under the auspices of the Royal Institute of International Affairs (London: Oxford University Press, 1962).

JAMES E. MEADE, *Introduction to Economic Analysis and Policy* (New York: C. Y. Hitch, 1946).
——, *The Theory of Customs Union* (Amsterdam: North Holland, 1955).
V. A. SEYID MUHAMMAD, *The Legal Framework of World Trade* (London: Stevens, 1958).
GARDNER PATTERSON, *Discrimination in International Trade – the Policy Issues* (Princeton: Princeton University Press, 1966).
RAUL PREBISCH, *Towards a New Trade Policy for Development* (New York: United Nations, 1964).
M. W, REDER, *Studies in the Theory of Welfare Economics* (New York: Columbia University Press, 1947).
GEORGE C. REEVES, *Tariff Preferences for Developing Countries, Existing and Proposed Arrangements*, Staff Research Studies, U.S. Tariff Commission (Washington: U.S. Government Printing Office, 1971).
WERNER REICHWALD, *Die Deutschen Zollvorschriften* (Cologne: BFA, 1966), 'Sonderveroffentlichung des Zolldienstes'.
R. SANNWALD and J. STOHLER, *Economic Integration* (Princeton: Princeton University Press, 1959).
FRANCIS BOWES SAYRE, *The Way Forward – The American Trade Agreements Program* (New York: Macmillan, 1939).
TIBOR SCITOVSKY, *Economic Theory and Western European Integration*, rev. ed. (London: Unwin University Press, 1962).
L. W. TOWLE, *International Trade and Commercial Policy* (New York: Harper Brothers, 1947).
JACOB VINER, *The Customs Union Issue*, Carnegie Endowment for International Peace (New York and London: Stevens, 1950).
——, *Trade Relations between Free Market and Controlled Economies* (Geneva: League of Nations, 1943).
CLAIR WILCOX, *A Charter for World Trade* (New York: Macmillan, 1949).
ROBERT ZINSER, 'Das GATT und die Meistbegünstigung', *Handbuch für Europaische Wirtschaft*, Volume 24 (Baden-Baden and Bonn: Verlag Lutzeyer, 1962).

Index

NOTE: References to items in Notes at the end of chapters are shown by the number of the page on which the note appears, the letter 'n' and the note number. Authors of books referred to in the notes are only included in the index if mentioned in the text.

ad valorem part of duty
  in EC, 71, 78
  in USA, 103, 107, 111, 128
  specific tariff compared, 142–7
  see also Qualitative quota with *ad valorem* duty
Association Agreements, 29, 59, 62–5
Australia
  and the GATT, 3, 7, 28–9
  waiver, 4, 147, 179
  tariff quotas
    from point of view of importing countries, 147–8
    global, 147
    now used only as exception, 235
    trade under GSP (1966–71), 183
  see also GSP Australian scheme
Austria
  Treaty with Switzerland (1926), 6

Belgium
  ECSC and GATT, 19
  France, commercial agreement (1926), 6
  List G, 60
  Luxemburg re cast iron and salt, 60
  USA re wool and worsted, 16
  see also Benelux
Belgium & Luxemburg Economic Union, 69, 190
Benelux
  ECSC, 53–5
  GSP, 189, 190
  'harmonisation', 7, 56
  imports and MFN treatment, 203

tariff quotas
  aluminium and ferro alloys, List G, 60–1
  general allocation (1974), 205–6
  plywood, 205
  textiles, 206
  unroasted coffee, 59
Brasseur, M., 157
Brazil
  Japan, maximum amount limitation, 214
  USA agreement (1935) and MFN principle, 22
Bretton Woods monetary system, xxi
Brussels Tariff Nomenclature (BTN), 186, 189
Bulgaria
  Japan, maximum amount limitation, 214
butoirs, xxi

Canada–US Trade Agreements Programme, 8, 25, 104
Charter of Alta Gracia, UNCTAD Programme, 170–2
Chile
  Japan maximum amount limitation, 214
China
  USA stainless steel table flatware tariff quota, 133
Colombia
  Japan maximum amount limitation, 214
Common External Tariff (CET), 94

Cooper, Richard M., 192
Currency devaluation, 233
Customs unions and GATT
  effects on third countries,
    protectionist trend or freer trade, 37–8
    welfare gains or losses, 38–46
    interpretation problems, 34–7
    tariff quota for harmonisation, 7, 29–30
Customs unions in economic theory, 37–46
  trade diversion and trade creation, potential isolation of, 44–5
  welfare, gains or losses, 38–46

Definitions
  greyhound process or system, 3, 79
  harmonisation in customs union, 7
  'passive' finishing trade, 10
  prior licensing system, 3
  tariff quota, xix, 2–5
    allocated, 2
    global, 175n19
    national (EC), 96n8, 98n24
    unallocated, 2
    value added, 175n16
Demand schedule, reaction to shifts in, 141
Denmark
  adopted EC GSP on joining, 205
  tariff quotas
    general allocation (1974), 205–6
    plywood, 205
    textiles, 206
Developing countries
  Australian waiver, encouragement and non-discrimination, 3, 29
  demand for generalised preferences, 155–8
  EC scheme (1960), 159–60
  global quotas, 147–9, 160–72
  import requirement calculation, 166–7
  injustice of MFN, 156
  problems on preferences, 157–8
  tariff quotas promote more liberal conditions, 6–7, 151

  UNCTAD proposal (1964), 160–70
Development Decade, 161–70

Eisenhower, President, 115, 131
Escape-clause system
  EC GSP, 186, 187
  conditions for fixing tariff quotas, 56
  future possibilities, 232–3, 235
  Greek Association Agreement, 63
  Japan, 208
  safeguard with global quota, 170, 173
  USA stainless steel table flatware, 103, 131
European Coal & Steel Community (ECSC)
  EC GSP, 188
  harmonisation, 7–8
  national tariff quotas, 53–5, 65
  waiver under GATT, 19, 28
  West German coal duty-free quota, 23
European Commission, 206
  monitoring semi-sensitive product imports, 188
European Community (EC)
  Agreement of Accession (1974), 94
    external tariffs and common external tariff (CET), 94
  automotic licensing and US objections, xx
  butoirs, xxi
  Community reserves, 91–2, 95, 195, 203
    absence of, 203
    experts' opposition, 92
    suggested, 89
  discriminatory tariffs, 2–3
  General System of Preferences (GSP), 93
  Greece, Agreement of Association, 3, 10, 29, 30
  internal distribution of common quota, 4
  national imports by value and volume (1960), 68
  national tariff quotas (1961–70), 71

Index

European Community (EC) (contd)
   Nigeria, Agreement of Association, 29
   Protocols re tariff quotas, 59–63 passim, 84
   raw materials available from associated countries, 73
   rise in tariff, effect on product price, 73
   tariff quota applications (1961–6), 70
   tariff quotas bound in GATT, 5, 16–19, 21, 64–6
   Turkey, Agreement of Association, 3, 10, 29
   USA stainless steel table flatware, 133
   see also Rome, Treaty of
European Free Trade Association (EFTA), 93
   EC complications of preferential arrangements, 94
Export price, definitions affecting quota allocation, 225

Finland
   EC regulations for supervising imports from, 93
   USA trade agreement, 24
First-come, first-served basis of control, see Greyhound system
Foreign exchange earnings, maximising, 226–9, 235, 236–7
France
   Belgium, commercial agreement (1926), 6
   exports to USA, 124
   GSP allocation, 189
   least interested (EC) tariff quotas, world and non-member imports, 68–9
   Switzerland, Agreement re finishing trades replaced by EC agreement, 64
   tariff quota, general allocation (1974), 205
   unutilised imports at preferred duty rates, overall net excess share, 203

General Agreement on Tariffs and Trade (GATT)
   Article XI, 15, 25
   XII–XIV, 15
   XIII, 15, 25–6
   XV, 54
   XIX, 108, 161, 164
   XXIV, 28, 31, 34–7, 45, 234
   XXV, 30, 179
   XXVIII, 132
   XXXVII, 178
   automatic licensing, draft code, xxi
   discrimination against developing world, 156–7
   EC tariff quotas bound in GATT, 5, 16–19, 64–5
   Kennedy Round, xxi, 16–19, 215n16
   League of Nations Economic Committee, 15–16, 20–1
   national tariff quotas within customs unions, 29–30
   preference demands by developing countries, 155–8
   tariff quota rules have to be deduced, 31
   Tokyo Round, xxii
   waivers, 19–21, 28–9
      Australia, 3, 7, 20, 179
      ECSC, 28
      Italy to Libya, 9, 19
      refused to Greece re Soviet Union, 30
      USA, 19, 104, 107, 132
   see also Customs unions and GATT, MFN, and Tariff quotas and GATT
Generalised System of Preferences (GSP), 93, 155–77, 178–214, 231–5
   advantages, 169
   Australian Scheme (1966–73), 178–86
   calculation methods, 163–9
   central computer agency needed, 168
   criticism, 169–70
   developing countries' exports of manufactures and semi-

Generalised System of Preferences (GSP) (*contd*)
  manufactures only, 162
  Development Decade, 161–70
  ECE scheme (1960), 159–60
  EC scheme, 186–207, 231–3
  escape clauses, 170, 173, 208, 233
  exceptions list, 164
  Japanese scheme, 207–14, 233
  Latin-American countries' proposal (Charter of Alta Gracia), 170–2
  UNCTAD scheme, 155–8, 160–70
Geneva Reservation to GATT Agreement (1947) – US tariff concession to UK (and others under MFN) re woollen and worsted fabrics, 16–17, 21, 22, 28, 207–26
Germany, West
  GSP share allocation, 189
  'combined procedure', 189–90
  harmonisation, 56, 93
  imports and MFN, 203
  intention to seek other tariff quotas, 61n22
  Italy, agreement re maraschino, 6
  legislation, 93
  Switzerland, agreement re finishing trade, 64
  tariff quotas
    allocation by 'combined procedure', 189–90
    by unified greyhound type system, 88
    aluminium, unwrought, List G, 7, 60
    bananas, 9, 59, 84, 192
    coal, 23
    example of greyhound system, 90
    of proportional share negotiation, 23
    ferro alloys, List G, 60
    general allocation (1974), 205–6
    imports from world and non-members, 68–9
    lead and zinc, List G, 60, 61
    meat, frozen, non-discriminatory quota failed, 7
  pre-fabricated wooden houses, 58
  prunes, 74–6
  textiles, 206
  wine, 63
Global quotas, 147–9, 160–72 passim, 175n19
Greece
  Association Agreement, 29, 59, 62–3
  citrus fruits, grapes and peaches, 3, 10, 29, 30
  collophony and turpentine oil, 62–3
  olives and tobacco, 62
  wine to Germany, 63
  Soviet Union Agreement, 30
Greyhound (first-come first-served) process
  and maximum amount limitation, 189
  change from prior licensing, 93
  contrast with prior licensing, 80–1, 83, 184, 224
  dangers, 168
  definition, 3, 79
  European Council of Ministers specifies 13 products for greyhound, 92
  Germany, West, 88, 190
  global tariff quotas
    licensing authority policy, 223
    suggested unfair advantages, 168
  Japan, 208–9
  tariff quota larger than demand, 143
  telephone procedure, 79, 93
  treatment of products on arrival, 196
  USA elaborate arrangements, 105–6
Guillotine quota, 140

Haberler, Gottfried, 37, 12n33
Haimi-Cohen, R., 236–7
Harmonisation in a customs union, 7–8
  definition, 7

Harmonisation in a customs union (*contd*)
  EC
    in transition period, 29–30
    individual administration needed, 82
    national legislation, 93
    national tariff quotas to promote harmonisation, 53
    possible harm, 56
    purpose, 54
  Havana Charter, 37
  Hawkins, H. C., 23
  Heuser, H. K., 6
Hong Kong
  benefit and disadvantage from Australian scheme, 180–1, 184
  EC GSP plastic and rubber footwear, 206
  Japan maximum amount limitation, 214
  USA stainless steel table flatware, 132–3
Hungary
  USA whisker brooms and brushes quota, 103

India
  benefit from Australian scheme, 184
  EC
    GSP tobacco quota, 207
    handicrafts tariff quota, 7
  Japan, maximum amount limitation, 214
International Trade Organisation (ITO)
  Charter (1948), 23, 25
  tariff duties considered liberal method of trade restriction, 27
Iran
  EC
    raisin tariff quota, 92
    telephone procedure, 93
Ireland
  adopted EC GSP on joining, 205
  tariff quota general allocation (1974), 205

Italy
  EC
    List G ferro alloys, 60
    telephone procedure, 93
    exports to USA, 124
    GATT waiver (Libya), 9, 19, 28–9 (Somalia), 59
    greyhound system, 93, 190
    intention to seek other tariff quotas, 61n22
    Switzerland, finishing trades agreement replaced by EC Agreement, 64
  tariff quotas
    ferro alloys, List G, 60
    general allocation (1974), 205–6
    textiles, 206
    tunny, 76–8
    unroasted coffee, 59
    Treaty with West Germany re maraschino, 6
    Wool and woven cloth exports to USA reduced (1960–67), 117–22 passim, 128–9

Jackson, John H., 15, 27
Jaenicke, G., 35
Japan
  exports to USA
    licensing control scheme, 124
    stainless steel flatware, 132, 133
    wool and worsted, 117–19, 122, 129
    woven cloth, 125
  GSP scheme, 7, 207–14
    products imported (1970) under ceilings, 211

Korea, Republic of, 129, 132, 133
  Australian preference scheme, 184
  Japan, maximum amount limitation, 214

Laurel and Langley, revised trade agreement (USA 1955), 102
League of Nations
  border trade tariff quotas, 6
  Economic Committee, 3, 10

League of Nations (*contd*)
   MFN and tariff quotas, 15–16, 20–2 passim

Libya
   GATT waiver – Italy, 9, 19, 28–9, 59
   Licence fees for quantities over quota (oil – USA), 104

Lipsey, Richard, G., 43

List G, 59–62, 83

Luxemburg
   Belgium
      agreement re cast iron (1839), 6
      duty-free salt quota, List G, 60
      Benelux quota equally divided between Netherlands and Belgium/Luxemburg, 190
      European Coal and Steel Community and GATT, 19
      greyhound system, 190
      see also Benelux

Manufactures and semi-manufactures, agreed definition discussion, 162

Maximum amount limitation
   EC
      GSP, 189, 194, 198–200
      proposed (1975) changes re semi-sensitive lists, 206–7
      reduction as protective device, 200
   Japan GSP, 208, 210–14

Meade, James E., 38–40, 44, 48n29, 48n34

Mexico
   Australian GSP, 185
   USA tariff quotas, 103, 104

Morocco
   EC Association Agreement, fish and fish products, 64

Most-favoured-nation clause (MFN)
   absolute equality of treatment, 26
   allocation of country quotas, 23
   border trade tariff quotas compatible but exceptions, 6, 29
   customs unions, 29–30, 44
   EC
      Semi-sensitive, sensitive and non-sensitive products, 188
      tariffs inside quota usually below MFN common external tariff, 78
   exceptions from, 29–31
   GATT and tariff quotas, 15–31 passim, 34
   injustice to developing countries, 156
   League of Nations Economic Committee, 20–2 passim
   preferential treatment for developing countries incompatible, 179
   quantitative restrictions and tariff quotas incompatible, 20, 23
   Swiss surcharge duty, 9
   tariff quotas,
      an evasion, 15
      compatible with MFN, 31
   unallocated, 21
      distinguished from tariff and ordinary quota, 20
      prohibitive, 4
   USA wool and worsted, 16, 22

Muhammad, V. A. Seyid, 15, 28, 32n27

Netherlands
   Administrative instruction for EC tariff quotas, 93
   Benelux quota equally divided between Netherlands and Belgium/Luxemburg, 190
   European Coal and Steel Community and GATT, 19
   harmonisation, 93
   imports from world and EC non-members, 68–9
   List G, lead and zinc, unwrought, 60, 61
   pressure for GSP changes, 206
   prior licensing system, GSP, 190
   see also Benelux

New Zealand, 105

Nigeria
   Association Agreement with EC, 29

Non-discrimination principle, 24, 25, 44

Index

Non-sensitive products, GSP, 188, 200–1
future possibilities, 232–3, 235
Norway
pre-fabricated wooden houses, 58

Organisation for Economic Co-operation and Development (OECD) and Japanese GSP, 207
Special Group on Trade with Developing Countries, 173–4
Organisation of American States (OAS), 170

Pakistan
Australian preferences scheme, 184
EC handicrafts tariff quota, 7
Paraguay
Japan – maximum amount limitation, 214
Paris, Treaty of (1952)
Benelux transitional tariff quotas, 54–5
Peru
Japan – maximum amount limitation, 214
Philippines
Australian preferences scheme, 184
Japan – maximum amount limitation, 214
USA trade agreement, 3, 102, 104
Poland
USA tariff quota, brooms and brushes, 103
Portugal
Japan – maximum amount limitation, 214
Preferential tariff quotas, 94
example of benefit, 147
see also Generalised Scheme of Preferences
Price fluctuation
against unified tariff (USA importers), 129
effect of currency devaluation, 233
if developing countries' exports below tariff quota, 151
import fluctuations concealed if tariff quota in value terms, 233
primary products vulnerable, 156
rise reduces real value preferential imports in basic quota, 192
value of quantitative quota, 146
UK wool exports to USA, 123
with effective qualitative quota, 146–7
Prior licensing
advantage over greyhound system, 184, 224
Australia, 183–4
attempted introduction (1930s), 22
change to greyhound system, Iran, Italy and Turkey, 93
contrast with greyhound system, 80–1
definition, 3
discriminatory, 3
EC GSP, 80–1, 83, 189
Japan GSP, 209
Processing industries 'consequences prejudicial to', 57, 60–1
Products and raw materials
brooms and brushes, USA Tariff Schedule Amendment Act, 102, 103, 241
chemicals
collophony and turpentine oil, EC – Greece, Association Agreement, 62–3
dyeing and tanning extracts, high exports to developed countries, 175n12
ethyl alcohol, Italy's intention to seek tariff quota, 61n22
eucalyptus extrali, tariff quota bound in GATT, 18
gelatine and glues from bone, Japan GSP, subject to duty, 208
oil, USA import limits, 103; Japan, petroleum, crude, spirits and gases, GSP no preferential treatment, 208
organic chemicals, Japan ceiling, 211

Products and raw materials (*contd*)
  clothing, knitted outer garments, Japan ceiling, 211
  food and drink
    agricultural (dairy and meat)
      bovine meat, EC (1964) tariff quota, 65
      cattle, EEC, 64; USA, 102, 104, 238; USA and Canada, 8, 104
      cream and whole milk, USA and Canada, 8
      dairy products, USA, 102, 105, 239–40
      frozen meat, EC, 66; West Germany discriminatory tariff failed, 7
      List G, EC, 61
      new products, EC, 206
      processed products, EC GSP, 187
      whole milk, USA, 105, 239
    beer and spirits, Australia, 185
    coconut oil, USA – Philippines agreement, 3, 102, 242
    coffee, unroasted, Benelux – Italy tariff quota to be phased out, 59
    fish, miscellaneous, EC tariff quota bound in GATT, 18
    Morocco – Tunisia, Association Agreements, 64
    USA tariff quota 102, 104; imports greatly exceed quota, 105, 106
    West Germany and Italy, intention to request tariff quota, 61n22
    tunny, 76–8
  fruit and nuts
    bananas, West Germany GATT waiver and EC Protocol, 9, 59, 84, 192
    citrus fruits, EC discriminatory quota, Association Agreement, Greece, 3, 10, 29
    figs, Turkey, Association Agreement, 92
    grapes, Greece, Association Agreement, 29, 62
    hazel nuts, Turkey, Association Agreement, 92
    mirabelles, Belgium – France, Commercial Agreement, 6
    nuts and peanut oil, USA GATT waiver, 19
    olives, Greece, Association Agreement, 62
    peaches, Greece, Association Agreement, 29
    prunes, EC consideration and decision, 74–6
    raisins, Iran, EC discriminatory quota, 92; Turkey, Association Agreement, 10, 92
    strawberries, Belgium–France, Commercial agreement, 6
  maraschino spirits, Italo-German Treaty (1925), 6
  potatoes, USA trade agreement concessions, 102, 240
  salt, Belgium – Luxemburg duty-free quota, List G, 60
  wine, EC tariff quota for German imports from Greece, 63
footwear
  EC GSP, 188, 197–8, 200, 202, 206
  Japan GSP, no preferential treatment, 208
  glassware, EEC imports subject to quota, 195
handicrafts
  Australian imports GSP, 183
  EC India and Pakistan import tariff quota, 7
leather
  Japan GSP clothing and accessories subject to duties, 208
  sheep and lamb, ceiling, 211
minerals, metals and metal manufactured goods
  aluminium
    European Commission's (1969) proposals, 92
    Japan, ceiling, 211

Index

Products and raw materials (*contd*)
  Unwrought, tariff quota bound in GATT, 18; EC List G, Benelux and Germany, 7, 60–1
  bicycles
    EC imports subject to tariff quota, 195
  calculating and statistical machines, 184
  Cast iron
    Belgium – Luxemburg agreement, 6
  coal
    West Germany, non-discriminatory quota duty-free, GATT and European Coal and Steel Community, 23
  copper and copper scrap
    Japan GSP ceiling, 211; duty-free on MFN basis, 212
  electrical machinery and equipment
    Japan ceiling, 211
  ferro-alloys
    EC List G, Benelux, West Germany and Italy, 60–1
    and ferro-manganese, Japan ceiling, 211
    ferro-chromium and ferro-silicon, quota bound in GATT, 18
  iron and steel products
    EC GSP, 187n28, 197 8, 200
    Japan ceiling, 211
  lead and zinc unwrought
    EC List G, West Germany and Netherlands, 60, 61; Belgium lead only, 60, 61
  machinery and mechanical appliances
    Japan ceiling, 211
  magnesium
    EC tariff quota in one allocation, 92
    unwrought tariff quota bound in GATT, 19
  silver, unalloyed
    Japan ceiling, 211
  stainless steel table flatware
    USA tariff quota escape-clause investigation, 102–3, 130–6
  steel and pig iron
    EC escape clauses, 65
  steel ball bearings, precision ground, 184
  paper
    newsprint
      EC tariff quota in one allocation, 18, 92
  pulp
    EC List G – members could open tariff quotas free of duty or at reduced rate, 61
  pearl or shell buttons
    USA – Philippines trade agreement, 3, 102, 242
  precious and semi-precious stones
    Japan ceiling, 211
  rubber
    articles – flexible administration system, 213
    tyres and tubes
      EC imports subject to tariff quotas, 195
      MFN rate re-established, 220n95
  textiles, fibres and cloth
    coir and jute products
      EC customs exemption envisaged, 187
    cotton
      EC GSP customs exemption conditions, 187, 188, 197, 200, 202; quantitative tariff quota and different tariff rates, 230n6, tariff quotas and ceilings (1971–3), 197; cotton and substitutes, 188, 197, 200, 202
      Japan ceiling, 211
      yarn; Japan ceiling, 211; USA allocated quotas, 2
    finishing trade
      EC – Switzerland, bilateral agreements, 10, 64
  League of Nations Economic

Products and raw materials (*contd*)
   Committee, definition of 'passive', 10
  flax or ramie yarn
   EC tariff quota bound in GATT, 18
  silk, raw, and woven fabric
   Japan GSP subject to customs duties, 208
  textiles other than cotton
   EC GSP, 188; tariff quotas and ceilings (1971–3), 197, 200; unspecified fibres, 197, 200, 202, 205–6
   USA man-made, 112–13
  wool and worsted fabrics –
   Geneva Reservation
   USA tariff quota, 2, 4, 8, 16–17, 102, 107–30; problems in application, 22
  tobacco and cigars
   Australia – revenue duties, 185
   EC – Greece, Association Agreement, 62
   increased quota to India (1975), 206
   USA tariff quotas, 3, 102, 104, 241–2
  wigs
   Japan ceiling, 211
  wood
   plywood
    EC GSP, 205
    Japan GSP, subject to customs duties, 208
   prefabricated houses
    EC – West Germany, national tariff quota, 58
   sheets of Lauan etc.
    Japan ceiling, 211

Qualitative quota with *ad valorem* duty
  advantages to importers, 142–3, 145
  global quota, 149
  higher export quantity may be permitted under export control, 147
  larger imports in price ranges below free trade equilibrium, 142
  world price rises, 146

Quantitative quota
  and foreign exchange earnings, 225–9, 236–7
  examples, 141–3, 145
  favours developing countries, 148–9
  preference to highest price exporters, 225
  size, 145–6
  with specific duty, least advantage to importer, 145
  world price rises, 146

Regional integration schemes, 163
Reichwald, Werner, 15
Reserve quota
  EC, 89, 91–2, 95, 195, 203
Rome, Treaty of
  references to specific Articles: *3* 85; *4* 66; *18* 66; *21* 62; *25* 55–69 passim, 73, 75, 76, 85; *25 and 28*, 4, 65; *28* 58–9, 85; *29* 56, 72–5 passim; *42 and 43*, 65; *111, 113 and 114*, 85
  tariff quotas
   and ECSC, 54
   and EC, 55
   and legal point of view, 83
   West Germany, banana tariff quota, 9

Safeguards
  Alta Gracia proposal, 171–2
  and over-expansion by any particular country, 158, 161, 167
  Australia, GSP 185
Scitovsky, Tibor, 40–3
Semi-sensitive products, 188, 196–205 passim
  and 'maximum amount limitation', 206–7
  future possibilities, 232
  unutilised ceilings and imports at MFN rates (1970), 201–2
Sensitive products, 188, 196–205, passim

Index

Sensitive products (*contd*)
  future possibilities, 232
  national tariff quotas but no EC reserve, 194–5
  overall tariff quotas not fully used (1970), 201–2
  proposed alterations (1975), 206
  restrictiveness of tariff quotas, 200–1
Singapore
  Australian preference scheme, 184
  Japan, maximum amount limitation, 214
  Small country enjoying preferred tariff quota, example, 144
Somalia
  GATT waiver, Italy, 59
Soviet Union
  bilateral agreed tariff quota, 11n11, 30, 62
Spain
  Australian GSP, 185
  Japan, maximum amount limitation, 214
Specific tariff cf. *ad valorem* tariff, 142–7
Switzerland
  Austrian Treaty (1926), 6
  EC bilateral agreements re finishing trade replacing agreements with West Germany, France and Italy, 10, 64
  GATT tariff quota agreed re certain types of cow, 64
  protective tariff quota, 9

Taiwan, 132
  benefit from Australian scheme, 184
Tariff quotas and GATT
  discriminatory to developed countries, 3
  EC 'bound in', 5, 16–19, 21, 64–6
  individual opinions on, 15, 21, 23, 27, 28
  League of Nations Economic Committee on, 15–16, 20, 21
  MFN
    administrative form, 21

    Brazil/USA Agreement (1935), 22
    country quotas, 22, 23–8
    customs union and national tariff quota, 29–30
    equal and equitable treatment, 21–3, 26
    equitable, not equal, treatment, 23
    for third country not in conformity, 234
    geographic proximity, 21, 37
    licensing procedure, 26
    overall quotas, 26, 27
    past-trade principle, 24
    unallocated quotas, 21–8 passim
    under exceptions from MFN, 29–31
    waivers, 28–9
    USA Geneva Reservation, 16–17, 22, 107–26, 132
Tariff quota cf. guillotine quota or tariff quota of equal size, 140–1
Tariff quotas – exporting countries' responses, 223–9
  administrative policy
  greyhound procedure, 223
  quantitative, 225
  single exporting country, but production above quota, 223–4
  maximising net foreign exchange earnings with tariff quota, 226–9
  maximising total foreign exchange earnings, 226–9, 235
Tariff quotas in EC
  annual, 91
  community, Commission's proposals to Council, 92–3
  contractual, 94
  experts' proposals, 88–91
  General Scheme of Preferences (GSP), 93 *and see* separate entry
  global, 93
  guidelines submitted to Council of Ministers, 86–8, 91–2

Tariff quotas in EC (*contd*)
  national, 71
    administration, 79–82
      greyhound system, 79, 83 *and see* separate entry
      prior licensing system, 80–1, 83 *and see* separate entry
    and EC institutions, 65–6
    basis for, 55–66
      Agreement (1960) re List G, 59–62
      criteria for granting and reasons for limitations, 55–9
      main legal basis, 58
      no limitations of time or to transitional period, 57, 58, 83
      Protocols affecting, 59–63 passim
      strictness in granting, 69
    definition, 96n8, 98n24
    differences in national administration and legislation and need for harmonisation, 81–2
    during transition period, 57, 58, 66, 82
      agriculture, 74–6
      industrial sector, 73
      initial problems, 66–71
      procedure for granting, 71–9
      right of appeal to Court of Community, 74
    evaluation, points for, 84
    in Association and Trade Agreements, 62–5
    justified only during transition period, 69
    purposes, 56, 84
      to facilitate harmonisation, 53
    summary, 82–5
      types of national quotas, 78–9
    types of community quotas, 93–4
    unallocated, 33n44
    undesirable, 56
    used in enlargement of EC, 96n2
    see also Association Agreements
Tariff quotas in favour of one exporting country and effect on demand in importing country, 150
Tariff quotas in USA
  administration, 105–7
  and rates of duty (1973), 238–42
  character differences, 103–4
  concept, 114–15
    and trade union support, 114
  experience in operation, 104–5
  global, 22
  results compared, 134–5
  stainless steel table flatware, 130–6
    GATT and renewed application of tariff quota, 132
  woollen and worsted fabrics, 2, 4, 8, 16–17, 22, 102, 107–30
    ad valorem part of duty, 107, 128
    developments after tariff quota termination, 128–30
    difficulties in application, 22, 107–14
    dissatisfaction of all parties, 126, 127
    suggested changes, 126–8
    tariff quota invocation, 115–26
Tariff quotas – Partial Equilibrium Analysis, 140–51
Tariff quotas, size, effects of, 143
Tariff quotas – Summary of pros and cons, 150–1
  more liberal trade restriction tool than quotas or tariffs, 150, 234
Tariff quotas system cf. escape-clause system, 232–3
Tariff quotas – Types
  absolute, 5
  allocated, 2
  autonomous, 3, 94
  bilateral preferred, 3, 144
  contractual, 3, 94
  definition, xix, 2–5
  discriminatory, 2–3
  duty changing or fixed, 5
  EC, common or national, 4, 29–30, 78–9, 96n8, 98n24
  effective, prohibitive and ineffective, 4–5
  general, 3

Index 257

Tariff quotas – Types (contd)
  global, 2, 22–3, 93, 147–9, 160–72 passim, 175n19
  greyhound process, 3, 79–81, 83, 88–9, 92
  national 22, 23–5
  non-discriminatory, 2–3
  one-time, 5
  overall, 2, 26, 27, 88, 89
  permanent, 5
  preferential, 94, 147, 168
  prior licensing, 3, 80–1, 83, 93, 183–4, 189, 209
  qualitative, 142–9 passim
  quantitative, 141–9 passim, 225–9, 236–7
  relative, 5
  renewable, 5
  specific, 3, 30
  unallocated, 2, 21–3, 33n44
Tariff quotas – Uses, 5–11
  border trade, 6, 29
  customs union harmonisation, 7, 29–30
  domestic output, supplement, 7
  finishing trade 'passive', 10, 29
  helping consumer, producer or exporter, 84
  interim agreements, 29–30
  national specialities, 6
  new trade promotion, 6
  preferential treatment, 10, 158–9
  price reduction, 7
  protective purposes, 9, 56
  trade diversion, reduction or avoidance, 9
  trade liberalisation, 8, 84
Tariffs
  ad valorem, 5, 107, 128, 142–7 passim; see also ad valorem part of duty
  mixed, 5
  ordinary v. reduced, 5
  preferential, 157
  specific, 5, 141–7 passim
Telephone procedure re greyhound system, 79, 93
Thailand
  and Australian preference

scheme, 184
Tokyo Round, xxii
Transitional period, 30, 57, 58, 69, 83, 93
Tunisia
  EC Association Agreement re fish and fish products, 64
Turkey
  EC Association Agreement
  raisins, figs and hazel nuts, 3, 10, 29, 63, 92
  tobacco, 63
  telephone procedure 93

United Kingdom
  adopted EC GSP on joining, 205
  coal, negotiations re West German Draft Law, 23
  tariff quotas, general allocation (1974), 206
  USA – GATT quota, stainless steel table flatware, 133
  wool and worsted and woven cloth exports to, 117–29 passim
United Nations Conference on Trade and Development (UNCTAD)
  Charter of Alta Gracia, 170
  GSP, 155–8, 160–70
  discussions, 172–4
  Japan, 7, 210, 213
  trade flow calculations in relation to 44 analysed tariff quotas (for 1971), 203, 210
  New Delhi Conference, 173–4
United Nations Economic Commission for Europe (ECE), 155
  developing countries' exports of manufactures, tariff quotas
  1960 Scheme per product per year, 159–60
  1964 UNCTAD proposal, 160–70
United Nations Special Committee on Preferences, 174, 178, 192
United States of America
  Agricultural Adjustments Act and GATT, 19, 105

United States of America (*contd*)
 Brazil trade agreement (1935), 22
 Canada trade agreement (1934), 8, 25
 Federal Import Milk Act (1927), 105
 Finland trade agreement, 24
 Geneva Reservation, 16–17, 22, 28, 107–30
 Import monitoring, xx
 Importers hostile to tariff quotas, 127
 Kennedy Round, xxi, 16–19, 215n16
 Laurel & Langley Agreement, 102
 Philippines trade agreement, 3, 102
 stainless steel table flatware and escape clause investigation, 102–3, 130–36
 Tariff Act (1930), 16
 Tariff Commission, 102, 105, 116, 129, 131–4 passim
 Tariff Schedule Technical Amendments Act (1965), 102
 termination of tariff quotas, developments after, 128–30
 Trade Agreement Extension Act (1951), 102, 131
 Trade Agreement (Multilateral, 1947), 16
 Trade Agreements Programme, 8, 102
 Trade Expansion Act (1962), 131
 Woollen and worsted fabrics tariff quota, 2, 4, 8, 16–17, 22, 102, 107–30
 see also Tariff quotas in USA
Uruguay 129

Value added
 data based on calculations from ex-works price, 225
 definition (EFTA), 175n16
 GSP – minimum to be produced in developing country? 20%, 162 but 50%, 184
 optimising export receipts, 226–8, 230n12
Viner, Jacob, 8, 37–8, 44

Waivers under GATT, 9, 19–21, 59, 184
 Australian, 3, 4, 7, 28–9, 147, 179
 see also List G
Welfare, gain or loss from customs union, 38–46, 48n29, 48n34

Zinser, Robert, 15, 21, 33n46